Reappraising Special Needs Education

Special Needs in Ordinary Schools

General editor: Peter Mittler
Associate editors: James Hogg, Peter Pumfrey, Colin Robson
Honorary advisory board: Neville Bennett, Marion Blythman,
George Cooke, John Fish, Ken Jones, Sylvia Phillips, Klaus
Wedell, Phillip Williams

Titles in this series

Meeting Special Needs in Ordinary Schools: An Overview
Reappraising Special Needs Education

Concerning pre- and primary schooling:

*Primary Schools and Special Needs: Policy, Planning and
Provision*

Developing Mathematical and Scientific Thinking in Young Children
Encouraging Expression: The Arts in the Primary Curriculum
*Improving Children's Reading in the Junior School: Challenges and
Responses*
Pre-School Provision for Children with Special Needs

Concerning secondary schooling:

Secondary Schools for All? Strategies for Special Needs

Humanities for All: Teaching Humanities in the Secondary School
Responding to Adolescent Needs: A Pastoral Care Approach
Science for All: Teaching Science in the Secondary School
Shut Up! Communication in the Secondary School

Concerning specific difficulties:

Children with Hearing Difficulties
Children with Learning Difficulties
Children with Physical Disabilities
Children with Speech and Language Difficulties
*Improving Classroom Behaviour: New Directions for Teachers and
Pupils*
The Visually Handicapped Child in Your Classroom

Forthcoming:

Communication in the Primary School
Teaching Mathematics in the Secondary School

Reappraising Special Needs Education

Brahm Norwich

CASSELL

Cassell Educational Limited
Villiers House, 41/47 Strand, London WC2N 5JE, England

© Cassell Educational Limited 1990

First published 1990

British Library Cataloguing in Publication Data

Norwich, B. (Brahm)
  Reappraising special needs education. — (Special needs in
  ordinary schools).
  1. Great Britain. Special education
  I. Title II. Series
  371.90941

ISBN 0 304 32286 5

Phototypeset by Input Typesetting Ltd, London
Printed and bound in Great Britain by
Billings Ltd, Worcester

Contents

Acknowledgements   vi
Foreword   vii
Introduction   1
1 Abolishing categories of handicap   6
2 Identifying childhood disabilities and difficulties   18
3 The 1981 Education Act: its principles and some
   problems   33
4 Integration: the ideal and the reality   53
5 Curriculum in special needs education   72
6 Designing the curriculum: teaching and assessing   88
7 Professional issues   111
8 Philosophical considerations   130
9 Conclusion: the 1988 Education Reform Act and the
   future   150
References   168
Name Index   176
Subject Index   178

Acknowledgements

I would like to thank Harry Daniels, Daphne Earl, Jean Ware, Klaus Wedell and an anonymous reviewer for their constructive comments on the draft of the book.

Foreword: Towards education for all

AIMS

This series aims to support teachers as they respond to the challenge they face in meeting the needs of all children in their school, particularly those identified as having special educational needs.

Although there have been many useful publications in the field of special educational needs during the last decade, the distinguishing feature of the present series of volumes lies in their concern with specific areas of the curriculum in primary and secondary schools. We have tried to produce a series of conceptually coherent and professionally relevant books, each of which is concerned with ways in which children with varying levels of ability and motivation can be taught together. The books draw on the experience of practising teachers, teacher trainers and researchers and seek to provide practical guidelines on ways in which specific areas of the curriculum can be made more accessible to all children. The volumes provide many examples of curriculum adaptation, classroom activities, teacher–child interactions, as well as the mobilisation of resources inside and outside the school.

The series is organised largely in terms of age and subject groupings, but three 'overview' volumes have been prepared in order to provide an account of some major current issues and developments. Seamus Hegarty's *Meeting Special Needs in Ordinary Schools* gives an introduction to the field of special needs as a whole, whilst Sheila Wolfendale's *Primary Schools and Special Needs* and John Sayer's *Secondary Schools for All?* address issues more specifically concerned with primary and secondary schools respectively. We hope that curriculum specialists will find essential background and contextual material in these overview volumes.

In addition, a section of this series will be concerned with examples of obstacles to learning. All of these specific special needs can be seen on a continuum ranging from mild to severe, or from temporary and transient to long-standing or permanent. These include difficulties in learning or in adjustment and behaviour, as well as problems resulting largely from sensory or physical impairments or from difficulties of communication from whatever cause. We hope that teachers will consult the volumes in this section for guidance on working with children with specific difficulties.

The series aims to make a modest 'distance learning' contribution to meeting the needs of teachers working with the whole range of pupils with special educational needs by offering a set of resource materials relating to specific areas of the primary and secondary curriculum and by suggesting ways in which learning obstacles, whatever their origin, can be identified and addressed.

We hope that these materials will not only be used for private study but be subjected to critical scrutiny by school-based inservice groups sharing common curricular interests and by staff of institutions of higher education concerned with both special needs teaching and specific curriculum areas. The series has been planned to provide a resource for Local Education Authority (LEA) advisers, specialist teachers from all sectors of the education service, educational psychologists, and teacher working parties. We hope that the books will provide a stimulus for dialogue and serve as catalysts for improved practice.

It is our hope that parents will also be encouraged to read about new ideas in teaching children with special needs so that they can be in a better position to work in partnership with teachers on the basis of an infomed and critical understanding of current difficulties and developments. The goal of 'Education for All' can only be reached if we succeed in developing a working partnership between teachers, pupils, parents, and the community at large.

ELEMENTS OF A WHOLE-SCHOOL APPROACH

Meeting special educational needs in ordinary schools is much more than a process of opening school doors to admit children previously placed in special schools. It involves a radical re-examination of what all schools have to offer all children. Our efforts will be judged in the long term by our success with children who are already in ordinary schools but whose needs are not being met, for whatever reason.

The additional challenge of achieving full educational as well as social integration for children now in special schools needs to be seen in the wider context of a major reappraisal of what ordinary schools have to offer the pupils already in them. The debate about integration of handicapped and disabled children in ordinary schools should not be allowed to overshadow the movement for curriculum reform in the schools themselves. If successful, this could promote the fuller integration of the children already in the schools.

If this is the aim of current policy, as it is of this series of unit texts, we have to begin by examining ways in which schools and school policies can themselves be a major element in children's difficulties.

Can schools cause special needs?

Traditionally, we have looked for causes of learning difficulty in the child. Children have been subjected to tests and investigations by doctors, psychologists and teachers with the aim of pinpointing the nature of the problem and in the hope that this might lead to specific programmes of teaching and intervention. We less frequently ask ourselves whether what and how we teach and the way in which we organise and manage our schools could themselves be a major cause of children's difficulties.

The shift of emphasis towards a whole-school policy is sometimes described in terms of a move away from the deficit or medical model of special education towards a more environmental or ecological model. Clearly, we are concerned here with an interaction between the two. No one would deny that the origins of some learning difficulties do lie in the child. But even where a clear cause can be established — for example, a child with severe brain damage, or one with a serious sensory or motor disorder — it would be simplistic to attribute all the child's learning difficulties to the basic impairment alone.

The ecological model starts from the position that the growth and development of children can be understood only in relation to the nature of their interactions with the various environments which impinge on them and with which they are constantly interacting. These environments include the home and each individual member of the immediate and extended family. Equally important are other children in the neighbourhood and at school, as well as people with whom the child comes into casual or closer contact. We also need to consider the local and wider community and its various institutions — not least, the powerful influence of television, which for some children represents more hours of information intake than is provided by teachers during eleven years of compulsory education. The ecological model thus describes a gradually widening series of concentric circles, each of which provides a powerful series of influences and possibilities for interaction — and therefore learning.

Schools and schooling are only one of many environmental influences affecting the development and learning of children. A great deal has been learned from other environments before the child enters school and much more will be learned after the child leaves full-time education. Schools represent a relatively powerful series of environments, not all concerned with formal learning. During the hours spent in school, it is hard to estimate the extent to which the number and nature of the interactions experienced by any one child are directly concerned with formal teaching and learning. Social interactions with other children also need to be considered.

Questions concerned with access to the curriculum lie at the heart of any whole-school policy. What factors limit the access of certain children to the curriculum? What modifications are necessary to ensure fuller curriculum access? Are there areas of the curriculum from which some children are excluded? Is this because they are thought 'unlikely to be able to benefit'? And even if they are physically present, are there particular lessons or activities which are inaccessible because textbooks or worksheets demand a level of literacy and comprehension which effectively prevent access? Are there tasks in which children partly or wholly fail to understand the language which the teacher is using? Are some teaching styles inappropriate for individual children?

Is it possible that some learning difficulties arise from the ways in which schools are organised and managed? For example, what messages are we conveying when we separate some children from others? How does the language we use to describe certain children reflect our own values and assumptions? How do schools transmit value judgements about children who succeed and those who do not? In the days when there was talk of comprehensive schools being 'grammar schools for all', what hope was there for children who were experiencing significant learning difficulties? And even today, what messages are we transmitting to children and their peers when we exclude them from participation in some school activities? How many children with special needs will be entered for the new General Certificate of Secondary Education (GCSE) examinations? How many have taken or will take part in Technical and Vocational Education Initiative (TVEI) schemes?

The argument here is not that all children should have access to all aspects of the curriculum. Rather it is a plea for the individualisation of learning opportunities for all children. This requires a broad curriculum with a rich choice of learning opportunities designed to suit the very wide range of individual needs.

Curriculum reform

The last decade has seen an increasingly interventionist approach by Her Majesty's Inspectors of Education (HMI), by officials of the Department of Education and Science (DES) and by individual Secretaries of State. The 'Great Debate', allegedly beginning in 1976, led to a flood of curriculum guidelines from the centre. The garden is secret no longer. Whilst Britain is far from the centrally imposed curriculum found in some other countries, government is increasingly insisting that schools must reflect certain key areas of experience for all pupils, and in particular those concerned with the world of work (*sic*), with science and technology, and with economic awareness. These priorities are also reflected in the prescriptions for teacher education laid down with an increasing degree of firmness from the centre.

There are indications that a major reappraisal of curriculum content and access is already under way and seems to be well supported by teachers. Perhaps the best known and most recent examples can be found in the series of Inner London Education Authority (ILEA) reports concerned with secondary, primary and special education, known as the Hargreaves, Thomas and Fish Reports (ILEA, 1984, 1985a, 1985b). In particular, the Hargreaves Report envisaged a radical reform of the secondary curriculum, based to some extent on his book *Challenge for the Comprehensive School* (Hargreaves, 1982). This envisages a major shift of emphasis from the 'cognitive–academic' curriculum of many secondary schools towards one emphasising more personal involvement by pupils in selecting their own patterns of study from a wider range of choice. If the proposals in these reports were to be even partially implemented, pupils with special needs would stand to benefit from such a wholesale review of the curriculum of the school as a whole.

Pupils with special needs also stand to benefit from other developments in mainstream education. These include new approaches to records of achievement, particularly 'profiling' and a greater emphasis on criterion-referenced assessment. Some caution has already been expressed about the extent to which the new GCSE examinations will reach less able children previously excluded from the Certificate of Secondary Education. Similar caution is justified in relation to the TVEI and the Certificate of Pre-Vocational Education (CPVE). And what about the new training initiatives for school leavers and the 14–19 age group in general? Certainly, the pronouncements of the Manpower Services Commission (MSC) emphasise a policy of provision for all, and have made specific arrangements for young people with special needs, including those with disabilities. In the last analysis, society and its institutions will be judged by their success in preparing the majority of young people to make an effective and valued contribution to the community as a whole.

A CLIMATE OF CHANGE

Despite the very real and sometimes overwhelming difficulties faced by schools and teachers as a result of underfunding and professional unrest, there are encouraging signs of change and reform which, if successful, could have a significant impact not only on children with special needs but on all children. Some of these are briefly mentioned below.

The campaign for equal opportunities

First, we are more aware of the need to confront issues concerned with civil rights and equal opportunities. All professionals concerned with human services are being asked to examine their own attitudes and practices and to question the extent to which these might unwittingly or even deliberately discriminate unfairly against some sections of the population.

We are more conscious than ever of the need to take positive steps to promote the full access of girls and women not only to full educational opportunities but also to the whole range of community resources and services, including employment, leisure, housing, social security and the right to property. We have a similar concern for members of ethnic and religious groups who have been and still are victims of discrimination and restricted opportunities for participation in society and its institutions. It is no accident that the title of the Swann Report on children from ethnic minorities was *Education for All* (Committee of Inquiry, 1985). This too is the theme of the present series and the underlying aim of the movement to meet the whole range of special needs in ordinary schools.

The equal opportunities movement has not itself always fully accepted people with disabilities and special needs. At national level, there is no legislation specifically concerned with discrimination against people with disabilities, though this does exist in some other countries. The Equal Opportunities Commission does not concern itself with disability issues. On the other hand, an increasing number of local authorities and large corporations claim to be 'Equal Opportunities Employers', specifically mentioning disability alongside gender, ethnicity and sexual orientation. Furthermore, the 1986 Disabled Persons Act, arising from a private member's Bill and now on the statute book, seeks to carry forward for adults some of the more positive features of the 1981 Education Act — for example, it provides for the rights of all people with disabilities to take part or be represented in discussion and decision-making concerning services provided for them.

These developments, however, have been largely concerned with children or adults with disabilities, rather than with children already in ordinary schools. Powerful voluntary organisations such as MENCAP (the Royal Society for Mentally Handicapped Children and Adults) and the Spastics Society have helped to raise political and public awareness of the needs of children with disabilities and have fought hard and on the whole successfully to secure better services for them and for their families. Similarly, organisations of adults with disabilities, such as the British Council of Organisations for Disabled People, are pressing hard for better quality, integrated education, given their own personal experiences of segregated provision.

Special needs and social disadvantage

Even these developments have largely bypassed two of the largest groups now in special schools: those with moderate learning difficulties and those with emotional and behavioural difficulties. There are no powerful pressure groups to speak for them, for the same reason that no pressure groups speak for the needs of children with special needs already in ordinary schools. Many of these children come from families which do not readily form themselves into associations and pressure groups. Many of their parents are unemployed, on low incomes or dependent on social security; many live in overcrowded conditions in poor quality housing or have long-standing health problems. Some members of these families have themselves experienced school failure and rejection as children.

Problems of poverty and disadvantage are common in families of children with special needs already in ordinary schools. Low achievement and social disadvantage are clearly associated, though it is important not to assume that there is a simple relation between them. Although most children from socially disadvantaged backgrounds have not been identified as low achieving, there is still a high correlation between social-class membership and educational achievement, with middle-class children distancing themselves increasingly in educational achievements and perhaps also socially from children from working-class backgrounds — another form of segregation within what purports to be the mainstream.

The probability of socially disadvantaged children being identified as having special needs is very much greater than in other children. An early estimate suggested that it was more than seven times as high, when social disadvantage was defined by the presence of all three of the following indices: overcrowding (more than 1.5 persons per room), low income (supplementary benefit or free school meals) and adverse family circumstances (coming from a single-parent home or a home with more than five children) (Wedge and Prosser, 1973). Since this study was published, the number of families coming into these categories has greatly increased as a result of deteriorating economic conditions and changing social circumstances.

In this wider sense, the problem of special needs is largely a problem of social disadvantage and poverty. Children with special needs are therefore doubly vulnerable to underestimation of their abilities: first, because of their family and social backgrounds, and second, because of their low achievements. A recent large-scale study of special needs provision in junior schools suggests that while teachers' attitudes to low-achieving children are broadly positive, they are pessimistic about the ability of such children to derive much benefit from increased special needs provision (Croll and Moses, 1985).

Partnership with parents

The Croll and Moses survey of junior school practice confirms that teachers still tend to attribute many children's difficulties to adverse home circumstances. How many times have we heard comments along the lines of 'What can you expect from a child from that kind of family?' Is this not a form of stereotyping at least as damaging as racist and sexist attitudes?

Partnership with parents of socially disadvantaged children thus presents a very different challenge from that portrayed in the many reports of successful practice in some special schools. Nevertheless, the challenge can be and is being met. Paul Widlake's recent books (1984, 1985) give the lie to the oft-expressed view that some parents are 'not interested in their child's education'. Widlake documents project after project in which teachers and parents have worked well together. Many of these projects have involved teachers visiting homes rather than parents attending school meetings. There is also now ample research to show that children whose parents listen to them reading at home tend to read better and to enjoy reading more than other children (Topping and Wolfendale, 1985; see also Sheila Wolfendale's *Primary Schools and Special Needs*, in the present series).

Support in the classroom

If teachers in ordinary schools are to identify and meet the whole range of special needs, including those of children currently in special schools, they are entitled to support. Above all, this must come from the headteacher and from the senior staff of the school; from any special needs specialists or teams already in the school; from members of the new advisory and support services, as well as from educational psychologists, social workers and any health professionals who may be involved.

This support can take many forms. In the past, support meant removing the child for considerable periods of time into the care of remedial teachers either within the school or coming from outside. Withdrawal now tends to be discouraged, partly because it is thought to be another form of segregation within the ordinary school, and therefore in danger of isolating and stigmatising children, and partly because it deprives children of access to lessons and activities available to other children. In a major survey of special needs provision in middle and secondary schools, Clunies-Ross and Wimhurst (1983) showed that children with special needs were most often withdrawn from science and modern languages in order to find the time to give them extra help with literacy.

Many schools and LEAs are exploring ways in which both teachers and children can be supported without withdrawing children from ordinary classes. For example, special needs teachers increasingly are working alongside their colleagues in ordinary classrooms, not just with a small group of children with special needs but also with all children. Others are working as consultants to their colleagues in discussing the level of difficulty demanded of children following a particular course or specific lesson. An account of recent developments in consultancy is given in Hanko (1985), with particular reference to children with difficulties of behaviour or adjustment.

Although traditional remedial education is undergoing radical reform, major problems remain. Implementation of new approaches is uneven both between and within LEAs. Many schools still have a remedial department or are visited by peripatetic remedial teachers who withdraw children for extra tuition in reading with little time for consultation with school staff. Withdrawal is still the preferred mode of providing extra help in primary schools, as suggested in surveys of current practice (Clunies-Ross and Wimhurst, 1983; Hodgson, Clunies-Ross and Hegarty, 1984; Croll and Moses, 1985).

Nevertheless, an increasing number of schools now see withdrawal as only one of a widening range of options, only to be used where the child's individually assessed needs suggest that this is indeed the most appropriate form of provision. Other alternatives are now being considered. The overall aim of most of these involves the development of a working partnership between the ordinary class teacher and members of teams with particular responsibility for meeting special needs. This partnership can take a variety of forms, depending on particular circumstances and individual preferences. Much depends on the sheer credibility of special needs teachers, their perceived capacity to offer support and advice and, where necessary, direct, practical help.

We can think of the presence of the specialist teacher as being on a continuum of visibility. A 'high-profile' specialist may sit alongside a pupil with special needs, providing direct assistance and support in participating in activities being followed by the rest of the class. A 'low-profile' specialist may join with a colleague in what is in effect a team-teaching situation, perhaps spending a little more time with individuals or groups with special needs. An even lower profile is provided by teachers who may not set foot in the classroom at all but who may spend considerable periods of time in discussion with colleagues on ways in which the curriculum can be made more accessible to all children in the class, including the least able. Such discussions may involve an examination of textbooks and other reading assignments for readability, conceptual difficulty and relevance of content, as well as issues concerned with the presentation of the material, language modes and complexity used to explain what is required, and the use of different approaches to teacher–pupil dialogue.

IMPLICATIONS FOR TEACHER TRAINING

Issues of training are raised by the authors of the overview works in this series but permeate all the volumes concerned with specific areas of the curriculum or specific areas of special needs.

The scale and complexity of changes taking place in the field of special needs and the necessary transformation of the teacher-training curriculum imply an agenda for teacher training that is nothing less than retraining and supporting every teacher in the country in working with pupils with special needs.

Although teacher training represented one of the three major priorities identified by the Warnock Committee, the resources devoted to this priority have been meagre, despite a strong commitment to training from teachers, LEAs, staff of higher education, HMI and the DES itself. Nevertheless, some positive developments can be noted (for more detailed accounts of developments in teacher education see Sayer and Jones, 1985 and Robson, Sebba, Mittler and Davies, 1988).

Initial training

At the initial training level, we now find an insistence that all teachers in training must be exposed to a compulsory component concerned with meeting special needs in the ordinary school. The Council for the Accreditation of Teacher Education (CATE) and HMI seem set to enforce these criteria; institutions that do not meet them will not be accredited for teacher training.

Although this policy is welcome from a special needs perspective, many questions remain. Where will the staff to teach these courses come from? What happened to the Warnock recommendations for each teacher-training institution to have a small team of staff specifically concerned with this area? Even when a team exists, they can succeed in 'permeating' a special needs element into initial teacher training only to the extent that they influence all their fellow specialist tutors to widen their teaching perspectives to include children with special needs.

Special needs departments in higher education face similar problems to those confronting special needs teams in secondary schools. They need to gain access to and influence the work of the whole institution. They also need to avoid the situation where the very existence of an active special needs department results in colleagues regarding special needs as someone else's responsibility, not theirs.

Despite these problems, the outlook in the long term is favourable. More and more teachers in training are at least receiving an introduction to special needs; are being encouraged to seek out information on special needs policy and practice in the schools in which they are doing their teaching practice, and are being introduced to a variety of approaches to meeting their needs. Teaching materials are being prepared specifically for initial teacher-training students. Teacher trainers have also been greatly encouraged by the obvious interest and commitment of students to children with specal needs; optional and elective courses on this subject have always been over-subscribed.

Inservice courses for designated teachers

Since 1983, the government has funded a series of one-term full-time courses in polytechnics and universities to provide intensive training for designated teachers with specific responsibility for pupils with special needs in ordinary schools (see *Meeting Special Needs in Ordinary Schools* by Seamus Hegarty in this series for information on research on evaluation of their effectiveness). These courses are innovative in a number of respects. They bring LEA and higher-education staff together in a productive working partnership. The seconded teacher, headteacher, LEA adviser and higher-education tutor enter into a commitment to train and support the teachers in becoming change agents in their own schools. Students spend two days a week in their own schools initiating and implementing change. All teachers with designated responsibilities for pupils with special needs have the right to be considered for these one-term courses, which are now a national priority area for which central funding is available. However, not all teachers can gain access to these courses as the institutions are geographically very unevenly distributed.

Other inservice courses

The future of inservice education for teachers (INSET) in education in general and special needs in particular is in a state of transition. Since April 1987, the government has abolished the central pooling arrangements which previously funded courses and has replaced these by a system in which LEAs are required to identify their training requirements and to submit these to the DES for funding. LEAs are being asked to negotiate training needs with each school as part of a policy of staff development and appraisal. Special needs is one of nineteen national priority areas that will receive 70 per cent funding from the DES, as is training for further education (FE) staff with special needs responsibilities.

These new arrangements, known as Grant Related Inservice Training (GRIST), will change the face of inservice training for all teachers but time is needed to assess their impact on training opportunities and teacher effectiveness (see Mittler, 1986, for an interim account of the implications of the proposed changes). In the meantime, there is serious concern about the future of secondments for courses longer than one term. Additional staffing will also be needed in higher education to respond to the wider range of demand.

An increasing number of 'teaching packages' have become available for teachers working with pupils with special needs. Some (though not all) of these are well designed and evaluated. Most of them are school-based and can be used by small groups of teachers working under the supervision of a trained tutor.

The best known of these is the Special Needs Action Programme (SNAP) originally developed for Coventry primary schools (Muncey and Ainscow, 1982) but now being adapted for secondary schools. This is based on a form of pyramid training in which co-ordinators from each school are trained to train colleagues in their own school or sometimes in a consortium of local schools. Evaluation by a National Foundation for Educational Research (NFER) research team suggests that SNAP is potentially an effective approach to school-based inservice training, providing that strong management support is guaranteed by the headteacher and by senior LEA staff (see Hegarty, *Meeting Special Needs in Ordinary Schools*, this series, for a brief summary).

Does training work?

Many readers of this series of books are likely to have recent experience of training courses. How many of them led to changes in classroom practice? How often have teachers been frustrated by their inability to introduce and implement change in their schools on returning from a course? How many heads actively support their staff in becoming change agents? How many teachers returning from advanced one-year courses have experienced 'the re-entry phenomenon'? At worst, this is quite simply being ignored: neither the LEA adviser, nor the head nor any one else asks about special interests and skills developed on the course and how these could be most effectively put to good use in the school. Instead, the returning member of staff is put through various re-initiation rituals ('Enjoyed your holiday?'), or is given responsibilities bearing no relation to interests developed on the course. Not infrequently, colleagues with less experience and fewer qualifications are promoted over their heads during their absence.

At a time of major initiatives in training, it may seem churlish to raise questions about the effectiveness of staff training. It is necessary to do so because training resources are limited and because the morale and motivation of the teaching force depend on satisfaction with what is offered — indeed, on opportunities to negotiate what is available with course providers. Blind faith in training for training's sake soon leads to disillusionment and frustration.

For the last three years, a team of researchers at Manchester University and Huddersfield Polytechnic have been involved in a DES funded project which aimed to assess the impact of a range of inservice courses on teachers working with pupils with special educational needs (see Robson, Sebba, Mittler and Davies, 1988, for a full account and Sebba and Robson, 1987, for a briefer interim report). A variety of courses was evaluated; some were held for one evening a week for a term; others were one-week full time; some were award-bearing, others were not. The former included the North-West regional diploma in special needs, the first example of a course developed in total partnership between a university and a polytechnic which allows students to take modules from either institution and also gives credit recognition to specific Open University and LEA courses. The research also evaluated the effectiveness of an already published and disseminated course on behavioural methods of teaching — the EDY course (Farrell, 1985).

Whether or not the readers of these books are or will be experiencing a training course, or whether their training consists only of the reading of one or more of the books in this series, it may be useful to conclude by highlighting a number of challenges facing teachers and teacher trainers in the coming decades.

1. We are all out of date in relation to the challenges that we face in our work.
2. Training in isolation achieves very little. Training must be seen as part of a wider programme of change and development of the institution as a whole.
3. Each LEA, each school and each agency needs to develop a strategic approach to staff development, involving detailed identification of training and development needs with the staff as a whole and with each individual member of staff.
4. There must be a commitment by management to enable the staff member to try to implement ideas and methods learned on the course.
5. This implies a corresponding commitment by the training institutions to prepare the student to become an agent of change.
6. There is more to training than attending courses. Much can be learned simply by visiting other schools, seeing teachers and other professionals at work in different settings and exchanging ideas and experiences. Many valuable training experiences can be arranged within a single school or agency, or by a group of teachers from different schools meeting regularly to carry out an agreed task.
7. There is now no shortage of books, periodicals, videos and audio-visual aids concerned with the field of special needs. Every school should therefore have a small staff library which can be used as a resource by staff and parents. We hope that the present series of unit texts will make a useful contribution to such a library.

The publishers and I would like to thank the many people — too numerous to mention — who have helped to create this series. In particular we would like to thank the Associate Editors, James Hogg, Peter Pumfrey, Tessa Roberts and Colin Robson, for their active advice and guidance; the Honorary Advisory Board, Neville Bennett, Marion Blythman, George Cooke, John Fish, Ken Jones, Sylvia Phillips, Klaus Wedell and Phillip Williams, for their comments and suggestions; and the teachers, teacher trainers and special needs advisers who took part in our information surveys.

SOME IMPLICATIONS OF THE EDUCATION REFORM ACT:
AN EDITORIAL POSTSCRIPT

Full access to the curriculum is the central theme of this series of
books and the fundamental challenge posed by the 1988 Education
Reform Act. What are the implications of this Act for children with
special educational needs? Will it help or hinder access to the
national curriculum? How will they fare under the proposed
assessment arrangements? What degree of priority will be given
to these children by the new governing bodies, by headteachers,
by LEAs and by the community? Will the voice of parents be
heard when priority decisions are being taken on how the schools'
resources will be used? What are the implications of local management, financial delegation and open enrolment? Is there a risk that
children in ordinary schools will be denied access to the national
curriculum? Will there be increased pressure to provide them with
the 'protection of a statement' and to press for them to be sent to
special schools? Will ordinary schools welcome children whose
needs call for additional resources and for a fully accessible curriculum? Will they be welcome in grant-maintained schools? What is
the future of the strong links which have been established between
special and ordinary schools during the last few years and which
are enabling an increasing number of special school pupils to be
timetabled to spend periods in a neighbouring ordinary school?
Will the Act make it harder for children in special schools to be
integrated into ordinary schools?

These and many other questons have been asked with growing
urgency ever since the publication of the first consultation paper
on the national curriculum. There was concern and anger that the
government appeared to have overlooked children with special
educational needs both in its consultation document and in the
early versions of the Bill and because it appeared to be ignoring
the strong representations on this subject which were being made
during the consultation process. The early Bill contained only one
special needs clause concerned with exclusion from the national
curriculum, accompanied by reiterated official references to the
need to be able to exempt children from a second language when
they had not yet mastered English.

There seemed to be little recognition of the risks to the principles
and practice of the 1981 Education Act, to the needs of the 18
per cent of children in ordinary schools and to the dangers of
inappropriate exclusion. For many months it was not clear
whether grant-maintained schools would be subject to the 1981
Act. At a general level, there was concern over the reduced powers
of LEAs, given their key role in consultation with parents and
their overview of planning and monitoring of special needs pro-

vision over the authority as a whole. This last concern was most acutely reflected in relation to the abolition of the ILEA, which had not only developed good authority-wide provision but has published far-reaching plans for improved integrated provision in ordinary and special schools. Where are these reports today?

The extent to which these anxieties are justified will depend in part on the way in which the legislation is interpreted in the schools and LEAs, and on the kind of guidance issued from the centre. In this latter respect, there are grounds for optimism. Although it was only when the Bill was in its final parliamentary stages that there was evidence that special needs issues were beginning to be considered, there is increasing evidence that these special needs concerns are receiving a much higher degree of priority. New members with special needs interests were added to the National Curriculum Council and the School Examinations and Assessment Council. Clear statements of policy and principle from ministers, from the DES and from HMI are establishing the rights of all children to the national curriculum. Exceptions, exclusions, disapplications and modifications can only be made in individual cases for children with statements, with the full participation of parents and professionals and subject to appeal. There will be no blanket exemptions for groups of children, far less for types of school. Each modification will have to be fully justified by reference to the needs of the individual child, and against the background of a policy which is designed to ensure the fullest possible access to the curriculum. Exemptions for children not on statements can only be temporary. In all cases, schools have to indicate what kind of alternative provision is to be made. Modifications can be made in respect of single attainment targets, programmes of study or assessment arrangements. For example, it seems that children may be on programmes of study leading to attainment targets but might need a modified approach to assessment — e.g. oral instead of written, computer-aided rather than oral, etc. All these issues will need to be debated in relation to individual children rather than to 'categories' of pupils.

The national curriculum documents in science, maths and English as well as interim reports on design and technology and Welsh are all firmly committed to the principle of the fullest possible access for all children. The Report of the Task Group on Assessment and Testing (TGAT) went a long way towards meeting special needs concerns with its suggestion that attainment targets should be reported in terms of ten levels and that they should be formative, criterion-referenced and in profile form. These ten levels, which are linked to programmes of study, are designed to ensure progression and continuity and to avoid children being seen to 'fail the tests'. Children will be able to progress from one level to another for any of the attainment targets, even though they may be several years behind the attainments of other children of the same age. Finally, the specifications and terms of reference given to the development agencies charged with producing Standard Assessment Tasks (SATs) — initially for Key Stage 1 at the age of about seven — clearly specify that SATs must be suitable or adaptable for pupils with special educational needs.

Although the emphasis so far has been largely on children in ordinary schools, the challenge of implementing the national curriculum in all special schools will also need to be addressed. It is clear that special schools are without exception subject to the national curriculum and to the assessment arrangements but a great deal of work needs to be done to develop programmes of study and assessment arrangements which are suitable and age-appropriate for the whole range of pupils with special needs in special schools, without departing in principle from the framework provided by the national curriculum.

At the beginning of 1989, special needs provision is clearly at a highly critical stage. A pessimistic forecast would be that children with special needs, whether in ordinary or special schools, could be marginalised, isolated and excluded from developments in mainstream education. They might be less welcome because priorities may lie with children whose needs are easier and cheaper to meet and who will not adversely affect the school's public performance indicators. Such progress as has been made towards integration of special school pupils could be halted or reversed and an increasing number of children already in ordinary schools could become educationally and socially segregated in their own schools or inappropriately sent to special schools. The ethos of schools could become divisive and damaging to vulnerable children.

Because these remain real and potentially disastrous possibilities, it is essential to develop determined advocacy at all levels to ensure that the national curriculum and the new legislation are exploited to the full in the interests of all children, particularly those with special educational needs. Such advocacy will need to be well informed as well as determined and will be most effective if it is based on a partnership between professionals, parents and the pupils themselves.

Professor Peter Mittler
University of Manchester
February 1989

REFERENCES

Clunies-Ross, L. and Wimhurst, S. (1983) *The Right Balance: Provision for Slow Learners in Secondary Schools*. Windsor: NFER/Nelson.

Committee of Inquiry (1985) *Education for All*. London: HMSO (The Swann Report).

Croll, P. and Moses, D. (1985) *One in Five: The Assessment and Incidence of Special Educational Needs*. London: Routledge & Kegan Paul.

Farrell, P. (ed.) (1985) *EDY: Its Impact on Staff Training in Mental Handicap*. Manchester: Manchester University Press.

Hanko, G. (1985) *Special Needs in Ordinary Classrooms: An Approach to Teacher Support and Pupil Care in Primary and Secondary Schools*. Oxford: Blackwell.

Hargreaves, D. (1982) *Challenge for the Comprehensive School*. London: Routledge & Kegan Paul.

Hodgson, A., Clunies-Ross, L. and Hegarty, S. (1984) *Learning Together*. Windsor: NFER/Nelson.

Inner London Education Authority (1984) *Improving Secondary Education*. London: ILEA (The Hargreaves Report).

Inner London Education Authority (1985a) *Improving Primary Schools*. London: ILEA (The Thomas Report).

Inner London Education Authority (1985b) *Equal Opportunities for All?* London: ILEA (The Fish Report).

Mittler, P. (1986) The new look in inservice training. *British Journal of Special Education* 13, 50–51.

Muncey, J. and Ainscow, M. (1982) Launching SNAP in Coventry. *Special Education: Forward Trends* 10, 3–5.

Robson, C., Sebba, J., Mittler, P. and Davies, G. (1988) *Inservice Training and Special Needs: Running Short School-Focused Courses*. Manchester: Manchester University Press.

Sayer, J. and Jones, N. (eds) (1985) *Teacher Training and Special Educational Needs*. Beckenham: Croom Helm.

Sebba, J. and Robson, C. (1987) The development of short, school-focused INSET courses in special educational needs. *Research Papers in Education* 2, 1–29.

Topping, K. and Wolfendale, S. (eds) (1985) *Parental Involvement in Children's Reading*. Beckenham: Croom Helm.

Wedge, P. and Prosser, H. (1973) *Born to Fail?* London: National Children's Bureau.

Widlake, P. (1984) *How to Reach the Hard to Teach*. Milton Keynes: Open University Press.

Widlake, P. (1985) *Reducing Educational Disadvantage*. London: Routledge & Kegan Paul.

Introduction

Why write a book about special needs education? There are two sides to this question. One concerns the changing education scene resulting from the passing of the Education Reform Act 1988. To write a book while the framework for education is being changed might be considered premature and therefore poor timing in view of uncertainties about the exact form and effects of the changes. However, this could also be seen as an appropriate time to reappraise current ideas and practices in the special needs field in preparation for implementing the 1988 Act. The other side to the question of writing a book is more personal and concerns whether there is something significant and interesting to communicate; what difference could it make to those who read it, and has it been done mainly because it is expected and required of university lecturers to write books?

Although it would be hard to deny that publications are relevant to my personal interests, I have written this book partly because of a growing conviction that there are things about special needs education which need to be said. I have been involved for several years in teaching about special educational needs at the London University Institute of Education. Since arriving at the Institute from a post as a professional educational psychologist, I have worked closely with colleagues in developing advanced courses for teachers on the changing ideas and practices in this field. In the course of lectures, seminars, supervisions and informal chats, I have had the time to listen to a wide range of experiences, ideas and ideals. I have had the privilege to spend time with others interested in the field to reflect, criticise and construct. The urge to write this book developed from these experiences. Of course, what is written in the following chapters are my interpretations and commentaries, but I recognise and appreciate how much I have derived from my colleagues and the course members with whom I have worked.

I realise that the ideas expressed in this book may not agree in significant respects with some current and influential conceptions in the field. Perhaps this is one of my main reasons for embarking on the project. My intentions are not to persuade or preach a particular line about special needs as many recent books have. I have wished, rather, to present some of the difficulties and dilemmas which exist. My goal is to try to resolve difficulties where possible and to point out the weaknesses of current positions and assumptions. The overriding purpose is to broaden some of the current conceptions about special educational needs by linking issues to more basic ethical and knowledge concerns in the field of education and social and human affairs more generally.

I am aware when expressing views in written form that such expressions derive partly from my own personal history and experiences. I am one of those professionals who have been criticised for dominating the lives of those with difficulties, one whose livelihood depends on the hardships of others. Can what I say relate in a constructive and meaningful way to the needs of individual children with difficulties, their families and their teachers? Can someone in my position understand what is involved in meeting special educational needs? Though I have had my share of personal difficulties, these have not affected my life in any severe or long-term way. I am a member of that white, able-bodied, middle-class male group which has been accused of discriminating against those with difficulties and disabilities. Can my views escape from the influence of my social and personal background? I raise these questions not because there are simple answers, but to underline the fact that I have written in a spirit of enquiry and open dialogue. The ideas here are presented as part of a continuing interchange; as such they may cast some light for some readers, while for others they may provoke criticism.

This book is not intended as a textbook or an introduction to the field of special needs education. There are many such books currently available. In some respects it is a polemical book and is written in an abstract and theoretical style. It is written for those who wish to consider some of the fundamental issues. Although it will be assumed that the reader has some familiarity with special needs education, the argument relates to wider educational, health and social issues. The book could, therefore, be of interest to those who work with children from other professional and service perspectives. I am aware that the style could make it unappealing to a wider readership but hope that those who are interested in this field will find that their effort is rewarded.

One of the main themes of the book is the tendency for the various changes and developments in special needs education to be presented in oversimplified and polarised terms. This is apparent, for instance, in the representation of special educational needs as a concept distinct from traditional disability and handicap. In this, as in other respects, the interdependence of concepts and orientations is overlooked. In the case of the concept of special educational needs, for example, I will argue that explicit recognition of the concept of disability is required. I have interpreted this polarising trend as an expression of the promotional and persuasive means used by special educational proponents. It can be seen as part of the attempt to establish authority for new conceptions and practices.

The 1981 Education Act represents in this respect the culmination of an era which was based on developments towards a common curriculum in common schools. With the 1988 Education Reform Act some of these basic assumptions about education and therefore special education have been called into question. This book was planned as the consultation process for the Education Reform Act 1988 was starting. It was written while the Reform Bill was passing through Parliament. This is one reason for not focusing explicitly or at length on the basic changes in the education system resulting from the Act. However, where the prospects of integrating children with special educational needs could be affected, as with the introduction of the local management of schools, there is some discussion of the changes. In the concluding chapter there is also some discussion of the future prospects under the 1988 Act and its relationship to the principles of the 1981 Act.

Another reason for not dealing at greater length with the new changes is that the book focuses on some basic underlying issues, in particular those concerned with the explanation of learning difficulties and with social and educational values. More specifically, I discuss throughout the current emphasis on and use of environmental explanations in behavioural theories at the individual psychological level of analysis and in conflict theories at the sociological level. The position adopted here is informed by a general systems approach (von Bertalanffy, 1968) which finds an explanatory place for the biological, the psychological and sociological levels of analysis. The general systems framework provides an integrative framework and adds to the sophistication of explanatory accounts. Its limitation is in guiding decisions about how to combine different levels of analysis and when different levels take precedence. It is in this context of explanatory uncertainty that established value positions have a major impact on the preference for different theories at different levels of analysis. This can be seen in the preference for social and environmental explanations among those with strong egalitarian value orientations. Their assumption is that the problems associated with special educational needs do not derive, or derive only very marginally, from the individual's conditions of impairment or disability; rather they result from obstacles placed by mainstream society. Such accounts seem to promise the possibility of change and improvement because environmental factors are thought to be alterable.

The relationship between what can be attained and what is sought as an ideal is critical in this field as in other areas of human endeavour. The ideals of equal opportunity and participation in mainstream education are basic to the recent moves in this and other aspects of education. These egalitarian values are discussed in different chapters in relation to the content, organisation and methods of schooling. My position is that there tends to be an overemphasis on an unanalysed notion of equality which can undermine what is good about equality and other important values such as autonomy. Again, as in the discussion about explanatory accounts and levels, there is a very delicate balance to be struck, in this case between related and different values which have far-reaching consequences for the question of integration.

Throughout the book there is an explicit critique of certain features of current thinking in the special needs field. Part of this critique is of the relative lack of conceptual clarity and precision; the other part is of a reluctance to work constructively and positively within the constraints which operate. This reluctance is more apparent among theorists and commentators than among practitioner special educators. However, theoretical conceptions do have some influence and it is to this sphere of thinking that much of the argument in this book is directed.

In concluding this introduction I would like to draw attention to the place of special needs education in relation to other needs and services for children with difficulties, in particular, health and social welfare services. One of the main dilemmas in the field concerns the relationships between special educational, health and social welfare needs. This has been concealed to some extent by the recent emphasis on a common education for all in special needs education. However, this only shifts the question to how differences in individual needs are conceptualised. Some of these issues are discussed in connection with the division of responsibilities for children between different professionals organised within different services.

Finally, it is important to realise that in writing about SEN there can be a tendency, as with all general concepts, to overlook crucial differences between different areas within the wide field. The assumptions and orientations found in areas such as severe learning difficulties and specific learning difficulties vary considerably. It is also critical to guard against stereotyping special needs education; for example, it is not equivalent to educational failure in general nor to low intellectual ability and achievement or socio-economic disadvantage. Special educational needs is an educational concept which arises in the context of the compulsory schooling of all children. What unifies the different examples of special educational needs and the different broad areas is the provision of different or additional educational resources for some children on account of some degree of disability or impairment. It is when this notion is explored more fully that the different interpretations and positions crystallise out: for example, the issues connected with identification, what counts as different/additional resources and what are the goals for which the resources are to be used. The question of when additional resources are required also depends on what is available in ordinary schooling and teaching. For this reason what counts as special education varies with the nature of ordinary education. So in discussing special educational needs as a general concept, we must be aware of the diversity and indeterminacy of this aspect of education.

—1—

Abolishing categories of handicap

INTRODUCTION

This chapter is about the move away from handicap categories in the special educational field over the last two decades. Abolishing categories of handicap, such as maladjustment and educational subnormality, was one of the key recommendations of the Warnock Committee (DES, 1978), which investigated the state of special education during the mid–1970s. This chapter is not about the full range of the 200-plus Warnock recommendations. Nor will it cover the main themes of the Report which focused on assessment, pre-school and 16-plus provision, teacher training and the organisation of special education provision in special and ordinary schools. The chapter explores the arguments for and against the Warnock perspective on categories. The reason for considering this aspect of the Report is that it is at the heart of the switch in framework to that of special educational needs. In examining this issue in detail, some of the wider and underlying issues in the special needs field will be exposed. This is a useful way to enter the range of issues to be considered in this book.

PROBLEMS WITH CATEGORIES

Although the Warnock Committee was appointed to review provision for children and young people handicapped by disabilities of body and mind, it approached the issue of special education by questioning the relevance of the term 'handicap' in this field (DES, 1978, p. 36). The basic position was that special education is concerned with meeting special educational need and not with the education of handicapped children and young people. Handicap was no longer to be seen as a useful concept in an educational context. This represents an educational starting point where disabilities and difficulties are considered from the perspective of the wider issues of learning and development which make up education.

A distinction was then drawn between handicap and educational handicap, which implies that a variety of conditions can act as obstacles in an educational sphere. It was argued that there is no simple and direct relationship between the severity and permanence of a disability and educational handicap. For example, a boy with one leg may be excluded from many activities, but it may not prevent him, it was argued, from making academic progress. The educational impact of a disability may also depend on the stage of the child's development. For example, a conductive hearing loss affects language development more adversely at a younger than an older age. Another area in which Warnock thinking separated disability from educational handicap was the impact of school and other environmental factors on whether a disability constituted an educational handicap. For example, the impact of a severe physical disability may depend on the encouragement and support offered at home and school.

The force of these points led the Committee to conclude that there were no precise criteria for defining a handicap and that the distinction between handicap and non-handicap did not deal with the complexities of individual need. When these points were taken with the assertion that the kind of handicap conveyed 'nothing of the type of educational help' needed, we can follow how the Committee concluded that:

> We wish to see a more positive approach, and we have adopted the concept of special educational needs, seen not in terms of a particular disability which a child may be judged to have, but in relation to everything about him, his abilities as well as his disabilities — indeed all the factors which have a bearing on his educational progress.
>
> (DES, 1978, para. 3.6, p. 37)

THE WARNOCK CASE AGAINST CATEGORIES

My aim is not to reject this line of thought but to comment on some of the difficulties and ironies in the Warnock approach. To focus on Warnock thinking is to consider views which were current and dominant in the 1970s and the 1980s. The Warnock approach crystallised prior views and influenced subsequent ideas which were the basis for parts of the 1981 Education Act.

It is interesting to see how the Warnock Report, having just renounced the usefulness of the handicap concept, was willing to base its estimates of the extent and forms of special educational needs on certain well-known studies of childhood disorder and handicap, such as the Isle of Wight study (Rutter, Tizard and Whitmore, 1970) and the Inner London Borough study (Rutter et al., 1975). Although Warnock thinking does not refer explicitly and critically to it, many of the current proponents of an educational needs approach are critical of the so-called 'medical model' (Barton and Tomlinson, 1984; Ainscow and Tweddle, 1979, p. 9). The Warnock approach is more diplomatic, but uses similar arguments for abandoning medically based categories:

- many children suffer from more than one disability, producing categorisation difficulties which affect school provision;
- categories confuse what special education is needed, in promoting the idea that all children in the same category have similar educational needs;
- categories as the basis for special provision draw resources away from children who do not fit categories;
- categories have the effect of labelling children and schools in negative ways which persist beyond school and stigmatise unnecessarily.

In arguing for the new system, two points in favour of statutory categories were recognised:

- categories helped to focus attention on the needs of different groups of handicapped children;
- categories offer a valuable safeguard for the rights of handicapped children to an education suited to individual needs.

Nevertheless, the weight given to these two latter points was small, and on balance the third and fourth points above were the determining issues. Weighting the points in this way can be seen as an expression of a general social concern with the adverse effects of labelling on the rights and opportunities available to individuals and minority groups. The Warnock Committee recommendations were in this respect very much in tune with current ideas in educational circles.

ALTERNATIVES TO CATEGORIES

The force of some of the arguments against categorisation does not, however, lead to any simple alternatives. This is shown clearly in the way that Warnock then goes on to introduce the concept of 'children with learning difficulties':

> We recommend that the term children with learning difficulties should be used in future to describe both those children who are currently categorised as educationally subnormal and those with

educational difficulties who are often at present the concern of remedial services.

(DES, 1978, para. 3.26, p. 43)

To argue that a category like educationally subnormal is imprecise and then to substitute for it an even less clearly defined concept of 'moderate learning difficulties' is a strange form of reasoning. This is not abandoning categorisation, but changing labels for the categories. Perhaps it was seen as preferable to have categories with no direct reference to subnormality and with an educational rather than a medical origin. This interpretation is consistent with a position pursued in other chapters of this book, that many of the changes in special education can be seen as the expression of a developing process in which special education becomes more professionally oriented.

A CONFUSION ABOUT CATEGORIES

A more significant issue which arises from an analysis of the Warnock approach is the confusion between categories of educational provision and categories of child difficulty and disorder. In rejecting the division between the handicapped 2 per cent in special schooling and the non-handicapped in other forms of schooling, Warnock argues that about 18 per cent of children require some form of special provision. This is sometimes referred to as the broader concept of special education, as if there had been little appreciation before the Warnock Report of the needs of the 16 per cent not in special schools.

From a historical perspective, it had been recognised early in this century that there were many handicapped children who should and would receive special provision within ordinary schools (Wood Committee, 1929; Education Act, 1944). It has been easy in recent years to forget that special help has been offered to children with difficulties who were not officially categorised as handicapped in the educational system. 'Handicapped' therefore had two distinct meanings pre-Warnock:

- having a disability, disorder or difficulty which required special educational methods other than that normally given in ordinary schools;
- having a disability, disorder, or difficulty which was sufficiently marked and prolonged adversely to affect life activities.

Despite reference in the Warnock Report to the work of Rutter et al. (1970) as grounds for a broader concept of special education, his distinction between psychiatric disorder and maladjustment was not recognised. Psychiatric disorder was defined by Rutter as 'abnormality of behaviour, emotions or relationships sufficiently marked and prolonged to cause a handicap to the child or distress or disturbance in the family or community' (Rutter et al., 1970, p. 124). Maladjustment was defined in the 1962 Handicapped Pupils and Special Schools' Regulations as 'evidence of emotional instability or psychological disturbance that requires special educational treatment in order to effect personal, social and educational readjustment'. It is possible that a child can have a psychiatric disorder in the above sense but not require special educational 'treatment'. There are children who have attended a Child Guidance or a Psychiatric Centre for a particular emotional or behavioural difficulty and are not seen to need placement at a special school for children with emotional and behavioural difficulties (maladjusted children).

This distinction between handicap and handicap which requires special educational methods applies across the different forms of special education. For example, there are children with epilepsy who may or may not require educational methods which are different from those available in ordinary schools. Figure 1.1 illustrates the way in which the Warnock Committee identified the term 'handicapped' with those in special schools (A). The term had in fact been associated with a broader group of children (B), some of whom had been in ordinary schools (C).

ANALYSING THE WARNOCK ARGUMENTS AGAINST CATEGORISATION

It is notable that three of the four points made by the Warnock Report against categorisation can be questioned because they do not take account of the distinction between handicap and handicap in need of special educational methods.

Categories and multiple disabilities

Let us first take the point that many children suffer from more than one disability and that this is supposed to present intractable classification problems. Firstly, it is important to get the extent of the classification problem into perspective. Surveys indicate that fewer than half of those children with special educational needs have more than one major difficulty: about 25 per cent in the Isle of Wight study (Rutter et al., 1970) and about 40 per cent in a more recent study (Croll and Moses, 1985). Secondly, there is

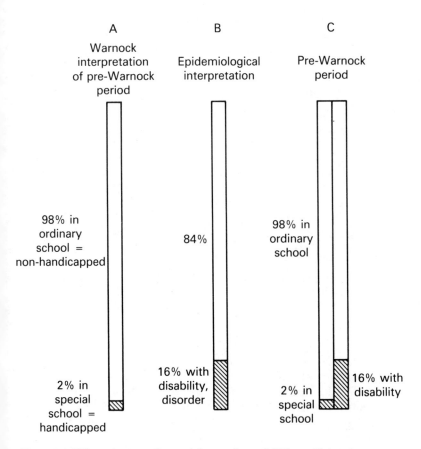

Figure 1.1 *Different interpretations and the prevalence of children with learning difficulties*

nothing in a medical classification which prevents a child from having more than one disorder or disability: for example, deafness and physical disability, intellectual retardation and psychiatric disorder. Problems arise for the educational administrative categories because these categories relate to specialised schools or units for children with different difficulties. It can be difficult for a Local Education Authority to maintain school provision covering the ten different categories (1962 Regulations). To maintain specialised school or unit provision which would also cover the overlap between categories, such as a school or unit for maladjusted children with partial hearing, is administratively quite unviable.

Categories and individual needs

The second Warnock argument against categorisation, that it promotes the idea that all children in the same category have similar educational needs and gives little indication of how best to help the child, raises some very complex questions. Firstly, there is a continuing risk that general categorisation of any kind, whether of health disorders or kinds of educational need, will lead to stereotyping in which significant differences between cases subsumed under a category are overlooked. This applies as much to the new categories of moderate learning difficulties and emotional and behavioural difficulties as to the categories of educational subnormality and partial sightedness.

Secondly, it is mistaken to believe that in the pre-Warnock period special educators did not appreciate the complexity of issues involved in determining the appropriateness of special schooling. For instance, the committee of inquiry into problems relating to partially sighted children (Board of Education, 1934) laid down several general principles to be adopted in this field. One stated that 'The actual amount of myopia should not be the sole factor in determining whether a child be sent to special school'. The loss of education by normal methods was balanced in this situation against the presumed risk of increasing myopia in the ordinary school. The advantages and disadvantages of segregated schooling were also considered (Lightfoot, 1948), even if the conclusions were different from those drawn nowadays.

The explanatory value of categories

A medically based category of disability or difficulty, or even an educational administrative category, may give little direct indication of how best to help an individual child. But this is not in itself sufficient grounds for denying the value of a general category as one important factor in deciding on the direction for developing an individual educational programme. Rejection of categorisation as a valuable activity in health and education arises when the purposes of categorisation become obscure and the use of categories does not serve the interests of individuals. Categorisation or classification schemes are conceptual means of organising information about any kind of phenomenon. Classifications of human phenomena are not fixed and given absolutes, but arise in particular historical and professional contexts and reflect dominant social interests.

Classifications comprise features which are common to different people, situations or methods. In the process of abstracting common features, specific features related to the individual cases are left out. In a medical classification the aim is to identify common features across individual cases in order to achieve some understanding of the relationships between these features and other conditions. The medical category used to describe a child's difficulty or disorder will not, therefore, convey important information about how the particular child differs from others with the same difficulty (Rutter, 1977).

A medical categorisation is designed primarily to identify causal factors associated with a condition, in order that effective medical treatment can be developed and some prediction of future outcomes can be made. As a medically based scheme it does not have any overriding implicatons for educational programmes. Medical categories can and do have a bearing on educational decision making for children with special educational needs, but this does not justify their use in place of educational categories. The traditional dominance of medical categories needs to be understood in terms of the historical role of medical practitioners in educational decision making for children with special educational needs.

The Warnock criticisms of categorisation can be seen to be based on a conflation of medical and educational categorisation. These criticisms are also mistaken in assuming that categorisations of any kind relate directly to individuals and can inform decision making for individual children without taking into account other information about the individual. It is mistaken to believe, for instance, that knowing a child has cerebral palsy or Down's syndrome leads directly to the selection of particular kinds of educational objective and method. This is analogous to the mistaken belief that knowing a child is a boy of junior school age has direct implications for selecting particular educational objectives and methods. The relation between any general category and its use for individuals is a complex one. It becomes more important to appreciate this complexity when the category is used in significant decision making about individuals.

Categories and resource allocation

The third Warnock argument against categorisation was that it draws resources away from children who need help but do not fit the category. This point is not about medical categorisation but about the use of educational categories in the allocation of resources. The criticism is aimed at the difference in resources available for those children who were sufficiently handicapped to be in special schools and those who had special educational needs which did not require special school — the difference between what is often called the 2 per cent and the 18 per cent.

What is at issue here is not the principle of categorisation as such, but its form and use in the context of scarce educational resources. Resource allocation decisions involve giving additional resources to certain children. This requires establishing some means of identifying which children to include and which to exclude. Where extra resources are mainly allocated through placement at a special school or unit, it is likely that the identification will involve from an administrative viewpoint an all or none categorisation — handicapped or not. This has led to the difficulties identified by the Warnock Report. However, these difficulties arise from the way in which additional resources are allocated to separate institutions, not from categorisation as such. Without some categorisation of children with special educational needs who are not in special schools, there would be no basis for asserting that certain children were not receiving the additional provision they needed.

Labelling and stigma

The fourth Warnock argument against categorisation involved the effects of identifying and labelling children as handicapped. This position recognises that stigma and stereotyping have adverse effects on people with disabilities. However, it is too simple to attribute these problems only to statutory categorisation schemes which are operated for service purposes. As we have seen, categorisation schemes are an administrative means designed to facilitate resource allocation for educational provision. The use of statutory categories can accentuate negative prejudices and stereotypes, but they are not the only source of discrimination. There are also non-statutory, social and interpersonal sources.

The Warnock Report's criticisms of categorisation also need to be seen in the context of the Committee's own recommendations for a set of educationally relevant categories: children with specific, mild, moderate and severe learning difficulties. It was not made clear in the Report to what extent it was expected that these categories would lessen the negative effects of labelling. Perhaps the Committee considered that the term 'special educational needs' would become a statutory concept which would operate as an administrative category for allocating additional resources.

A POSITIVE APPROACH WHICH INCLUDES CATEGORIES

What is very valuable about Warnock thinking is the move to recognise, firstly, the particular social sphere in which handicap arises and, secondly, the influence of factors in the child's environment, in addition to the factors which the child brings to the learning situation. By starting from an educational perspective, handicaps or obstacles to educational progress can be considered directly without presuming that there are obstacles or handicaps which operate similarly in all spheres of activity. By recognising assets and deficiencies in the environment and in the child (Wedell, 1980), it is also possible to avoid simplistic conceptions that the only handicapping effects derive from the child's deficiencies.

Working from these assumptions about the specificity of handicap to different spheres of social activity and the range of factors which contribute to handicap, it is possible to outline an approach to learning difficulties which includes significant aspects of current thinking and a role for educational categories.

The identification of child characteristics, both assets and deficits which are relevant to learning in an educational sphere, depends on what counts as worthwhile educational goals. What counts as normal and handicapped in an educational sense depends on which educational goals are emphasised (Wilson and Cowell, 1984). If, for example, social–emotional goals, such as the ability to make friends and show patience, were valued more highly than intellectual goals, then emotional and character traits would feature more highly in the identification of learning difficulties. Form this perspective we can understand how Warnock thinking can claim that 'a boy with one leg suffers a gross and obvious physical disability which excludes him from many activities, but which may not prevent his making as good academic progress as his non-handicapped fellows' (DES, 1978, para. 3.3, p. 36). The validity of this claim depends on distinguishing between academic and educational progress. The significance of a physical disability for educational progress depends on the nature of the disability and what counts as educational progress. If physical education were as highly prized as academic education in schools, then physical disability would be seen as preventing educational progress.

It is also assumed in this approach that other personal characteristics can increase or reduce the educational implications of a difficulty or disability (Wedell, 1980). Environmental factors can similarly operate in a compensatory or aggravating way. This complex interaction of personal and environmental factors — compensatory interaction — within the context of differing educational values is sometimes taken to imply what is called a relativity of educational handicap or special educational needs (Wedell, 1983).

A problem with the term 'relativity', in the phrase 'relativity of special educational needs', is that it can be taken to have different implications. The implication taken here is that special educational needs depend on an educational value framework and arise out of complex causal interactions. However, relativity of special educational needs is often taken to imply that there is also no educational handicap or special needs in any real or definitive sense; that it is merely a matter of subjective perspective. It is in this second sense that the relative approach is thought to replace a categorisation approach.

In the approach proposed in this book, it will be argued that an interactive perspective on special educational needs is not only consistent with the need to categorise but requires it. The mistake in the Warnock approach is to confound medical categories of child disorder and disability with categories of special educational need and provision. The value of categories is borne out by the Warnock proposal to differentiate between different kinds or forms of learning difficulty. I will argue in later chapters that the effective use of an interactive approach also requires categorisation of the child and environmental causal factors underlying special educational needs.

The popular view that categories have been abandoned has been welcome to many educators who place great value on the individuality of a child's needs. The interpretation of the relative, interactive approach which sees special educational needs as a matter of subjective perspective is associated with this emphasis. It promises an escape from what are seen as inappropriate scientific attempts to categorise people's deficiencies as a basis for mechanistic treatments or interventions. This interpretation of the relative, interactive approach is based on assumptions about what and how it is possible to know about human beings — a view of the human sciences which gives precedence to the individual case over generalities. The philosophical assumptions underlying this position will be taken up in later chapters, though it is relevant to refer here to another orientation which gives greater weight to the use of generalities and the prospects of knowing about human beings. In this orientation, an interactive approach requires general classification and categorisation as a basis for explanation, but of both child and environmental characteristics which contribute to learning difficulties.

CONCLUSION

In concluding this chapter on abolishing categories of handicap, it is interesting to ask how the Warnock Committee and others made the mistaken identification of the handicapped with special schooling and the non-handicapped with ordinary schooling. There was much historical evidence, quoted in the Report itself, that there had been children with difficulties and disabilities in the ordinary school (Galloway, 1985).

One way of understanding this confusion of an educational administrative definition of handicap and a more broadly based definition is to see it in the light of the move towards integrating children with more severe difficulties and disabilities in ordinary schools. A broader concept of special was introduced by rejecting the concept of handicap associated with special schools and 'discovering' the 18 per cent of children with difficulties in ordinary schools. The advantage of this broader concept is that it enabled the similarities between children in special schools — 'the handicapped' — and children in ordinary schools — 'the non-handicapped' — to be highlighted. An integrated conceptual framework was, therefore, set up by associating the term 'handicapped' with special schools, then rejecting the term 'handicap' and introducing the term 'special educational needs', which spans ordinary and special schools. Such a reconceptualisation promotes the idea that appropriate education for children with special needs would be in the ordinary school.

I have argued that behind the Warnock rhetoric of abolishing categories lie complex issues which need to be explored and not taken as easily resolved. As the argument in this chapter illustrates, the central importance of values in education is evident in an educational perspective on disability and in the social movement towards educating children with special educational needs in ordinary schools. The distinction between categories of child disorder and categories of special educational need and provision opens up questions about the nature and the relationship between different categorisation systems. Underlying this are questions about the dependability and usefulness of using categories in identifying childhood disorders and disabilities. These questions are addressed in the next chapter.

2

Identifying childhood disabilities and difficulties

INTRODUCTION

In suggesting a place for medical and educational categories in Chapter 1, I need to consider the criticism that some categories of childhood disorder and special educational need are not definable and dependable, that they are non-normative. I will discuss the dependability issue in this chapter mainly in terms of the reliability of assessment in the areas of emotional, behavioural, intellectual and reading difficulties. I will try to show that there are some problems with dependability for moderate or intermediate degrees of these conditions. These problems are not, however, only for non-organic or non-normative conditions, such as learning or emotional difficulties. There is evidence that the more severe or marked degrees of these conditions can be identified in fairly dependable ways. This conclusion is significant because it casts doubt on the position that the so-called non-normative conditions merely reflect value judgements. It also calls into question causal models which focus exclusively on biological or social factors. It will be argued that there are value judgements involved in assessing all conditions. The case is also made for a bio-psycho-social causal model, which considers the multiple role of biological, psychological and sociological levels of causal analysis. The chapter concludes with a discussion of the contribution which such a model can make to the co-ordination of different services for children with special educational needs.

NORMATIVE AND NON-NORMATIVE CONDITIONS

Tomlinson (1985, p. 269) has argued that 'the whole concept of special needs is ambiguous and tautological. It has become part of the rhetoric that serves little educational purpose'. Her point is that, while the concept of special educational needs has expanded the system of special education, the identification problem of deciding who has special needs has not been overcome. The kind of sociological analysis from which this argument derives will be discussed in Chapter 4, but the point that the concept of special educational needs conflates normative — the definable — and non-normative — the less definable — difficulties will be addressed here. To quote:

> [T]here can be some normative agreement about certain categories of handicap or need — such as blind, deaf, epileptic, severe mental handicap. These conditions affect children from all social classes and occupational groupings. On the other hand, categories such as educationally subnormal, maladjusted, disruptive are not normative. There are no adequate measuring instruments or agreed criteria to decide on these particular categories — for example, the inclusion of children in a category of 'disruptive' depends on value judgements, and there can be legitimate arguments between professionals, parents and others as to what constitutes the category.
> (Barton and Tomlinson, 1984, p. 7)

The above distinction parallels one made in medicine between organic and functional disorder. In organic disorders, the disorder is attributed to organic defects or pathologies, whereas in functional disorders, psycho-social factors are considered to predominate.

By separating out some conditions as non-normative, certain sociologists are trying to highlight that some assessment is not based on objective considerations and derives from value judgements over which there can be disagreements. To examine these claims it is necessary first to consider some of the evidence about the dependability of assessing functional or so-called non-normative conditions.

THE DEPENDABILITY OF ASSESSMENT

There has been a notable lack of systematic research into the reliability and validity of assessing childhood difficulties, though there has been more from a medical than an educational perspective. In this section I will discuss some of the issues involved in assessing childhood emotional, behavioural, intellectual and reading difficulties. The reason for considering these conditions is that they are supposed to be less definable and there is also some relevant and detailed evidence from the classic Isle of Wight study (Rutter et al., 1970).

From a health service perspective it is important to distinguish between the identification of children who are referred to a clinic setting and those identified in the wider community — a community diagnosis, sometimes referred to as an epidemiological approach (Yule, 1981). The significance of an epidemiological approach for this discussion is in revealing the difficulties in drawing the dividing line between normality and disorder in intermediate cases for a whole population. This is why the Isle of Wight study is so relevant to this discussion.

Psychiatric disorder

Psychiatric assessment usually differs from school-based assessments of emotional and behavioural difficulties in also taking parental reports into account. It follows from this that the concept of psychiatric disorder does not relate directly to education-based categories, such as 'disruptive' or 'behaviour difficulties'. Psychiatric assessment also involves a clinical interview, while education-based assessments usually depend on anecdotal reports and inventories completed by teachers and sometimes co-ordinated and interpreted by educational psychologists in a school setting.

Rutter (1977) interprets the reliability data from the Isle of Wight study to indicate 'quite high levels of reliability' for community diagnosis of the presence/absence of disorder. Agreement between two psychiatrists in this study was 90 per cent for definite or marked disorder, but only 51 per cent for less marked or intermediate degrees of disorder. A similar discrepancy was found between marked and intermediate ratings of parental interview schedules. This discrepancy is significant because research indicates that there can be a large minority of childen at these intermediate levels (Rutter et al., 1970; Davie et al., 1972). Even for different kinds of disorder there are difficulties in identifying pure types of neurotic and conduct disorder. In the Isle of Wight study, for example, about 25 per cent of those assessed as having a neurotic or conduct disorder had mixed signs and symptoms.

The relatively low reliability of intermediate degrees of psychiatrically assessed difficulties has also to be seen in the context of the differing incidences of difficulties between home and school settings. Surveys show that difficulties are specific to certain situations (Rutter et al., 1970). Children who, for example, are aggressive at school may not be so at home and vice versa. There is also a tendency for the incidence of difficulties assessed to be higher in school settings than in clinical settings (Davie et al., 1972). One interpretation of this difference is that the psychiatric perspective takes information about behaviour and emotional reactions at home into account. Another complementary interpretation is that health and education professionals take different starting positions. Health professionals work from the most severely disordered end of a continuum of difficulties. Ordinary school teachers start from the average child end of a continuum. These different starting points and perspectives are associated with their different areas of responsibility.

Intellectual difficulties

There are parallel assessment issues in the area of intellectual difficulties. The usual cut-off in this field has been an IQ of 70 or below. As in the case of emotional and behavioural difficulties, there are doubts about the reliability of assessment for the relatively large proportion of children with IQs around the 70 level. Despite the availability of technical psychometric data about reliability and validity, the interpretation of these data raises as many questions as they settle. High retest correlations of 0.80 conceal considerably more instability than is apparent. For example, such correlations are consistent with changes of between 15 and 30 IQ points in 58 per cent of a sample (Honzik et al., 1948). Longitudinal studies also reveal changes. For example, there were changes between the ages of 5 and 11 years of up to 15 IQ points for a quarter of a sample studied (Hindley and Owen, 1978).

Like the assessment methods for psychiatric disorders, the IQ method is not a measure of an underlying causal mechanism. It is a direct index of current intellectual functioning, and is at the same level of analysis as the school and other educational skills and knowledge. It is an aggregate measure which is made up of specific areas of functioning which can vary considerably in the same child. For example, 20 per cent of 8½-year-olds were found to have at least 17-point IQ differences between their scores on the verbal and performance scales of the WISC-R test (Kaufman, 1980).

There has been a movement, particularly in the USA, to define a notion of intellectual retardation in terms of significantly sub-average intellectual functioning and deficits in adaptive behaviour (American Association of Mental Deficiency). The move towards assessing adaptive behaviour is relatively recent and can be seen as one way of resolving aspects of the IQ controversy. However, although adaptive assessment introduces a wider range of domains than those covered by IQ tests, such as physical development, economic activity and domestic activity, the problems of reliability, validity and cut-off points are in principle no different. The effects of using the adaptive behaviour criterion is to reduce the number of children identified in the mild range, where most children scoring below 70 IQ are found. In a US study, for example, only 35 per cent of 300 children scoring between 50 and 70 IQ levels were below the cut-off for adaptive behaviour, thus reducing the proportion of children with mild intellectual retardation by 65 per cent (Mastenbrook quoted in Sattler, 1982).

The practice in this country has been to use IQ tests, which is based on a traditional school curriculum notion of intellectual functioning. From the broader school curriculum viewpoint, the range of intellectual operations included in the IQ tests has been limited, both in terms of psychological classifications of intellectual operations, e.g. there are few items covering divergent cognitive operations (Guildford, 1967), and in terms of curriculum concepts of worthwhile areas of school learning and experience, e.g. artistic and technical design skills. These limitations are hardly surprising given the historical and administrative context of the design of IQ tests as a method for fine tuning the practice of selecting children assessed as unable to benefit from ordinary schooling.

There are a number of specific uncertainties about the use of IQ tests in this field, some of which will be mentioned briefly. In using a cut-off point on the IQ scale, the way in which the average scores are initially set or standardised is critical. As the average score varies, so will the number of children falling above or below the cut-off. If the average is based on a group which does not adequately represent all children for whom the test may be used, then the test will not be suitable for subgroups not included in the original standardisation of the test. Some IQ tests have not included certain ethnic minority and special school groups, and are therefore suspect for identifying low scorers from these groups as having intellectual difficulties.

Reading difficulties

As in the other two areas considered, there are similar issues about the identification of reading difficulties. One influential approach to reading difficulties has been to distinguish between two groups, those whose reading levels are significantly below their expected age level — reading backward (RB) — and those whose reading levels are significantly below the level expected given both their age and intellectual levels — specific reading retardation (SRR) (Rutter and Yule, 1975). The reading retardation group can be seen as representing unexpected reading difficulties, which have been associated with terms like 'dyslexia' and 'learning disability'.

Rutter and Yule (1975) ground their two-way classification of children with reading difficulties on associated differences between the RB and SRR groups: differences in sex ratio, occurrence of neurological and motor abnormalities, language complexity and future educational progress in reading and mathematics. Although this classification has avoided certain assessment difficulties by using sophisticated regression methods, there has been little evidence that the method identifies a stable group of children across age and reading tests. For example, in a recent

New Zealand study by Share and Silva (1986) it was found that of the 44 children identified at age 7 as having SRR, only 57 per cent (25 children) were also identified two or four years later. For the children at the ages of 9 and 11, 25 per cent and 36 per cent identified as having SRR were not identified at other ages. The authors concluded that the findings indicate 'substantial stability' across ages. Another interpretation, however, is that there is a core of children who show a stable pattern of SRR, the ones with the most severe reading difficulties, and that some children show a different pattern which takes them outside the cut-offs for the SRR group. This interpretation is consistent with the view that there is a continuum of reading difficulties which cannot be classified simply in two distinct groups.

Recent Dutch researchers (van der Wissel and Zegers, 1985) argue that there are strong grounds for abandoning the SRR/RB distinction and that most of the reported differences can be explained by fairly general principles. Their argument relates to the hump at the tail of the normal distribution of difference scores (the difference between expected and actual reading levels), where Rutter and Yule identified the SRR group. The hump is attributed to a ceiling in the reading test used and is not taken to indicate the presence of a distinct group of reading underachievers. The difference in sex ratios in the two groups can be explained in terms of the mean differences in reading between the sexes. Although there is some current disagreement about whether other differences between the SRR and RB groups can also be explained, this work does indicate that there are problems with this IQ-based classification of reading difficulties. Research may yet lead to meaningful classification of children's reading difficulties, but this is likely to be based on work into the processes which cause failure (Frith, 1985).

Social and ethnic bias

In discussing the dependability of assessment it is important to consider issues concerned with cultural relevance and fairness. This cannot be dealt with in depth here, but is relevant to the overselection of children from lower socio-economic backgrounds to special schooling (Tomlinson, 1982; Coard, 1971). Though there has also been some concern in connecton with behaviour difficulties, it will be considered here in terms of intellectual functioning. The use of IQ tests as measures of children's intelligence assumes that all children are equally familiar with the materials and have had similar opportunities to develop test-related skills and abilities. This question is about the culture fairness of tests, which is at the heart of the IQ controversy.

It is often argued that if there have been different opportunities for development, then different IQ scores are not attributable to 'real abilities'. Consider the case of a child with an IQ score of 65, who comes from a cultural background which places a different value compared to the dominant cultural group on those character-istics sampled in IQ tests. One position is that an IQ score of below 70 does not mean that she is really 'retarded' as her score can be attributed to the background differences. One of the diffi-culties with this position is that it is caught between two critically distinct interpretations of IQ performance: (a) as a measure of current intellectual functioning (a current outcome), and (b) as a measure of true basic intellectual potential or ability (inherent starting potential).

The importance and implications of this distinction will be pur-sued in the discussion on equality in Chapter 8. For the present it is important to be clear that the evidence, some already referred to briefly, is consistent with the first current functioning interpre-tation. Although IQ measures are predictive of future school learn-ing outcomes, they are not particularly good predictors compared to other predictors, such as prior spelling and mathematics mea-sures (Woods, 1987). There is a widespread and profound misconception that IQ is a measure of true basic intellectual potential. This interpretation is implicit in the importance given to traditional psychological assessment of IQ and its use in identifying children and others who have the ability to benefit from particular oppor-tunities and experiences.

What is involved in this traditional practice is not just a system of testing as such, but the complex process of meeting the needs of particular social systems to match individuals to different oppor-tunities and kinds of social provision. In part the system of employing psychologists to use IQ tests developed historically in order to meet such system needs. Special schools were established to satisfy what were seen as the needs of ordinary schools at an administrative level and the needs of individual children who were not making satisfactory progress. Whether system and individual needs were effectively met, and which were predominant, are important issues. But, given that the education system functioned in this separatist way, some procedure for deciding which children could cope and be coped with in the ordinary school was required.

A new set of procedures, operated by the emerging professional psychologists, came to replace the means used by medical officers and by ordinary school teachers. To justify these new procedures they needed to be more systematic and predictive of school coping than the prior methods. One way of gaining acceptance for the procedures was to interpret the test results as a measure of basic or natural potential to benefit from ordinary school. This interpretation was in tune with the meritocratic ethos at the turn of the last century which equated merit with ability/intelligence (Sutherland, 1984). To establish the legitimacy of the use of IQ tests it was therefore useful to treat them as measures of basic potential. Yet it is interesting to note that even at that time there were some doubts in educational circles about this assumption (Sutherland, 1984).

The above discussion implies that it is crucial to be clear about the implications of attributing low ability or intelligence to someone. The problem is complicated by the fact that it is difficult to set a limit to an ability of potential. It is hard to know if an as yet unfound condition may reveal some potential. Let us return to the case of the girl with an IQ score of 65 from a minority or lower socio-economic background. From the previous argument, it follows that there is no known way of assessing her basic potential. Even if there were, or if based on other evidence she was found to have potential for higher achievements, the environmental means of enabling her to realise it would have to be found.

To realise potential requires educational opportunities and resources which are scarce or possibly unavailable. Relevant resources could be unavailable through economic scarcity and/or lack of know-how. The result may be that the girl does not develop to her full potential. This may be a major factor in her having moderate learning difficulties. Initial constitutional factors or personal factors acquired during development may in addition contribute to the moderate learning difficulties There are also no simple ways of altering either type of broad casual factor, environmental or personal, without some cost to others.

Not to be overlooked in this discussion is the social value placed on intellectual functioning and, by implication, the low valuation or devaluation of intellectual difficulties. What is valued socially about human functioning determines what individual characteristics have low evaluation. Although different societies might value different characteristics, they differ not in whether value is placed on individual characteristics; they differ in which characteristics are valued, the manner and style of evaluation and the degree of tolerance for deviations from valued characteristics.

This means that the extent, significance and social implications of how low intellectual functioning is evaluated can vary, not that evaluating ceases to be a social possibility. It is a matter of much concern that the bearers of characteristics with low evaluation, such as intellectual difficulties, become devalued or stigmatised as persons generally. But this is distinct from the low evaluation of particular characteristics, such as low intellectual functioning. The distinction is between a person and his or her particular characteristics. It is central to the point that medical and other classification systems are of features and characteristics common to different people, and not of people as individuals (Rutter, 1977).

What has emerged from the discussion so far is that there is most disagreement in identification in the moderate or mild ranges of the continuum of functioning. This disagreement also relates to other childhood difficulties and not just to intellectual ones. The question of identifying difficulties and disorders also depends on what counts as the particular area of functioning in question. With the assumption of a continuum of functioning, a cut-off or threshold has also to be set along this continuum. This will be discussed in the next section.

CUT-OFFS AND VALUE JUDGEMENTS

Gipps et al. (1985) have pointed out that the categories of mental deficiency (Burt, 1921), intellectual retardation (Rutter et al., 1970) and educational subnormality have been based on administrative criteria which are related to the number of available places at special schools. Burt is quoted to support this position: 'mental deficiency must be treated as an administrative category rather than a psychological one' because the cut-off 'corresponded with the general practice of the more experienced teachers and school medical officers, when nominating or certifying cases in need of education at special school' (Burt, 1921, p. 81). The Gipps point is that the setting of cut-offs has always been arbitrary and that problems arise when these cut-offs are treated as having 'substantive rather than statistical justification' (Gipps et al., 1985, p. 6).

There seems to be no basis for asserting that cut-offs are arbitrary and without substance because they are based on administrative criteria. As the above discussion has suggested, there is some uncertainty about identifying children with moderate difficulties. This uncertainty does not imply, however, that applying a cut-off is arbitrary in the sense of being random or that any cut-off could be chosen along the continuum. An IQ cut-off of 70 which corresponded to the general identification practice of experienced teachers and medical officers was a criterion which had a certain rationale, even if there were variations between these professionals.

There is a clear distinction to be made between the number of children considered to be in need of special schooling and the number of children actually offered such schooling. The difference could be attributed to several factors, in particular the resources available to meet the demand for such schooling. When the cut-off is based on the actual number of available places, then this can be criticised for not taking account of the number of children considered to be in need as a result of difficulties in the ordinary schools. A cut-off which is based on the number of children having difficulties in ordinary schools does not correspond, therefore, to the number of available places.

When cut-offs are called arbitrary, this is a criticism of the unjustified and negative aspects of identifying children for special education. It is understandable that we find it disturbing to use categories with strong undignified connotations, particularly when these descriptions are taken to refer to natural and unalterable negative characteristics of individual children. What also underlies these concerns about cut-offs are value judgements about the children which teachers in ordinary schools should or should not be expected to teach (Galloway, 1985). The cut-offs represent the means by which the ordinary school system withdraws responsibility for teaching certain children. It is to be expected, therefore, that the way schools cope with children with special needs will be judged according to positions taken on the responsibility issue.

MEDICAL MODELS

The discussion, to summarise, has led to the view that there are grounds for questioning some aspects of the reliability of the identification of childhood disorders and difficulties. This is mainly for the intermediate degrees of emotional, behavioural, intellectual and reading difficulties. On the other hand, with more severe degrees of these difficulties there is evidence of higher reliability. It is important at this stage in the discussion to distinguish between the reliability and the validity of identification. Reliability is easier to establish but does not guarantee validity, which depends on showing that the condition identified has a particular pattern of causation and outcome. For this reason it is inaccurate, strictly speaking, to equate the organic–functional distinction with the normative–non-normative one. The latter distinction refers to reliability and the former to causation. This implies that the idea that normative conditions are organically based and non-normative ones are psychologically and/or socially based is too simple.

This norm-based distinction is associated with an attempt to restrict the so-called 'medical model' to clear-cut cases of organically caused conditions. It is ironic that those who wish to criticise the medical model resort to such a tight categoric distinction while rejecting categories of disorder and difficulty. The reality of medical models is that they attempt to include organic and social factors in their classification schemes. For example, the Court Report on child health services (DHSS, 1976) distinguished between:

- a disability: as an impairment, imperfection, or disorder of body, intellect or personality; and
- a handicap: as a disability for a substantial period which adversely affects or retards normal growth, development or adjustment to life.

One implication of this distinction is that disabilities may not always be handicapping and that social factors can contribute to a handicap. Secondly, other medical writers have commented that there is no sharp dividing line between order and disorder (Graham, 1980; Quay, 1980; Yule, 1981). Thirdly, modern medical classification systems, such as the World Health Organisation's International Classification of Diseases (ICD9), involve explicit inclusion of psycho-social factors in its multi-axial system.

A norm-based distinction between childhood disorders is untenable for a more basic reason. All disorders, whether they have clear-cut biological causation or not, are identified in the first instance against a set of social norms and values (Kennedy, 1980). In this sense all disorders are normative. What underlies the alleged distinction between normative and non-normative disorders is not the role of social norms and values, but whether there is consensus about the norms used in identifying 'deviance'. Such a consensus is easier to achieve with the most severe instances of disorder or difficulty than it is with more moderate and mild difficulties.

What is at issue here is the inherent evaluative aspect of identifying disorder, disability or special needs. Those commentators who reveal the hidden evaluative aspects of some areas of difficulties are missing the crucial point that all special needs have inherent evaluative aspects. This issue does not divide those who are alleged to support a 'medical model' from those who do not. This is evident in the current interest in social and psychological approaches to health which are critical of an exclusively biological orientation to causation (Morgan et al., 1985).

THE CASE OF PSYCHIATRY

The perennial crises of psychiatry and its use of medical models of disease highlights some of the classificatory and causal questions discussed above. The question of whether medicine in general should concentrate on 'real' disorders which have organic causes or get involved in the psycho-social aspects of malfunctioning has been responded to in two ways in psychiatry. One way is to exclude psychiatry from medicine (exclusionist), while the other is to confine the field strictly to emotional and behavioural disorders caused by brain dysfunctions (reductionist). Szasz (1961) represents the view that mental illness is a myth since illness strictly applies only to conditions with organic causation. People with psychiatric illness or disorders are taken to have 'problems in living' which require re-education and not medical psychiatric treatment. The contrasting view is that emotional and behavioural deviations from the norm are diseases when they have biochemical or neurophysiological causes.

These different responses to mental and behavioural difficulties represent different philosophical assumptions about causation. The reductionist assumption is that real causes are at the biochemical or neurophysiological level of analysis, whereas the exclusionist assumption is that malfunctioning has causes at the psychosocial level of analysis. Engel (1977) argues that the current dominant model of illness or malfunctioning is the reductionist one — or what is called the biomedical model. It has achieved this status through its success in certain areas of malfunctioning, but takes on the role of a dogma because it is thought to be applicable to all areas of malfunctioning.

Engel points out, from a wider historical and social perspective, that malfunctioning has always been behavioural, psychological and social in nature at a descriptive stage. Societies have typically evolved institutions and nominated individuals to describe, evaluate and intervene correctively. Current classification systems in the biomedical tradition are an attempt not only to classify conditions in terms of presenting difficulties, but to seek organic causes and so to move from a descriptive to a particular kind of causal scheme. The main thrust of Engel's position is that there is a need to broaden the current dominant medical approach to malfunctioning to include psycho-social and biological levels of causal analysis — to be neither exclusionist nor reductionist. To do this the organic and functonal, the somatic and the mental or psychological disorders need to be considered in the same terms within a common framework. When biological or psycho-social analyses of both kinds of disorder are excluded, according to Engel, this will interfere with effective service delivery. Psychosocial factors are seen as critical in several ways: in explaining how biochemical defects come to be manifest as experienced illness, when the manifest illness develops, whether the person comes to see him/herself as sick and whether biochemical treatment restores functioning

THE BIO-PSYCHO-SOCIAL MODEL

This line of argument leads towards a bio-psycho-social model which takes fuller account of the social and professional role of the medical practitioners. The cut-off between functioning and malfunctioning is not seen as clear and sharp, as it is affected not only by biological characteristics but also by psychological and social factors. This does not imply, however, that it is arbitrary in the sense that it could be drawn anywhere. Biological indices are not the only criteria used in defining disorder or disease. Social and psychological criteria are also factors in identifying illness. Whether a person experiences a condition as an 'illness' or a 'problem in living' is from her or his perspective to do with whether she or he accepts the sick role and seeks entry into a health care system. Some people deny illness when there are organic signs of disorder, others may accept illness when there are no organic signs, and in some borderline conditions it is not clear whether the signs of a negative condition like grief are indicative of disorder or not. In the case of the borderline conditions it depends on what the needs are seen to be, what social arrangements there are for meeting the needs of persons concerned and which occupational group takes responsibility for such provision — whether medical doctors, religious officials, educators, therapeutic professionals or social workers, for example.

The borderline conditions are those in which negative experiences and behaviours can be accounted for in terms of psychological and social levels of analysis, yet there may be bodily disturbances which run their own course. Whether such conditions are seen as illnesses or not depends as much on the social arrangements for coping with the person's experiences as on the severity of a condition like a grief experience. From a historical viewpoint, the medical profession came to take an increasing responsibility for provision in certain areas of human welfare and malfunctioning, such as mental health and disability, and coping with birth and death. This is a reflection of changing patterns of care provision, e.g. from religious to secular agencies, and of the power and social position of the medical profession. It has less to do with the medical profession having exclusive access to the knowledge and skills relevant to provisions in these fields.

A GENERAL SYSTEMS APPROACH

The relevance of the bio-psycho-social model of medical practice to special needs education is in its adoption of a general systems framework (von Bertalanffy, 1968; Weiss, 1969). In a general systems framework it is possible to consider the multiple levels of describing human malfunctioning and relate these to different levels of causation. Human phenomena can be conceptualised as a hierarchy ranging from, for example, nation states to cellular molecules. Each level of the hierarchy is stacked or embedded in the next level; for instance, a single person is the highest level of the organismic hierarchy from cells to organ systems, and at the same time the lowest unit of the social hierarchy. Each level in this hierarchy represents an organised dynamic whole — each unit is therefore a whole from one perspective and a part from another. This framework enables us to consider disability, difficulties and special educational needs from different but related perspectives — organic, personal/psychological and social — without necessarily treating these perspectives as strict alternatives.

In advocating a cross-disciplinary explanatory framework for special needs education, there is a need to guard against expecting it to resolve all long-standing questions. In using a framework which accommodates and relates different levels of description and explanation, there are still problems in knowing which levels to select. These problems can be understood partly in terms of:

- whether causal processes can be identified in operational or concrete terms within a level of analysis or across several levels of analysis;
- whether the aims of interventions are seen as preventive, restorative/remedial or rehabilitative;
- the effectiveness of the interventions in terms of the aims;
- the practicablity of mounting the interventions in the short and longer term;
- the availability of financial and human resources.

Uncertainties and disagreements in these broad areas — for example, in the accurate identification of causal processes or the practicability of an intervention — would be expected. In these circumstances, there are likely to be different views about the appropriateness of different levels of analysis.

CONCLUSION

Despite its limitations, a general systems framework does at least open up the possibilities of a more complex, multi-level orientation. This framework makes it more difficult to see causal perspectives that are often posed as dichotomies (for example, social versus biological) as strictly incompatible and opposite. The strength of the systems orientation is in requiring that more than one level of description, analysis and intervention be considered. As such this framework provides a basis for a more common and integrated explanatory approach within which different particular causal analyses can be located and pursued.

One major implication of this chapter is that there is no incompatibility between medical and educational models for children with disorders and difficulties. This position depends, however, on having a cross-disciplinary explanatory framework, like the general systems one. For medical and educational approaches to be complementary, it is also necessary to be clear about the relative importance of developmental and remedial/rehabilitative goals for these children. This question will be discussed in more detail in Chapter 4, which concerns the curriculum for special educational needs.

By aiming for a more integrated descriptive and explanatory scheme, it becomes possible that different professional groups can locate and co-ordinate their own schemes with each other. A systems framework promises to provide the basis upon which different professional groups can co-ordinate the services they offer children with difficulties. These issues are at the heart of some of the professional problems in this field, which will be discussed in more detail in Chapter 7.

3

The 1981 Education Act: its principles and some problems

INTRODUCTION

It is not my intention in this chapter to discuss the detailed provisions, contexts and implementation of the 1981 Education Act. This has been done thoroughly in many other texts (Goacher et al., 1988; Welton et al., 1983; Select Committee Report, 1987). I will identify those aspects of the Act which express some of the conceptual issues raised in the previous chapters which are at the heart of special needs education. By pursuing the arguments about abandoning categories and about the relativity of special educational needs, I will argue that some of the problems associated with implementing the 1981 Act can be attributed to the Warnock approach to categorisation. Criticisms of and alternatives to individual statements of special educational needs as a means of additional resource allocation will also be discussed. The chapter concludes with some proposals about the respective roles of central and local government in determining special educational practice. There will also be some mention of the Education Reform Act 1988, as it might affect the operation of the 1981 Act. Other aspects of the 1988 Act will be discussed in the concluding chapter.

BACKGROUND AND PRINCIPLES OF THE 1981 ACT

There have been varied interpretations of the background of the Act. Some commentators see the Act as representing a significant advance in the principles and practices of education for those with special educational needs (Wedell, 1988a). The Act in this interpretation largely incorporates the key principles about the nature of special educational needs recommended by the Warnock Report (1978). Russell (1986) considers its significance in terms of being the first time that special education legislation included a broad concept of civil rights and a recognition of the role of parents in educational decision making. Other commentators from a more critical social perspective see it less as a radical departure and more as a reformulation of previous underlying assumptions and social practices (Tomlinson and Barton, 1984).

One characteristic of the Act as an expression of government policy derives partly from the tradition of general legislative formulation in which details are presented in the form of circulars which only have the force of recommendations. It is not clear, therefore, what kinds of sanction would be taken against non-compliant LEAs. This aspect of the 1981 Act has been portrayed positively as an example of enabling legislation which is based on good practice and goodwill (Goacher et al., 1988). As such this style of legislation represents the end of an era of educational policy which has now been replaced by more directive and pre-scriptive educational legislation. The conditional duty on LEAs to educate children with special educational needs in ordinary schools can be seen as an expression of the ideals of comprehensive schooling which arose and crystallised in the 1960s and 1970s. Although there had been prior legislation which recognised the integration principle, in the 1976 Education Act, it had not been a central part of previous legislation.

The most significant aspect of the context of implementing the 1981 Act was that its enactment occurred at a time when the government was cutting back on local government spending. This can now be seen as part of an attempt to restructure local government finance and the public services, including the education system itself. This wider context of the administration of education in England and Wales is also relevant to the impact of the 1981 Act. The Act depended for its implementation on the commitment of semi-autonomous LEAs and the system of partnership which existed between central and local government. The other main contextual aspect was the interdependence of the education, health and social services for the implementation of the Act, in terms of both the assessment procedures and the provision of services.

Goacher et al. (1988) have analysed the principles and content of the legislation in terms of three broad headings: (a) the nature of special educational needs; (b) the rights of those with special educational needs and of parents; and (c) concern for effectiveness in identifying, assessing and meeting special educational needs. Section 1 of the Act is about definitions and the nature of special educational needs. These will be discussed in more detail later in this chapter. Sections 2 and 3 are about provision of special education. Section 2 also includes a subsection about the duty of LEAs to secure special education provision in ordinary school. The issues involved here will be discussed in more detail in Chapter 4. Section 2 also places duties on LEAs and school governors in relation to the provision for children with special educational needs. Sections 4 to 10, the largest part of the Act, are about the identification of individual children with special educational needs. It is in these sections that the rights of parents are recognised in relation to statutory assessment procedures and appeals about the provision offered in a statement. These rights were limited, however, by not making the appeal committee's decisions binding on LEAs and by denying parents the same rights of school choice as other parents under the Education Act 1980.

AN EVALUATION OF THE 1981 ACT

A DES-funded evaluation of the implementation of the 1981 Act concluded that there was fundamental agreement with the principles underlying the legislation and that serious attempts were made to put it into operation (Goacher et al., 1988). Awareness about children with special educational needs had increased in LEAs and there had been a substantial increase in the number of children with special educational needs receiving education in ordinary schools. This finding contrasts with previous assertions about the increasing numbers of children going into special schools (Swann, 1983). There was evidence, too, of flexible and experimental responses to individual needs, increases in pre-school provision and some notable examples of LEAs reviewing their overall policy and practice in this field (Fish Report, 1985). However, there was a major concern amongst those responsible for the effectiveness of services that there had been inadequate resourcing to carry out their full duties for children with special educational needs.

The main difficulties which were identified in the study have been summarised recently as part of a two-year follow-up to the evaluation project (Evans et al., 1989). This project, 'Decision making for special needs', was concerned with designing resources to promote organisational and management development in the services for children with special educational needs. These findings were organised under six general themes.

1. A shared understanding

There was a widespread lack of understanding of certain key ideas about the nature of special educational needs: for example, whether the term 'special educational needs' included children with less severe difficulties, what types of provision came under the umbrella of 'special' educational provision and whether children had to have a statement to have access to such provision. There were also disputes about whether some special provision, such as speech therapy, was 'educational'.

2. Communication difficulties

Communication difficulties were found at several levels, about individuals, about services and about policies. Failures to communicate effectively about children could be attributed partly to the lack of a shared understanding of ideas about special educational needs mentioned above. Such communication is also dependent on effective cross-service interaction between education, health and social services. There was also some lack of knowledge about what other agencies could offer. Another difficulty was communication about policies developed in one service, e.g. LEAs, which would have consequences for the delivery of another service, e.g. speech therapy by the health authority.

3. Recording of needs and demands for provision

One of the most significant findings was that the demand for resources was being masked because education and health services were not always explicit about children's needs and the shortfalls in resources to meet these needs. There were difficulties in recording which arose out of the context of the new notion of special educational needs and which made it more difficult to keep systematic records of those children receiving special education provision. This highlighted the need for a central system of LEA records which could co-ordinate with systems used by school health and social services.

4. Statutory assessment procedures

The statutory assessment procedure laid down in the 1981 Education Act is designed to ensure a multi-disciplinary assessment of children's special educational needs. It is also intended to ensure the rights of parents and to safeguard the accountability of decision-makers to parents and to the community. A common finding was that statements were worded in vague generalities. This undermines the function of the statement as a means of ensuring parent and child rights for the effective monitoring of provision. It can also affect adversely the quality of information available for planning and delivering special services. Another major finding was of delays in completing the statutory procedures in some LEAs. These delays are related to the requirements to consult and inform parents. However, delays have also been attributed to the slowness of professionals in submitting their advice. In most LEAs the time to completion was more than three months on average. Despite the requirements to involve parents, the question of how parents can be supported and how professionals can be more open with them was also a continuing problem.

5. Distribution of resources

It was very difficult to change the pattern of special education resourcing. Despite the move towards supporting more children with special needs in ordinary schools, there was opposition from some teachers and heads who wanted to see the old system continue. It was found that few LEAs had undertaken a review of their special educational provision in the light of the new Act, such as the Inner London Education Authority had in the Fish Report.

6. Management of cross-service change

In requiring different services (LEAs, social services and district health authorities) to work together in providing services for the same client group, policy and practice in one service necessarily affects practice in the other services. It was found that there was insufficient cross-service review of practice and provision before changes were decided and implemented. The need for ways of managing change across services was highlighted.

THE 1981 ACT CONCEPT OF SPECIAL EDUCATIONAL NEEDS

At the heart of the 1981 Education Act is the new definition of special educational needs which derives from the principles laid out in the Warnock Report, some of which were discussed in Chapter 1. As I argued there, what underlies the 'abandoning of categories' in special needs education is the move towards integration. This involves separating the *delivery* of special education provision from the *location* of delivery in special schools. This is what mainstreaming or integration is about. In the 1944 Education Act, handicap categories were tied to the statutory provision of special education which took place in special schools and units. The move to mainstreaming requires the separation of categories of learning difficulty from the organisation and location of special provision. What is basically at issue is the nature of exceptional educational needs and the kinds of organisation of provision required to meet these needs. This was missed in Warnock's rejection of categories. As experience with implementing the Act indicates, problems with the definition of special educational needs are at the root of many of the practical difficulties summarised above:

- in communication between professionals, parents and education officers;

- in the sharing of a compatible understanding about special provision;
- in the recording of special educational needs and provision;
- in the delays and uncertainties of the statutory assessment procedure.

My contention in this chapter is that the 1981 Education Act has not abandoned categories but has replaced specific categories of educational handicap (1944 Act) by the more general categories of learning difficulty or special educational need. The change can be represented visually as in Figure 3.1.

The main change in the 1981 Act scheme is to loosen the connection between special education provision (SEP) and special schools and units. This is done conceptually by widening the reference of the term 'special educational needs' to include up to 18–20 per cent of children with less severe educational difficulties. As the figure indicates, there is no middle level of description of the different kinds of special need in the 1981 Act scheme, though this does not imply that the definition of special educational needs is relative or circular as is sometimes asserted (Wedell, 1988a). In the 1981 Act, a child is said to have special educational needs if he has a 'learning difficulty which calls for SEP to be made for him'. The term 'learning difficulty' is then defined in terms of:

(a) significantly greater difficulty in learning than the majority of children of his age; or

(b) a disability which either prevents or hinders him from making use of educational facilities of a kind generally provided in schools, within the area of the local authority concerned, for children of his age; or

(c) under the age of 5 years and is or would be if SEP were not made for him, likely to fall within paragraph (a) or (b) when over that age.

(Education Act 1981, section 1(i))

This definition of special educational needs in terms of learning difficulty and then in terms of age norms and disability, though general and not helpful directly in setting specific thresholds or criteria for decision making about special needs, is not circular. Special educational needs are clearly defined in terms other than just special education provision.

That this definition of learning difficulties is left in very general terms can be attributed partly to a particular interpretation of the nature of the concept. In this interpretation there is a reluctance to acknowledge that 'learning difficulties' is more than a description in relation to a specific time and situation, that it is a causal concept that can imply some future learning outcome effects. The

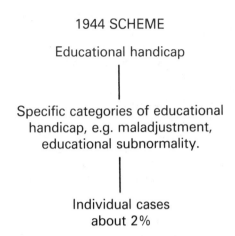

1944 SCHEME

Educational handicap

Specific categories of educational
handicap, e.g. maladjustment,
educational subnormality.

Individual cases
about 2%

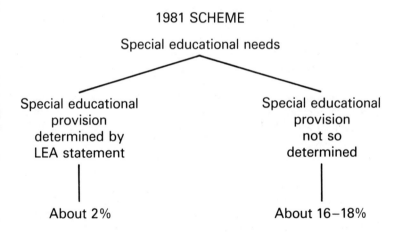

1981 SCHEME

Special educational needs

Special educational
provision
determined by
LEA statement

Special educational
provision
not so
determined

About 2%

About 16–18%

Figure 3.1 *Categories of educational difficulty before and after the 1981 Act*

discussion will now turn to examining some of the underlying
issues connected to this relative, interactive interpretation of learning difficulties.

THE INTERACTIVE APPROACH VERSUS CATEGORISATION: A FALSE OPPOSITION

It is often unclear whether the case for the 'interactive approach'
to special educational needs is the same as the case for the 'relative'

approach. When these terms are used interchangeably it is usually to offer an alternative to the 'categorisation' approach. There seem to be two main aspects to an interactive, relative approach. The first one is that learning difficulties (or special educational needs) have multiple causation in particular educational contexts. In this position special educational needs are thought to depend on inter-actions between personal resources (abilities, skills, motivations, dispositions) and deficits on the one hand, and resources and constraints in the environment on the other. By implication, two children with similar deficits but different personal resources and environment resources and constraints are likely to have different learning difficulties and therefore different special needs. In this position special needs are not necessarily taken as constant across different environmental conditions for a given deficit, from school to school, or class to class, on account of possible changes in environmental factors. Similarly, special educational needs are not necessarily constant over time; there can be changes in either environmental or personal factors.

The second position on the relative, interactive nature of learn-ing difficulties is more relevant to the implications of relativity. It relates to the perceptual or phenomenological view that whether a child has a learning difficulty depends on the perspective of the perceiver. A child may be said to have special educational needs or learning difficulty in one class or school but not in another class or school depending on the comparative performance of other children. When teachers in ordinary schools, for example, some-times refer to a child as having severe learning difficulties, these are not as severe as those found in special schools providing for 'severe learning difficulties'. The attribution of a learning difficulty and the severity of this difficulty can therefore depend on the perspective of the person making the attribution.

What underlies the move from a 'categorisation, within-child' to an 'interactive, relative' framework is a switch in theoretical model. Such theoretical models represent basic concepts and assumptions about the nature of human functioning, abilities and disabilities. They act as a framework which determines the kinds of explanation provided in a field of study. The 'interactive, relative' position involves a theoretical model in which educationally rele-vant causes are found mainly outside people, are considered in specific terms and are thought to be alterable. This conceptual scheme can have the function of fostering a more hopeful and action-oriented approach to disablities and difficulties. This has contributed to its acceptance in a social climate of extending oppor-tunities to disadvantaged groups including those with disabilities.

The appeal of this form of environmentalism rests on beliefs that environmental factors are alterable and that attributions to personal disabilities and deficits lead to despair. These assumptions need to be questioned. Positive actions or interventions to prevent, cure, teach or rehabilitate are by definition environmental actions, but the object of the action may be the environment and/or the person. There are no grounds for believing that altering environmental factors is any more effective or feasible than altering within-person factors. Although working with the alterable in teaching is a practical approach, the concept of what is 'alterable' needs to be based on sophisticated causal assumptions and empirical evidence. What is unalterable today may become alterable in the future. There may also be little commitment to alter what can be altered and this lack of commitment may itself be difficult to influence. As regards the second assumption, there are undoubtedly painful adjustments to be made when disabilities and difficulties are identified, but this does not lead inevitably to helplessness and despair. Even in cases of severe disabilities, positive and hopeful attitudes can be maintained despite the constant challenges of impairment.

A REDEFINED INTERACTIVE CONCEPT OF SPECIAL EDUCATIONAL NEEDS

The above points indicate that there is a false opposition between a 'categorisation, within-child' model and an environmentalist version of an 'interactive, relative' model. There is a third way which combines the better features of both models. I will discuss some of these underlying questions in more detail in Chapter 8. For the present discussion about the concept of special educational needs as part of the legislative framework, the following statements summarise the redefined concept:

- Attributing a learning difficulty depends on explicit or implicit educational objectives, varying as the objectives vary in kind and level.
- Learning difficulties are outcomes of the interaction of child and environmental causal factors.
- These causal factors are sometimes found to be stable over time and consistent across learning situations; at other times they change.
- Describing a causal factor as stable does not necessarily imply that it will be unalterable in the future with the development of new methodologies and techniques.
- The interaction of resources and deficits in the child and the environment can be compensatory or debilitating depending on the strength and severity of the factors. However, there

can be limits to the compensatory impact of resources on outcomes.

- Child factors — both resources and deficits — influence the range of outcomes within which environmental factors can have an impact. Child factors can therefore be useful in informing the selection of educational objectives. These factors are not the only influence on the selection of educational objectives, which should be set in terms of the common educational aims for all.
- In an interactive model the outcomes of an interaction of causal factors — child and environmental — can influence or act directly as entry factors for subsequent learning.
- The purpose of categorising child and environmental factors is to enable some degree of prediction or anticipation of possible future learning progress.

The purpose of proposing a reconstructed interactive model is to revive and endorse the positive and appropriate use of categories in the special needs field. This has to be distinguished from the negative use of categories, which involves:

- exaggerating the differences between children with ordinary and exceptional educational needs;
- treating all children who have a particular deficit as the same educationally;
- segregating, distancing and devaluing children as persons merely on account of their having a deficit.

Categories of resources and deficits are useful in so far as they inform educational decision-making about the selection of relevant objectives, methods and learning activities. There will inevitably be areas of uncertainty about the likely outcomes of the interactions of resources and deficits within the child and between the child and the environment. Where such uncertainties exist they need to be recognised openly and the resulting difficulties of prediction have to be taken into account in decision-making about appropriate educational provision. There are likely to be fewer uncertainties at the more severe levels of deficit, though even here the degree of uncertainty depends on the degree of specificity required and the time scale involved in predicting outcomes. In any case, using categories in description, explanation and prediction only gives indications to the extent that different individual cases show similar patterns of response. There remains the need for individual information to be taken into account to qualify these indications from the general case. In principle, ideas about the

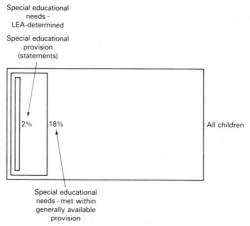

Figure 3.2 *Legal categories of special educational need*

general case will be modified in the light of information from individual cases.

LEGAL CATEGORIES OF SPECIAL EDUCATIONAL NEED

The effect of the general definitions of special educational needs in the 1981 Act is to establish two general boundaries which separate:

- those who have special educational needs from those who do not;
- those with special educational needs whose needs are met through 'generally available provision' in ordinary schools (section 13, Circular 1/83) from those whose needs are determined by the LEA (section 5(1), Act). (See Figure 3.2.)

In considering these two broad groups of children with special educational needs, it is important to be clear about who makes decisions about them at which level in the education service. Decisions about children whose special needs are met within generally available provision are made directly by ordinary schools, though no doubt these decisions are influenced by LEA policies, practices and resourcing for the 18 per cent. Decisions about children with special needs determined by the LEA are made through the statutory statementing procedures by professionals and officers with parental consultation about individual children. Circular 1/83 (sections 13 to 16) and the revised Circular 22/89 outline some of the broad factors and criteria to be used in the decision that a statutory statement of special educational needs will be made.

It is stated that decisions about what constitutes 'additional or otherwise different provision' will vary from area to area depending on provision available in the LEA's schools. Nevertheless, the circular does recommend some national uniformity in the criteria used:

> As a general rule the Secretary of State expects LEAs to afford the protection of a statement to all children who have severe or complex learning difficulties which require the provision of extra resources in ordinary schools, and in all cases where the child is placed in a special unit attached to an ordinary school, a special school, a non-maintained special school or an independent school approved for the purpose.
>
> (Circular 1/83, Section 14)

Special educational needs can be met according to the circular from provision available in ordinary schools where 'ordinary schools provide special educational provision from their own resources in the form of additional tuition and remedial provision, or in normal circumstances, where the child attends a reading centre or unit for disruptive pupils' (section 15).

It is evident that these guidelines depend on the precise meaning of the phrase 'ordinary schools provide special educational provision from their own resources'. The burden of the distinction between the two groups of special educational needs falls on the distinction between 'determined by the LEA' and 'ordinary schools provide from their own resources'. The guidance on when the LEA will determine special educational provision, and therefore make a statement of special educational needs, is still not specific enough to deal with the cases of children who are integrated in ordinary schools and do not have 'severe or complex learning difficulties'. These cases are particularly important as they represent a large proportion of the 2 per cent with special educational needs and are considered to need some protection of the additional resources allocated to them.

CONFUSIONS ABOUT SPECIAL EDUCATIONAL PROVISION

Another confusion which has arisen from the 1981 Act is the definition of the term 'special educational provision'. The Act refers explicitly to 'educational provision which is additional to or otherwise different from the educational provision made generally for children of his age in schools maintained by the LEA concerned' (section 1(3) (a)). Circular 1/83 uses the phrase 'generally available in ordinary schools in the area under normal arrangements' (section 13). The use and interpretation of these phrases was in question in the case of *R. v. Hampshire Education Authority ex parte J.* (1985). In this case, the judge refused to accept the interpretation of special educational provision in terms of provision which is additional to or different from what was available generally in schools.

The reasons for this refusal were that the term 'available' is not used in the Act, only the circular, and that the Act's definition of special educational provision is in terms of what is 'made generally for children of his age'. The phrase 'made generally' was interpreted to mean 'provided for the general run of normal children, to the normal majority'. This interpretation was judged to be necessary to avoid a paradox which arises if special educational provision is taken to mean provision which is additional to or different from what is available generally in ordinary schools. With this meaning the more this provision is available in ordinary schools, the less special educational provision there will be. That is, the more provision for children with, say, sensory difficulties available in ordinary schools, the less special educational provision there is for such children. This odd conclusion can be avoided by distinguishing between special educational provision and where it is available. The preferred definition of special educational provision is in terms of what is additional to or different from provision for the general run of normal children. This definition is also consistent with current ideas about describing special educational provision in terms of the different kinds of modification made to the ordinary curriculum — modifications of access to the curriculum, to the climate for learning and to the level of curricular goals. These broad types of adaptation are not required for the general run of normal or ordinary children.

DECISION AREAS FOR SPECIAL EDUCATIONAL PROVISION

It follows, therefore, that there is a distinction between the type of education called for and the location of the provision. The phrase 'made generally' refers to the *type* of provision, whether it is provided for the 'general run of normal children' or not. The phrase 'available generally' refers to the *location* of that provision, where it is available. There is a third factor implied in the 1981 Act framework which is concerned with the immediate *authorisation* of the resources for special educational provision, whether by the school or LEA. There are therefore three areas for decision making:

• Type of provision needed: what additional/different provision is needed?

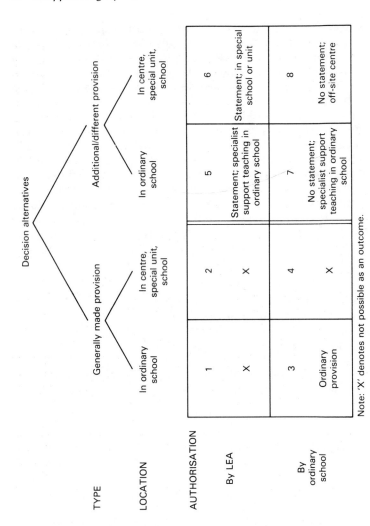

Note: 'X' denotes not possible as an outcome.

Figure 3.3 *Decision-making areas implied in the 1981 Act*

- Location of provision: where is provision available, in ordinary school or special unit/school?
- Authorisation of provision: who directly determines provision, ordinary school or LEA?

These decision areas can be represented as shown in Figure 3.3. For ease of explanation only, and at the risk of oversimplification, it is assumed that there are only two alternatives in each decision area.

By combining these decision alternatives, eight possible outcomes arise. Three of these (1, 2 and 4) are not possible in practice as generally made provision occurring in ordinary school is the immediate responsibility of ordinary schools. Outcome 3 (ordinary provision) is distinct from outcomes 5 to 8 in the kind of provision which is thought to be required. Outcomes 6 and 8 are different from outcomes 5 and 7 in the location of the additional provision. Outcomes 5 and 6 are distinct from outcomes 7 and 8 in the immediate authorisation of resources for the special educational provision.

Using this model it is possible to identify where greater clarification is needed in order to facilitate decision-making about special educational provision.

1. How will the phrase 'generally made provision' be interpreted and who will be counted in the 'normal majority' when it comes to decisions about the nature and allocation of additional provision? Even with 'normality' taken as a question of degree, what degree of 'normality' calls for 'generally made provision'?

2. Having decided on the need for additional/different provision, where will this provision be available: in ordinary classes, some mix of in-class support and withdrawal, a mix of ordinary school or separate centre, unit or school? This is the issue of the degree to which special educational needs can be met in ordinary schools — the integration issue. If it is decided to make the special provision available in an ordinary school through, say, a combination of setting up a resource centre and having in-class support, will such additional provision be considered *authorised* or determined by the school or the LEA? This is itself not a simple decision as an LEA may allocate its additional resources to ordinary schools to use for special educational provision. In this situation, are the resources to be considered as part of those of the ordinary school? If so, then the additional provision made available in the ordinary school will not be determined directly by the LEA and there will be no statutory procedure to protect this resource for the individual child with a statement. This situation is represented by outcome 7 in the model and is the practice in LEAs with low statementing practices.

3. A third area for clarification concerns the cases of young people mainly in secondary schools who attend off-site or on-site units on account of behaviour difficulties (disruptive behaviour). Placement at these units is seen as necessary when behaviour difficulties cannot be tolerated in ordinary schools and classes. The education provision received at these centres or units is different from what is generally made. It is located outside ordinary schools and is often resourced directly by the LEA, but it is not seen to call for the protection of a statement. So instead of being

outcome 6 in the decision-making model (with a statement in special unit or centre), it ends up as outcome 8, with no statement.

STATEMENTS OF SPECIAL EDUCATIONAL NEEDS

Some commentators have taken a critical attitude to the use of statements for allocating additional resources to children with special educational needs. In this respect, Dessent (1987) has argued that it is inconsistent with the idea of a continuum of special educational needs to introduce a statutory system of recording for some of these children. The effect, he claims, is to create a resource divide in which the 2 per cent receive considerably more resources than the 18 per cent.

The case against statementing is also based on the procedural difficulties which have been referred to above. The staffing of the procedural system, according to Dessent, has claimed an excessive amount of the limited resources available. The major criticism, however, is that difficulties arise from a statutory assessment procedure which focuses on the individual child. These difficulties are those identified in the 1981 Act evaluation project (Goacher et al., 1988): advice about individual needs is influenced by available provision, the tendency to fit individual children to existing special educational provision rather than the other way around.

Conflicts of interest can also arise in the statementing process between professionals, administrators and parents. However, these conflicts are to some extent inherent in a system which is matching needs to provision and where needs are likely to be greater than scarce resources. Another argument denies that statements secure and protect additional resources for children with special educational needs. This position represents a view that finds it hard to accept that one part of the LEA, the special education sub-system, may be designed to protect children from other parts of the LEA, the ordinary schools. However, conflicts of interest between parts of a system can arise in a situation where schools are relatively independent of the LEA. This is a situation which is likely to increase under provisions for local management of schools in the 1988 Education Reform Act. Mistrust can be found between ordinary schools and the LEA, between different parts of the same school and between parents as clients and the LEA. One of the functions of the 1981 Act was, as I have mentioned, to give parents of children with special educational needs additional client rights. However, this does not necessarily resolve the potential conflict of interests between providers and clients about the level, kind and location of the provision.

The relationships between parents, professionals and the LEA as regards the complex question of protection will be discussed in Chapter 7. For the present, I will focus on the function of the statementing procedures. Dessent's point is that the separation of the special education part from other parts of the LEA is based on the principle of protecting special education resources. This principle, as he recognises, can be most simply implemented by having an administratively separate system of special schooling, but it implies an unacceptable degree of segregation. What can be easily overlooked in this position, however, is the administrator's task of reconciling the principle of additional resource protection for special educational needs and the principle of the maximum ordinary school responsibility for all children.

ALTERNATIVE RESOURCE ALLOCATION APPROACH

The 1981 Act represents a considerable loosening up of the boundaries between special and ordinary schooling. Systems for protecting additional resource allocation for special educational needs are needed, which are compatible with ordinary school responsibility for special educational needs and which do not depend only on an individually based scheme of resource allocation. One possibility for reducing the lengthy statutory procedures would be to have two forms of individually based additional resource allocation. There would be assessments and decision-making about needs and provision but without the statutory procedures and statement. This would depend on parental willingness to short-circuit the formal decision-making procedures. If there were disagreements between parents, professionals and LEA officers, then the statutory procedures could be invoked by parents. LEAs would still have a duty to provide and review special educational provision, but decision-making in cases where there were compatible views and interests would be more rapid and flexible.

Another possible development, presented persuasively by Dessent (1987), would build on existing schemes of additional resource allocation to schools in which individual schools receive additional resources depending on a set of indicators, usually related to social disadvantage. Such a scheme, similar to that reported from Norway (Vislie, 1982), would allocate additional resources to individual schools based on the needs of the school's children with special educational needs. Dessent does not discount the possibility of individual resource allocations for a small minority with severe disabilities, but the overall effect would be to reduce the number of children going through the statementing system. The posibility of such developments illustrates the extent to which the 1981 Act embodies resource allocation procedures which belonged to an era when the management of the relationship of special needs and other provision was controlled centrally by LEAs.

With the devolvement to ordinary schools of responsibility for more children with special educational needs, additional safeguards are needed to protect provision for these children. One possible safeguard would be for the central government to amend the legislation to place more specific duties on schools to accept children with special educational needs. These would need to go further than sections 2(5) and 2(7) of the 1981 Act which relate to school governors and 'those concerned with making SEP for that child' in the ordinary school. Duties could be laid on headteachers and/or governors with the same stipulations as those placed on LEAs under sections 2(2) and 2(3) to provide for education in the ordinary school. A second area where safeguards are needed is in the decisions made by ordinary schools about the needs of and provisions for individual children with special educational needs. These decisions would have to be made in ordinary schools and by ordinary school-based professionals. There could arise a need for outside independent assessment and advice both when teachers are uncertain and when there might be disagreements between teachers and parents. A third area where the principle of protection would need to be operated is over the question of how the individual schools use their additional resources. LEAs would need to assess how the allocations were used by possibly requiring schools to submit regular evaluations about their use of the resources, which could be backed up by outside evaluations or inspections.

A final point about a school-based system of special education resource allocation is that it would entail differential allocation to different schools. This would involve establishing procedures for assessing individual schools' needs for additional special educational resources. This raises traditional problems about the validity and reliability of assessing the special educational provision needs of schools. In concluding this section, it can be noted that initial criticisms of the resource allocation scheme embodied in the 1981 Act have led to a consideration of other forms of allocation. As the discussion has shown, the challenge is in meeting the potentially conflicting principles of protecting additional resources, non-segregation, meeting individual needs and effective and efficient management of resources.

SIGNIFICANCE OF THE 1981 ACT

I have argued in this chapter that there are more continuities in the issues and difficulties which arise in this field between the pre- and post-1981 statutory frameworks than have often been recognised. We still need to use categories to summarise the similarities and differences between individual special educational needs and between the variety of curricular provision for individual children. Some of the previous problems identified by the Warnock Report persist in the 1981 Act framework. Firstly, the problem of individuals not fitting categories continues in the difficulties of matching currently available provision to the complex special educational needs of some children. Secondly, referring to a child as having a learning difficulty, whether moderate or severe, can still lead some people to treat all children having this general characteristic as having the same individual needs. Thirdly, when an LEA decides to determine an individual child's special educational needs and provide additional provision, this process can still draw scarce resources away from those children with special educational needs whose needs are met through resources available in ordinary schools. On the other hand, the 1981 Act does represent a significant change from the 1944 framework, in terms of the move towards integration. This has involved a reconceptualisation of special educational provision as something not available only in special schools or units. This, not 'abandoning categories of handicap', is the major conceptual change in the 1981 Act. Categorisation, as it has been argued, remains but in a different form and with different labels and connotations.

What underlies the concern about categorisation is the intention to avoid damaging, discrediting and devaluing those with difficulties and disorders. This intention cannot be realised without some form of categorisation, which is required in order (a) to identify those people who are going to receive additional or different provision, and (b) to protect the additional resources used. Avoiding stigma is a critical and delicate matter which is partly about *how* the additional resources are negotiated, allocated, used and protected. It follows from the identification process that criteria and thresholds will be needed to differentiate between those who will and those who will not receive additional or different provision, even when the learning difficulties are a matter of degree. Yet there are no simple procedures for 'discovering' criteria which would satisfy all parties concerned, parents, teachers, schools and LEAs. This gives rise to a major problem for which there is no simple solution. An appeal to the relativity of special educational needs represents a response to only one aspect of the problem. A more effective response is to establish a system for setting and revising specific criteria and thresholds for determining special educational needs and provision. This would have to be based on negotiation and feasible consensus, which takes account of resource availability and differing interests.

CONCLUSION

It is recognised in the 1981 Act that account needs to be taken of conditions in LEA schools, with the implication that these can vary from LEA to LEA. But, as Circular 1/83 and the revised Circular 22/89 imply, there are good reasons for having some degree of uniformity between different areas of the same country. One possible strategy is for there to be two levels of criteria setting — broad criteria at a national level which are more specific than at present, but still general enough to facilitate the setting of more specific criteria at LEA level. Similarly, central DES guidance could be more specific about the various kinds of special educational provision, clarifying what is different or additional in a 'modified' or 'developmental' curriculum. Within the current context of more central direction about the National Curriculum — i.e. generally made provision — there may be more inclination to make these specifications.

It is crucial that these specifications are not so constraining that they prevent LEAs from elaborating their own versions of criteria and thresholds to meet local conditions. LEAs could be expected to publish their criteria formally, and to review and update them with changing circumstances. Similarly, DES guidelines will need to be reviewed and updated in response to changing LEA and school conditions. It is an essential part of this strategy that any set of criteria or thresholds will not be expected to deal with individual cases in a simple routine way. The primary emphasis will be on individual needs which are assessed in terms of an individual's functioning in context. Local criteria, based on national ones, will be used in the general summary descriptions. However, the relationship between an individual case and general criteria is not a mechanical one, and in no sense is the individual to be seen as fully described in terms of general categories or descriptions. Regular action is also needed to guard against the tendency for a constructed scheme to become a fixed 'reality'. Such a scheme needs to be reviewed regularly, taking account of changing circumstances and value judgements.

4

Integration: the ideal and the reality

INTRODUCTION

The issue of integration has been and continues to be a central preoccupation in special needs education. Integration is a major theme in various parts of this book. The legislative framework within which practice was developed was discussed in the last chapter. Its relationship to questions about a common curriculum will be discussed in the next chapter. This chapter is basically about the organisation of the educational service from the perspective of provision for children with special educational needs. The chapter will begin with a brief discussion of the terminological and conceptual issues which are associated with different perspectives. This will lead to an examination of arguments used by different parties to the debate. Certain sociological perspectives will be considered in this context. The role of research in informing both policy and school practice will then be discussed. To conclude, there will be a consideration of the future of separate schools and units and what kinds of separation may be consistent with a set of common educational aims for all children.

CONCEPTIONS AND MISCONCEPTIONS

The principle of integration has become strongly associated with special educational needs over the last ten to fifteen years. Others have written in detail about the background history and current practices of educating children with special educational needs in ordinary schools (Hegarty et al., 1981; Booth and Potts, 1983). What emerges is a dissatisfaction with the term 'integration' itself. This is not surprising as one term is used to express a complicated set of ideas about which there are bound to be some disagreements. The term has been seen as inadequate to cover the issues of educating children with special educational needs who have not been in separate schools or units. It has focused attention on the 2 per cent and not the 18 per cent referred to by the Warnock Report (DES, 1978). Integration has therefore tended to imply a desegregation process. Hegarty (1987) has expressed this dissatisfaction and proposed that the issues are best dealt with in relation to the question of how to educate children with special educational needs in ordinary schools. What underlies this view is the belief that arguments for and against integration confuse means with ends. Arguments for integration, for example, often treat integration as an end in itself and overlook that it is, as Hegarty argues, a means to educating children with special needs. The question of whether integration promotes the effective education of children with special needs permits a more rounded evaluation of the complex issues involved.

These issues can also be seen in terms of extending the limits of the ordinary school. Dessent (1987) argues for the principle of non-segregation as opposed to integration based on the principle of a fully comprehensive education system. The difference between a desegregationist and a non-segregationist position is significant in drawing attention to the central concerns of the proponents. A desegregationist position works from the existing special school sub-system and asks whether this sub-system can be incorporated in or better linked to the main school system. Non-segregationism starts from the existing ordinary school system and asks whether this system can be extended and adapted to prevent the exclusion of children to the segregated system. By assuming a 'common schools for all' position, it is clear that non-segregationists would place the onus of proof on the opposition to show why schools cannot be for all. The desegregationist position, by contrast, mounts the case that ordinary-school-based provision for children with special educational needs has more advantages than disadvantages compared to special schools. The debate about integration can be better appreciated if these differing initial positions are recognised.

FORMS OF INTEGRATION

In advocating integration, the Warnock Committee noted that integration was part of a wider movement of 'normalisation' in western countries (Wolfensberger, 1972). What is involved are the rights of people with disabilities to participate in the activities of everyday life. The Warnock Committee proposed a three-way distinction between locational, social and functional integration. Though not considered as discrete kinds of integration, they were seen as forming progressive stages of association between children with special educational needs and others. Locational integration refers to the physical location of provision alongside ordinary schools. This can involve sharing the same site, the same building or the same physical facilities. For some proponents of integration, this hardly constitutes integration in the sense of providing constructive opportunities for mutual contact. This is what social integration is about. Usually this refers to social interchanges outside formal learning groups: for example, at lunchtime and playtime, and in general school activities. The third type, functional integration, which is usually considered as authentic integration, involves children with special educational needs joining and learning in ordinary classes as full participants. This kind of integration presents the greatest challenge to all concerned, teachers, children, parents and support and advisory professionals.

There have been more detailed schemes or classifications of integration which specify the various forms of provision in terms of their distance from mainstream classrooms in ordinary schools (Hegarty, 1987):

- pupils with special educational needs fitted into existing arrangements;
- mainstream placement with specialist support provided within the class;
- mainstream placement and withdrawal for specialist work;
- mainstream placement, attending special centre part time;
- special centre part time, mainstream class part time;
- special centre full time;
- special school part time, ordinary school part time.

This is a rough scheme, however, which does not deal with the possible variations in the conditions and modes of teaching for different children at any level in the scheme. Some proponents of 'integration' see the first two forms of provision as being 'real' integration, with any degree of withdrawal, even if only part time, as internal school segregation. Others take a more open approach in which integration is not merely the placement of a child in a particular kind of provision, i.e. a state; for them, integration is a process which requires a continued and planned interaction with contemporaries and the freedom to associate in different groups (Fish Report, 1985).

DIFFERENT UNDERLYING APPROACHES

The idea of integration as a process is similar to the idea mentioned above of integration being a means to an end. Though both ideas enable a more dynamic view of the process of bringing people who have been excluded into the mainstream of life, in this case ordinary school life, they leave open the crucial question of what are the ends of integration. The 'integration' debate, therefore, depends on larger questions about the aims of education within the context of individual differences. This dilemma is neatly summarised in Mittler's description of integration as 'reconciling the child's educational and learning needs with the need to maintain contact with ordinary children in the community' (1979, p. 81).

This 'reconciling' approach to integration contrasts with a more socio-political one in which integration is about advancing the interests of disadvantaged groups, not just those with disabilities: 'integration is essentially a political process, it is about the transfer of power' (Booth, 1988, p. 101). Special education and integration from this perspective is about interests and not needs (Barton and Tomlinson, 1984). It is about the conflict between different social interests, and not about meeting individual educational needs. Integration as a principle is interpreted as an expression of the more general principle of equality of value: 'In schools which operate according to such a principle attempts are made to reduce the devaluation of pupils according to their sex, background, colour, economic or class position, ability, disability or attainment' (Booth, 1988, p. 161). This principle derives its force from the negative experiences of individuals and groups who have felt devalued by being segregated. The equality of value principle can be interpreted as aiming to reverse the devaluation process with the eradication of discrimination and segregation as the means to this end. The strong feelings associated with the integration–segregation debate can be understood in these terms.

The special needs integration debate is therefore part of the wider equality of opportunity or equality of value debate. Committed arguments are to be expected, though whether the heat generated helps illuminate the issues and enables reasoned decisions is questionable. The climate of opinion has tended to be so pro-integration that the term 'segregation' itself has negative connotations. In many respects these issues have paralleled and derived force from the racial segregation–integration debate. It has been difficult to find a term to refer to different schooling for children with special educational needs without prejudging the issues — perhaps 'separate schooling' is a less emotive term, but even this has certain undesirable overtones.

THE ONGOING DEBATE

The integration movement, which in its radical version implies the closing of special schools or their merging with ordinary schools, has not been without critics. When integration is criticised by professionals, this can be more easily swept aside and attributed to professional self-interest. However, when criticisms come from parents, and especially from those who at some stage supported integration, then the debate assumes a different nature. Goodison (1987), for example, expresses a parent's concern for her child with special educational needs in a way that acknowledges the value of integration for younger children. She describes how as her child grew older she became increasingly 'left behind' in terms of academic progress, playground games and friendships. When transferred to a small village special school at 8 years old, she developed more confidence and made better academic progress. There was also access to additional resources, such as speech therapy and physiotherapy and small classes. Socially she formed close relationships with adults and children and she developed a sense of belonging.

An example like this can be discounted for several reasons: it is the mother's opinion and is not confirmed by independent assessment; it is not necessarily representative of other parents' experience of integration; or the integration was not adequately planned, resourced and reviewed. Yet Goodison's position is not that of someone who was unwilling to try integration. Nor is she alone in suspecting that integration can be an easy financial option for LEAs. Sandow and Stafford (1987) reported in a survey that 60 per cent of parents were not keen on integration. For many parents, integration could be seen as removing provision for suspect motives. This concern about closing or running down special schools and the placement of children with special educational needs in ordinary schools without substantial additional resources has been articulated in a recent 'Campaign for Choice in Special Education'.

One response to these developments is to assert that these fears will be allayed once established examples of integration in practice are clear to professionals and parents. This has been the experience in some integration projects in which doubtful teachers have come to change their initial positions (Helier, 1988; Hegarty et al., 1981). Yet there is a difference between the teachers' and the parents' perspectives, something which will be discussed in more detail in Chapter 7. Parents as consumers or clients of the service do not necessarily take the wider professional view of service providers. Goodison (1987) rejects the integrationist argument that children in special schools are 'put away', or are 'too sheltered, cosy and protected away from the hurly burly of ordinary life'. She has a sense that her daughter is privileged to receive the extra resources and opportunities which her special school offers. Life in special schools can offer challenge not over-protection, she asserts, and it can prepare for independence and provide opportunities for personal success and a sense of worth.

It is evident that this defence of special schooling confronts directly the alleged disadvantages of segregation. It calls into question the usual use of the term 'least restrictive environment'. A 'restrictive environment' may narrow intellectual and social opportunities and experiences, but it could also be outside the range of the social, emotional and intellectual resources of the child. As Goodison argues, the debate is about how equality is achieved; it is not about parents wanting to bar their children from ordinary schools: 'Sometimes, in order to achieve equality, disadvantaged groups feel the need for different situations and a level of separation to develop their own strengths and identities' (Goodison, 1987, p. 18). This defence of special schooling does not reject integration outright; indeed, it supports integration when the resources of the school and of the child are appropriate. However, this position does raise questions about whose assessments and what purposes prevail in judgements of appropriateness.

What some parents are demanding is a genuine choice which depends on there being some alternatives and implies that what is chosen may not be education in ordinary schools. The main differences in the integration debate can be seen now to be related to fundamental social value issues about the balance between individual choice and social equality. These issues will be discussed in relation to the curriculum in the next chapter. What partly underlies this balancing of individual choice and social equality is whether primacy is given to the individual's perspective or to the social, collective perspective. The egalitarian position is usually one which gives primacy to the social perspective; the libertarian gives primacy to the individual perspective. In the next section I will discuss the social perspective as expressed in a critique of individualistic approaches found in some sociological theories.

SOCIOLOGICAL PERSPECTIVES

The sociological perspective on special needs education has been relatively undeveloped over this century compared to the psychological one (Tomlinson, 1982). Some commentators have found this surprising since a sociology of education has developed considerably in relation to social class and social policy issues (Oliver, 1985). Sociological theories of differential school achievement and the relation between schooling and the wider society are best known in current educational thinking for their criticism of individualist assumptions about educational problems. Hargreaves (1982) expresses the perspective in what he calls the fallacy of individualism — the belief that, if only schools can successfully educate every individual in self-confidence, independence and autonomy, then society can be left to take care of itself. The corollary of this is that if individuals fail to learn in schools then this is because of individual characteristics. The approach offered by most of the sociologists in the special needs field is an extension of that used in accounting for social class differences — in terms of social structures and functions, and the power relations between different social groups. The Tomlinson and Barton position, for example, tends to favour accounts in terms of conflicts of interest and makes use of functional accounts when the functions relate to the interests of the dominant social groups or class at the expense of the disadvantaged.

Sociological theories, in the same way as psychological theories, have links with general value positions. The adoption of a particular social theory is likely to be influenced by fundamental value assumptions about what is socially just and legitimate. Conflict theories are often associated with a value orientation to social change based on some dissatisfaction with the social status quo. Functional and positivist theories seek to account for how the current social system maintains itself. They are often associated with a value orientation which is consistent with social differences in power and status. Asserting this link between social values and theories does not imply that social theories only reflect social values. Social theories are designed to account for certain social realities and as such should be based on a strong respect for empirical evidence. The point is rather that what has been presented as a sociology of special education represents only one strand of social thinking which has strong links with egalitarian social values. In the following paragraphs I plan to illustrate how much of the sociological thinking in this field, influenced by egalitarian values, has been preoccupied with the questions of differentiation and has assumed that this is damaging to the interests of children with special educational needs.

Educational differentiation

Oliver (1985) outlines five broad sociological approaches to special needs education — positivist, functionalist, interactionist/interpretive, conflict and neo-Marxian. In this discussion I will refer mainly to functionalist and conflict approaches. Tomlinson's work (1984) on the social construction of the ESN(M) category in the 1970s represents a combination of phenomenological and structural perspectives. Although the methodology and conclusions drawn from the empirical study can be criticised (Bunn, 1987), my intention is to examine the kind of social explanation offered. The basic perspective is that a social category like ESN(M), or SEN, is not a fixed objective category, but is socially constructed by professionals who have the social power to use such a category to place certain children in a particular stigmatised form of education. To account for the social use of the ESN(M) category, Tomlinson drew on the work of Bourdieu and Passeron (1977) which identified education as a mechanism for reflecting, reproducing and justifying inequalities in social status. In this view the education system demands a cultural competence which it does not provide, so advantage is given to those who possess this competence. Families of children categorised as ESN(M) are seen as not having this 'cultural capital' to pass on to their children. Children from the lower social classes will therefore find their way to ESN(M) schools, something which fits overall with the social class distribution at ESN(M) schools.

For Tomlinson, the development of this segregated system of schooling has served a dual social function: firstly, by removing potentially troublesome children from the ordinary school system, it ensures order in the mainstream system; and secondly, by placing some children in low-status non-credentialled schooling, it has contributed to the reproduction of a social class structure.

This account of special schooling as a form of educational differentiation and allocation is linked to other forms and devices for differentiating between children and for allocating them to different forms of education. Carrier (1984) likens it to within-school differentiation such as ability grouping and within-class allocations to different teaching goals and methods. His analysis includes reference to educational ideology, such as whether the education system should be egalitarian or not. By 'egalitarian' Carrier means the denial of fundamental social class or other ascribed differences between learners. His view is that all education systems involve some form of differentiation and allocation and that, although educational ideology does not cause differentiation and allocation, it does shape the form they take. The growth in special education services in England, both in ordinary and special schools, is seen as reflecting a shift in educational ideology from non-egalitarian to egalitarian with the advent of comprehensive schooling. This major reorganisation of secondary schooling increased the demands for alternative provision for certain deviant groups (Ford et al., 1982). These authors, concentrating on children with behavioural difficulties, focus on the systems of control used in dealing with problems. Control in such a system involves the use of the 'medical model' to defend the interests of the education service, by interpreting problem behaviour as individual illness amenable to individual treatment and care. The medical model functions as an ideology in making these problems appear natural and so deflects attention from their social origins.

Oliver's own perspective (1985) is concerned with the changing methods of social control in the move from institutional to community-based systems of provision. His analysis questions the two assumptions behind the move to integration: that special schools make matters worse for children with special educational needs, that integration is a better form of provision. His account is based on a change in the structure and function of the welfare and education systems. The increasing cost of provision in the context of cuts in public expenditure counts against special school placements, especially residential ones. Also, many of the professionals involved in special education are based not in institutions but in the 'community'. Another perspective on the move to integration, based on US experience, maintains that although locational integration has been achieved in many more schools, differentiation in key areas of children's experience is maintained (Shapiro, 1980). Shapiro suggests that reform can proceed only to the extent that it is consistent with the goals of the wider social and economic structure of society. The development of a 'resource base' or 'support department' in ordinary schools, which is designed as a means of providing for special educational needs without allocation to separate remedial classes or lower-ability groups, actually functions, he claims, in a segregating way.

A CRITIQUE OF THEORIES

Though it is not my intention to discuss these sociological theories in depth, several points are worth making. Most of these accounts refer to the functions of the separate special school system both for the mainstream schools and for the wider society. The development of special needs services and the shift to integrated services are invariably accounted for in terms of functions which do not recognise humanitarian interests and concerns as genuine. Tomlinson (1984) goes so far as to identify the culture of benevolent humanitarianism in special needs education as deriving from professional interests. My argument is that sociological perspectives do not necessarily imply that additional provision for children with special educational needs only serves the interests of the non-disabled. There are undoubtedly conflicting social interests involved in responses to those with disability, but the interests of the disabled can sometimes be compatible with those of the wider society. It is notable that sociological accounts which could highlight such compatibilities between different interests are absent from much of the current sociology of special needs education.

Sociological accounts which reduce categories such as learning and behaviour difficulties to power-based social attributions are about the fields of moderate learning difficulties and emotional and behavioural difficulties, the so-called 'non-normative' conditions. As I argued in Chapter 2, there is no clear-cut distinction between normative and non-normative special educational needs. All conditions have normative elements, though for some there is more social consensus than for others. Even in the case of children with severe disorders or difficulties with clear-cut organic origins there are still complementary psychological and sociological accounts of the individual's condition. Most of the above sociological theories represent an exclusive focus on the social–cultural aspects of human functioning. This is different from the general systems framework outlined in Chapter 2 which incorporates different levels of descriptive and causal analysis. Social theories which ignore or reduce other levels of analysis to the social are in one sense no different from some psychological or biological theories to the extent that they also opt for single-level accounts.

However, some sociological accounts in this field even conflate the biological with the psychological. For example, Tomlinson (1982) conflates individualist psychological explanations with innate biological explanations. Medical/biological and psychological approaches are treated as similar because they are presented as 'objective sciences'. One suggestion about what underlies this form of social determinism, a form of radical environmentalism, is that it reflects an inability to work in a positive way with human limitations and a reluctance to acknowledge different conceptions about human aspirations. This avoids the positive approach of recognising limitations in order to understand how they arise so that ways can be found to alter them. It is a position based on a conception that, if individual differences have some individual biological or psychological aspect, then this can be used to make educational differentiation appear legitimate. It is for this reason that psychology's status as a science is questioned. As a science, it is portrayed as naturalising and legitimising limitations on learning and development. In a radical social view such limitations are attributable not to individuals but to complex social processes. Theories which involve individualist explanations are then seen as constructed for social, usually negative, functions. The critique of the use of psychology to legitimise the process of educational differentiation can be understood in these terms.

This raises the question of why differentiation within education is a major topic of theoretical interest. One suggestion is that separate grouping or schooling is seen to deny access to high-status educational outcomes and to instil a sense of rejection and devaluation for some children. Having common grouping or schooling for all is thought to be a way of redressing these biases or discriminations. What underlies these conceptions is a commitment to the human values of equality. It is in this sense that much current sociology of special needs education is associated with a strong egalitarian position.

DIFFERENTIATION: NEGATIVE AND POSITIVE ASPECTS

This leads the discussion to issues which will be raised in the next chapter on the common curriculum. As I will argue there, a common curriculum is compatible with some degree of differentiation of specific goals and of the organisation of schooling and classes. Those proponents of a common curriculum which is taken to require common schools and classes tend to interpret differentiation in an unnecessarily negative way. Differentiation is equated in this view with the segregation and discrimination imposed on disadvantaged groups and individuals. There can be no denial that differentiation can have and has had these excluding and rejecting effects. However, there are examples of differentiation which do not involve the exercise of coercive power against the interests of such groups. Differentiation can also be the outcome of choice on the part of individuals or groups who wish to pursue their own conceptions of educational goals within their own separate organisations. Where choice is exercised, as in the case of religious, ethnic or even single-sex schools or classes, this does not necessarily lead to a denial of equal access or to a devaluation of learners.

Differentiation comes to be seen as negative because it is taken to result in low-quality and low-status educational provision and therefore in low educational attainment. Low attainment can be interpreted as educational failure with the consequent devaluation of 'failures'. There are, however, two related underlying assumptions in this evaluation of differentiation which need to be questioned. The first assumption is that educational attainments are relevant ways of assessing a child or young person's general worth — 'that contempt is the proper response to incapacity' (Midgley, 1981). The second is that lower levels of attainment are invariably a result of educational differentiation rather than differentiation *also* being a way of providing for different levels of attainment. Advocacy for disadvantaged groups and individuals can overlook that, particularly in the area of severe disability and difficulties, there are no known ways of altering or enhancing attainment to within the 'normal range'. To acknowledge these limitations is no reason to devalue and dismiss children with deficits. It can, on the contrary, release those involved to achieve the optimal progress in the prevailing circumstances.

My contention is that, although equality is an important educational value, it is not the only one. Educational aims are likely to be promoted not only through egalitarian policies and practices but also through policies based on values of autonomy, which involve the exercise of choice, and policies based on the values of fellowship or solidarity. These different values and policies are not in their radical interpretation fully compatible. Reasonable people can be expected, therefore, to place different emphases on these values. What can be overlooked in the debates about integration is that identifying current limits to educational attainment does not imply that personally significant progress cannot be made, nor does it necessarily lead to personal or group devaluation. Dignity in learning, as in other areas of activity, arises also from being treated as autonomous, as having genuine choices and through membership of and a sense of belonging to a valued learning community or group.

A COLLECTIVIST COMPARISON

Although it is difficult to make simple comparisons with the educational systems in other countries, it is illuminating to consider the different assumptions made about special education in the Soviet Union. The comparison is interesting in that the Soviet education system has traditionally had a key role in promoting the collectivist values of the state. According to Lubovsky (1981), although special education has the same duties as the general system, of which it is a part, it has also to provide the most favourable conditions for correcting abnormal development. Integration is the purpose of education in that anyone from 'a special school must enter society as a full member, capable of living independently, of interacting with people around him and engaging in productive activity' (p. 445).

The Soviet experience, according to Lubovsky, indicates that the most effective way to prepare children with disorders or difficulties for integration into society is instruction in special schools. The principle of integration is interpreted, therefore, in terms of common aims and is seen as consistent with some degree of differentiation in the organisation of the education service at the level of schools. Lubovsky summarises the basic principle of Soviet special education as being correction oriented. It is this principle which applies in the Soviet education service with respect to the organisation of special schooling. Integration at the level of schools and classes is seen to prevent a higher-level integration based on the potential for development. Such potential requires specialist teaching within separate provision for some conditions (Sutton, 1986; Vygotsky, 1978).

This perspective contrasts with most Western ones where there

is less confidence about the compatibility of educational differentiation and common educational aims and goals. The traditional
Soviet approach could be understood in terms of the powerful
influence of the state in securing a tight relationship between the
school system and other sectors of Soviet society. In Western
liberal democracies, the state does not operate in such a 'com-
mand' manner, nor does it promote such a strong ideology of
active social citizenship and a sense of collective belonging. In this
wider social context, the Western school system can become an
important institutional context in which certain social/political
groups can pursue arrangements designed to promote social solidarity. The challenge and ideal of the comprehensive school (Hargreaves, 1982) in Britain can be understood in these terms. So can
the Western movement towards the integration of children with
special educational needs in ordinary schools.

EVALUATING INTEGRATION

Some of the dissatisfaction with special schooling since the Second
World War has derived from research studies from the United
States and the United Kingdom which indicated that scholastic
performance was not enhanced by special schooling or remedial
teaching (Galloway and Goodwin, 1979). This picture fitted with
the growing commitment to comprehensive schooling and enabled
a switch in the climate of opinion to a pro-integrationist one.

The function of research studies in this field is an interesting
illustration of how research findings are generated and have an
impact within a particular climate of opinion and values. What
emerges from an examination of evaluation studies is that research
strategies can change depending on the purposes of the research.
Many of the studies which showed that children with various
kinds of special educational need in separate special provision
fared no better, and in some cases fared worse, than similar children in ordinary provision used group experimental or statistical
survey type methodology. However, in the United Kingdom the
preferred methodology used to evaluate integration projects has
been single case and qualitative (Hegarty et al., 1981). Although
there can be good research reasons for using qualitative or illuminative methodologies in some conditions, these might also have
been selected because they are more practical than experimental
or large-scale survey approaches for educational settings. They are
also less expensive financially and are in some ways more accessible to school teachers, and are therefore more likely to be influential in changing practice. Much of the funded research on inte-

gration in this country has used such qualitative approaches (Hegarty et al., 1982; Hodgson et al., 1984).

Single-case or qualitative methods fulfil an indispensable role in providing information about the conditions and outcomes of particular practices. However, they need to be used in combination with larger-scale projects which attempt to identify critical conditions which operate across a range of particular cases and which assess the incidence of these conditions and outcomes. There have been few systematic comparative evaluation studies of integration in the United Kingdom, of which methods or forms of organisation have what outcomes under what conditions and for which groups of children. Such research has even fallen into disrepute in some quarters, with a growth in uncertainty about whether the results of such designs can ever inform policy and practice at all. This scepticism has been less evident in other countries where research into aspects of integration has used experimental and large-scale survey designs. There is, for example, interesting research from Australia about teacher beliefs and attitudes to integration. One Australian study of educational services in the United Kingdom and the United States has indicated that, although there are negative attitudes to teaching children with moderate intellectual difficulties, these attitudes vary depending on other teacher characteristics and the ethos and support offered for integration (Thomas, 1985). Other Australian research indicates a lack of confidence among ordinary teachers in their instructional skills and the quality of support personnel available (Yola and Ward, 1987). There was a tendency to favour integrating only those children whose disability-related characteristics were not likely to require extra instructional or management skills. However, some of these attitudes were modified by the presence of pre-service training and the nature of subsequent professional experience.

In the United States there has also been more research interest in the comparison of ordinary and special placements of children with special educational needs. Despite the recurrent difficulties with experimental and statistical controls, some of the research points to different educational outcomes for different groups of children with special educational needs. Reviews and meta-analyses of many research projects indicate that ordinary class placement with well-designed support teaching is associated with all-round educational benefits compared to special class placement, for children with moderate learning difficulties (Madden and Slaven, 1983; Carlberg and Kavale, 1980). The Carlberg and Kavale meta-analysis also indicated that special class placement, by contrast, was associated with higher outcomes in terms of basic achievements and social–behavioural measures, for children with learning disabilities (specific learning difficulties) and emotional and behavioural difficulties.

Some recent UK research has focused on integration issues at the between-school and within-classroom levels. There has been some work on comparing different forms of collaboration between teachers to support children with special educational needs in ordinary classes (Thomas, 1986). Jowett et al. (1988) have surveyed examples of the growth of links between special and ordinary schools. Links were classified into the movement of staff, pupils and/or resources between special and ordinary schools. Links were found in 74 per cent of special schools in 1985, involving mostly the movement of pupils and teachers. However, there was restricted movement to special schools, and where it took place it was by ordinary staff in search of resources and experience. If, as seems likely, there will be special schools in the immediate future, there seems to be a need to evaluate these schools in terms of those conditions and processes which are associated with optimal outcomes, including social and academic benefits from ordinary school links. Such research could be done in the tradition of the school effectiveness studies of ordinary schools (Rutter et al., 1975; Mortimore, 1988), and could complement more detailed individual qualitative studies.

LEGISLATIVE PROVISION FOR INTEGRATION

I have not yet referred in this chapter to the legislative provision for integration, i.e. the duties placed on LEAs to secure the education of children with special educational needs in ordinary schools. In Chapter 3 I suggested that the conditional duties on LEAs may need to apply to school governors and heads if LEAs are to devolve more financial management responsibilities for special needs to ordinary schools. This suggestion does not imply that section 2(3) of the 1981 Act, with its reference to integration being compatible with the 'efficient education' of other children and the 'efficient use of resources', could be applied without alterations or specification in government circular. On the contrary, section 2(2) and 2(3) of the Act do not go far enough in promoting the effective development of more integrated schooling by virtue of their general formulation and the lack of specific circular guidance. However, the major obstacle to integration has been a lack of central government support, in terms of both finance and commitment (Select Committee Report, 1987). The low priority given to special needs integration was evident before the emergence of the Education Reform Act 1988. For a government which has not avoided a directive strategy within the education service generally, there has been a notable lack of action in special educational needs policy and practice. For example, Education Support Grants have been available to LEAs to support and promote developments of various sorts, such as records of achievement, the Portage pre-school programme and the low-achievers project. There have been no similar grants for LEAs to develop their policy and provision in line with the 1981 Act.

Central government initiative

The UK experience contrasts with that of Spain (Marchesi, 1986) where central government has initiated a large-scale development project. Spanish schools choose to take on responsibility for teaching a specific number of children with severe special educational needs starting with the first year. This is in return for secured additional resources in the form of specialist teachers, materials and equipment, reduced class size for all children and advisory and support services. Schools opt for this only with the majority support of staff and parents.

Such a project could not be directly imported into this country with its different administrative system for education. However, the principles are directly relevant to the question of how a central government, which is committed to testing out the extent of feasible and effective integration, could proceed. Even if central government were not inclined to such a project then it could in principle be operated on a smaller scale within an LEA which had a commitment to special educational needs developments. In considering the gradual redeployment of financial and teaching resources from certain special schools, an LEA could offer some of its ordinary schools the opportunity to opt to take extra responsibility for certain additional groups of children with special educational needs. The additional resources could be made available only if those schools met certain agreed conditions. This could give an impetus to the development of whole-school policies for special needs.

For such a theme to be effective there would need to be a climate of opinion in favour of positive action on behalf of those with special educational needs. Teachers would have to be willing to see the professional and personal rewards of making the extra effort. LEAs would have to be willing to take a more directive, pro-active role in managing such developments. Most of the integration projects in the United Kingdom have not derived from such policy initiatives, but have grown up from local areas of need in schools (Jones, 1983). This might involve having to accept that certain forms of integrated special provision be concentrated in certain schools for economic and organisational reasons. This last condition is a difficult one to support from a radical integrationist perspective which is opposed to any separate organisation forms in ordinary schools. It could be that a radical version of integration could turn out to be a major obstacle to the effective non-segregation of some children in ordinary schools.

Hegarty (1987), in considering whether ordinary school can be reformed sufficiently to build up the capability to educate more children with special educational needs, comes to the conclusion that special schools will not become redundant. His position seems to be that the principles of comprehensive schooling have to face up to practical realities. This contrasts with the argument in this book which examines the principles of a common curriculum and concludes that they do not always require common schools and common classes. Some degree of differentiation both in educational goals and in the organisation of services is compatible with a common curriculum framework. That some special schools will form part of special needs provision for the foreseeable future does not require apology but should be supported positively. Without this support they are unlikely to be effective in providing access to a common curriculum with the relevant adaptations.

Future forms of provision

In future there could be proportionally fewer special schools. The majority of children currently with statements, those with moderate learning difficulties, sensory and motor difficulties, could eventually be provided for within ordinary school settings, within resource departments and/or in ordinary classes with additional support. Those with severe and profound learning difficulties, multiple difficulties and some emotional and behavioural difficulties are more likely to be provided for in separate special units or schools. The special units or classes could be based in ordinary schools. Such developments could lead to the consolidation of special schools into generic special schools which are not organised along traditional disability lines. Although special schools have usually had children with more than one disability, schools have been designated in terms of primary disability. With the move to generic special schools there could be departments which specialised in different special educational needs.

One of the main difficulties in educating children with special educational needs in ordinary schools is to secure an efficient and effective means of making scarce services available there. A common means for the wider group of children with special educational needs has been to have an LEA-managed peripatetic service for children with special needs in ordinary schools. One drawback to this approach is that local schools within a certain proximity may not be served by the same personnel. These schools may also have little influence over how the services are organised. It is in this context that it has been proposed that a small number of schools in a locality — a cluster — work together to develop mutually supportive arrangements for special educational needs and to provide a focus for deploying support services (Wedell, 1986; Fish Report, 1985). The functions of a cluster of schools would include the sharing of responsibility for most children with special educational needs, continuity across phases of schooling, local decision making about provision and a focus for service delivery of health and social services. The core of a cluster could consist of a secondary school with feeder primary schools within close proximity.

There are likely to be many difficult issues to resolve in establishing schemes of local collaboration for special needs services: the grouping of schools, the initiative and incentives for such developments and whether schools can opt for or against this type of collaboration. A cluster or consortium of schools could also act as the focus for additional resources to enable the non-segregation and integration of the 2 per cent of children with more severe difficulties. As such, a cluster could act as an administrative unit for an extension of special needs resourcing into the ordinary school. Whether such a scheme provides a more effective and efficient means of special educational needs resourcing for ordinary schools than direct resourcing to schools depends partly on the overall availability of financial resources. The less finance available, the more would be the need to share limited resources between schools. However, whether sharing will be viable depends on the degree of financial autonomy granted to ordinary schools. The introduction of the local management of schools under the 1988 Education Reform Act is therefore directly relevant to the prospects of establishing more locally based special educational needs services. In fact, the principle of local management is critical for the development of more integrated services. This will be discussed further in Chapter 9.

CONCLUSION

It should be evident from the above discussion that making more provision for children with special educational needs in ordinary schools involves complex systems of resource allocation and monitoring. Separate provision is administratively less complex, but is not necessarily the most educationally worthwhile. As services become more expensive and complex it becomes more difficult to make them available in a range of locations. There comes a point, difficult as it is to define in advance, at which for a given amount of finance appropriate services are most economically provided in centres with specialist functions; that is, in specialist schools/units.

The argument in this chapter has been that separation does not in itself lead to inferior quality or devalued education, nor deny equal opportunities. Where separation arises from a tendency to exclude, deny or reject those who do not fit the ordinary system, and there have been many instances of this in special needs education, then it can have these restricting and damaging effects. But where separation is not imposed but negotiated with or chosen by parents and/or children with special educational needs, then it might be the optimal provision under certain circumstances. That separate provision is not the ideal from one point of view may partly reflect the fact that having a disability or difficulty is itself not ideal. This is the case whether the child is in special or ordinary school. Once parental choice is acknowledged, however, then there can be tensions between what is chosen and what schools and LEAs can provide. Individual choice can also conflict with other people's choice. From the provider's perspective this would require having genuine alternatives in special needs provision available for the parents. A policy with integration as an option, if it is to be carried out effectively with high-quality alternatives, is bound to require extra LEA expenditure. There seems to be no simple way of resolving the trade-off between alternative forms of special needs provision and their cost.

—5

Curriculum in special needs education

INTRODUCTION

In the previous chapters I have discussed the concept of special educational needs and its position in the legislative framework. In Chapter 4 I argued that the case for integration depends on how a common curriculum is formulated. This leads me to consider some relevant issues about a common curriculum for all. The current orthodoxy in special needs education has been described as a curriculum-based approach. This is significant because special education has historically had either a therapeutic base, as in work with children with emotional and behavioural difficulties, a custodial base, as in treatment of severe intellectual impairment, or a remedial base, as in work with children having literacy difficulties. In these conceptions special education was seen as apart from mainstream education, both locationally and in terms of goals and methods. The significance of a curriculum-based approach is to reaffirm educational aims — the all-round development of the child, not just focusing on the area of deficit. This leads inevitably to consideration of what children with special educational needs have in common with all children and what the general purposes of education are for all children, including those children with exceptional characteristics.

One implication of the curriculum approach is that issues in special needs education are similar to or represent examples of general educational issues: issues concerned with the purposes, organisation and methods of education. In this chapter I will discuss some general curriculum issues as they relate to special needs education. This will involve a discussion about the aims of education, whether these apply to all children, the organisation and conceptualisation of what is included in the curriculum, and the question of balance. The main issue to arise out of this discussion will be how some degree of curriculum modification or differentiation for special needs education can be accommodated within a common curriculum for all.

COMMON EDUCATIONAL AIMS FOR ALL

The Warnock Committee stated that the 'purpose of education for all children is the same. The goals are the same' (DES, 1978, section 1.4). This statement is made in the context of a general statement of the long-term goals or aims of education:

(1) to enlarge a child's knowledge, experience and imaginative understanding and thus his awareness of moral values and capacity for enjoyment;
(2) to enable him to enter the world after formal education is over as an active participant in society and a responsible contributor to it, capable of achieving as much independence as possible.

The Report continues:

We are fully aware that for some children the first of these goals can be approached only by minute, though for them highly signifi-cant steps, while the second may never be achieved. But this does not entail that for these children the goals are different.

(section 1.4)

As these excerpts show, this short section expresses the philo-sophical and ethical basis of current thinking about special needs education.

White (1982) has questioned whether the goals of education can be the same for all when it is recognised that some children, a very small minority with severe disabilities, may not attain these goals. This is relevant in the context of White's position that the demands of educatedness should not be pitched so high that large proportions cannot reach them. The point reflects the basic difficulty in reconciling the attainability of educational goals with having the same goals for all. A popular way of resolving this is to distinguish between long-term goals or aims, short-term goals and specific concrete objectives. Aims can then be taken as common to all, so long as they are formulated in sufficiently general terms to enable different schemes of goals and objectives to be construed as examples of the general aims. This would imply that the Warnock formulation of goals should be thought of as aims. But even as aims there is some doubt about whether they are applicable to all children. Another more general formulation, such as 'the maximum development of abilities and skills of which the individual is capable' (Hutt and Gibby, 1976), might have more comprehensive application. The problem, however, with making the formulation more general is that it reduces ultimately to a tautology. Alternatively, it ends up as an abstract definition of education and in so doing does not indicate what general abilities and skills are to be developed. The effect is that as formulations become more general they have an increasingly tenuous link to curriculum planning and actual educational practices. This can result in statements of aims being treated as token expressions of commitment which do not get translated into specific and practicable goals and objectives.

Nevertheless, there is still considerable social and educational significance in general statements of educational aims such as those of Hutt and Gibby (1976). To assert that education aims to develop the abilities of all individuals is to recognise a common educational humanity. It includes those children with severe difficulties who have been considered in the past as 'ineducable'. As such it expresses a value position which can be seen as egalitarian in the sense that it values equality of opportunity and equality of esteem. This egalitarian position is strongly associated with the comprehensive education movement which rejects the historical legacy of differentiated schooling. A recent example of this position illustrates some of the assumptions and values involved:

> Schools claim to be concerned to assist every individual to achieve her or his full potential, but by providing a differentiated curriculum they ensure that the claim remains a myth and that the opportunities for those labelled 'less able' are severely limited by denying them access to certain sorts of knowledge. If we genuinely believe in equality of opportunity we must provide a common basic curriculum as a logical extension of the comprehensive movement.
>
> (Reid and Hodson, 1987, p. 4)

These views express a rejection of a class-stratified society with clear separation between sections of society, the low status of separate curricula for the 'less able' and the denial of access via educational achievement to social and economic advancement. What is at the heart of this position is an avoidance of the indignities and sense of failure associated with a low-status curriculum (Hargreaves, 1982). Reid and Hodson continue: 'no child should be provided with an alternative inferior curriculum on the grounds of perceived differences from other children, no matter whether those differences relate to race, gender, social origins or intellectual attainment' (1987, p. 9). As much as this position deserves endorsement for its positive stance, other value positions on the aims of education also need to be considered.

SOCIAL VALUES AND EDUCATIONAL AIMS

There are several ways of representing different social ideologies which bear on the question of educational aims (George and Wilding, 1984; Lawton, 1988). For the present purposes a loose broad distinction will be drawn beween left-wing socialist or collectivist positions and right-wing individualist positions. The egalitarian position mentioned before is broadly associated with democratic and Marxist socialist ideas and values which emphasise equality, freedom and fraternity (fellowship). Of these values, equality is paramount and finds expression in the principles of democratic participation and humanitarianism. Right-wing positions, which have had a renewal over the last decade and which have guided most recent major social policy changes in the United Kingdom, have an anti-collectivist and anti-statist orientation. Fundamental values are related to freedom or liberty, individualism and inequality. Freedom or liberty is paramount, and is strongly linked to the principle of a free market economy. Freedom is taken to lead to inequality, with individualism as the basis for attributing achievements and difficulties to individual action. Though this simplistic representation of broad ideological positions could be disputed, it serves the purpose of underlining the extent to which debates about the aims of education generally reflect and express general differences about the nature of society and social justice.

Using this analysis of ideological positions, the Warnock dual aims of education can be interpreted as showing an individualist orientation by comparison with the socially oriented aims set out by Hargreaves (1982) in his book, *The Challenge of the Comprehensive School*. The Warnock aims include no reference to socially oriented attitudes and abilities such as the ability to co-operate with others in the interest of the group. In stating that the aims of education are the same for all children, the Warnock philosophy is expressing an egalitarian position but without the collectivist or social orientation of the Hargreaves philosophy. In this sense, the Warnock aims represent a broadly social democratic position which adopts elements of egalitarian and individualist values and rejects the purist values of individualist and collectivist positions. One reason for emphasising this relationship between general social value positions and educational aims is to point to the broad conceptual frameworks within which the current debates take place in this field. Another reason is that the field of special educational needs, and in particular the area of severe disability, provides a critical instance against which general formulations about the aims of education have to be tested.

A COMMON CURRICULUM AND SCHOOL SPECIALISATION

Educational aims which take account of egalitarian values need to be formulated in sufficiently general terms to apply to all children, but also to have sufficient content to be translatable into more specific goals and practicable objectives. Balancing these considerations involves a search for containing educational diversity within a unified and coherent set of common aims, to which there are no simple definitive solutions. One approach has been the concept that meaningful educational aims are the same for *virtually* all children (White, 1982; Tansley and Gulliford, 1960). Although this version is not all-inclusive, it is egalitarian in rejecting different educational aims for different sections of society (cf. Bantock, 1973). It is not radically egalitarian, however, in the sense of rejecting any conditions on a common curriculum for all.

The term 'curriculum' can be misleading because it is often used to refer to teaching intentions at different levels of specificity. In referring to a common curriculum, we need to distinguish between general aims and specific areas and fields of learning. Curricula can be differentiated, therefore, in terms of:

- general aims;
- areas and fields of learning;
- levels of progression within an area or field.

These distinctions are important in understanding the organisation of a common curriculum in an education system. Schools can specialise in different areas of knowledge and experience, or they can provide the same areas as each other. This is one of the continuing fields of educational debate — whether a common curriculum can accommodate some specialisation of school goals. It is pertinent to the current situation in which specialised City Technology Colleges are being established while a National Curriculum is being implemented. Though less contentious in education politics, the question of the continuation of special schools raises similar questions.

The extent to which some school specialisation can be accommodated within a national common curriculum framework depends on (a) the range of areas of knowledge and experience included in the common curriculum, and (b) the proportion of available school time which is required for these areas. A relatively loose and minimal common curriculum framework which takes up a small proportion of time would be compatible with some degree of differentiation between schools. With a tighter and extensive national common curriculum which takes up a high proportion of school time there would be less opportunity for specalisation in different schools.

The significance of these considerations for special needs education is that a school can follow specialised elements of the curriculum alongside common elements within a framework of common aims. Special schools could in principle have some specialised curriculum elements alongside curricular elements which are common to ordinary schools. Common educational aims for all are therefore compatible with special schooling which follows a flexible common curriculum framework. This position applies as much to specialist arts or science schools as to specialist schools for children with special educational needs.

SOCIAL ASPECTS OF CURRICULUM

Another important aspect of common curricula in common schools relates to social and emotional education and the membership of the schools and teaching groups. One of the main arguments for comprehensive schools and mixed ability classes is that social and personal educational goals are achieved not so much by explicit instruction and teaching as through the way schools and classes are organised and managed. This is sometimes referred to as the 'hidden curriculum', though this does not mean that these aspects of learning are unintended. On the contrary, this social and personal learning is a matter of considerable deliberation, but tends not to be formulated or documented in as much detail as the cognitive and intellectual parts of the curriculum. Of course, there is cognitive and social learning which is unintended, but I am not dealing with this kind of hidden curriculum now.

Schools can be organised to provide the same areas of knowledge and experience to learners with different characteristics, by limiting school entry on the basis of gender, ethnicity, religion, age, disability and so on. There would be little purpose in having different entry rules unless there were some additional or different educational intentions or methods for these groups, or there were grounds for believing that separation promoted achievement in the common curricular areas: for example, in the promotion of separate science teaching for girls. Yet this situation becomes more complicated if the curriculum is taken to include social and emotional educational aims. When learning the different areas of the curriculum, children could be learning about authority, decision making, collaboration, competition, self-reliance, self-determination and tolerance, for example. As members of a school community they are also learning about other children and their backgrounds.

One of the key arguments for the common school, the comprehensive school, for children from all backgrounds and with all personal characteristics is that it can and does promote the educational aims of respect, tolerance and mutual co-operation. These social aims of fellowship or fraternity are strongly valued by left-wing ideological positions, which place particular emphasis on including children from working-class and disadvantaged minority groups in common schools. The emphasis on inclusion is basic to such ideological positions, though for cognitive as well as social and emotional reasons.

The inclusion of more children over the last century in the school system has also been supported because it gives access to higher levels of cognitive achievement. This argument is one which right-wing positions can actively endorse, as it relates to the values of freedom and individuality. However, the individualist position is one which bases this access on the principles of the efficient use of resources: only those children with the personal resources and abilities to benefit from access to higher educational goals would be provided with this access. Right-wing positions also tend to place less value on the educational aims of fellowship and more on those concerned with individuality: self-reliance, self-determination and competition. This right-wing focus on individual achievements, both cognitive and social/emotional, assumes motivation and economic principles which are linked. The motivation principle is that individuals seek to benefit and improve themselves through achieving certain desirable goals. The economic principle is that these desirable ends are often in short supply relative to the demands for them and that this leads to some competition. Losing or failing is seen positively as a stimulus or challenge to seek future success and achievement or to adjust one's goals.

The validity and credibility of the individualist and collectivist ideological positions are not under consideration in this discussion. The point is that the arguments for common schools for all on social and emotional grounds depend partly on ideological assumptions and values. Those who argue for the integration or the non-segregation of children with severe difficulties on social and emotional grounds are expressing fundamental social values of fellowship and equality which may not be widely shared. That there has been some consensus about the policy of comprehensive or common schooling should not hide the fact that behind the consensus there have been different ideological positions.

SPECIAL NEEDS CURRICULA

If special education involves additional or different provision, then it is important to be clear about the nature of this difference. Starting from the discussion about a common curriculum in the previous sections, it would be unacceptable to attribute additional or different aims to some children: for example, to aim to enable them to overcome their special learning difficulties. The reason is that it is inconsistent to assert common aims for all and then to assert additional aims for some, even when these additional aims are for children with disadvantages. However, if the common aims are taken as basic, then any additional intentions could be formulated in terms of additional goals. This could be in the form of additional goals for children with learning difficulties, which could be compatible with common aims and be a means of fulfilling these common aims. This would involve some differentiation at the level of educational goals and objectives, with the same basic goals for most of the curriculum and additional goals for some children. However, time constraints may make it impractical to encompass both the basic and the additional goals in actual school programmes. Basic common goals would need to be limited in order to make time available for the additional goals. This implies a potential competition between common and additional goals for scarce time.

However, there are other objections to having any additional goals concerned with overcoming learning difficulties. These relate to the implication of the term 'overcoming'. It could be argued that overcoming implies that these children have a deficit which can be treated or remedied and that this additional goal raises traditional problems of identification. To many special educators this could be seen as a return to a 'within-child medical model'. As I argued in Chapters 1 and 2, and will argue later in this chapter, this is too simple a view and closes off consideration about the nature of special educational needs and the relationship between special needs education and other professional services for children with difficulties and disablities.

CURRICULA DIFFERENTIATION OR MODIFICATION

The reason for discussing the issue of accommodating additional goals for some children within a common curriculum is that this is one of the central curricular difficulties in this field. The recent trend, however, has been to emphasise the common educational needs of all children. This is understandable in view of the separateness of special from ordinary schooling. Yet the emphasis on

	Aims	Goals	Objectives	Classroom methods
1	C	C	C	C
2	C	C	C	D
3	C	C	D	D
4	C	D	D	D
5	D	D	D	D

Note: C = common to all; D = different for some.

Figure 5.1 *Different combinations of differentiation in curricular intention and classroom methods*

common educational aims can be mistakenly taken to imply that differentiation is only possible at the level of classroom methods. Figure 5.1 illustrates that this is not a sufficiently complex view.

Of the five possible combinations represented in the figure, examples 1 and 5 represent pure cases of similarity and differentiation, both of which are outside the range of possibilities which are usually considered. It is apparent that examples 2, 3 and 4 represent different mixes of common and different elements. Similarity in aims, goals and objectives with differences in methods is only one possibility. There are within this simplified model at least two other possibilities which represent increasing degrees of differentiation in intention, short of differences in aims.

This analysis of the elements of curriculum differentiation can be used to illustrate the poverty of official conceptions of special needs curricula in the 1980s. The DES (1984) classified curriculum in terms of:

- mainstream plus support;
- modified curriculum;
- developmental curriculum.

Mainstream plus support refers to a curriculum compatible in breadth and objectives with that in ordinary schools but with the provision of additional, possibly specialist teaching support, and resources. The modified curriculum is defined as:

a curriculum similar to that provided in ordinary schools [which], while not restricted in its expectations, has objectives more appropriate to children whose SEN would not be properly met by a mainstream curriculum. Children requiring such a curriculum may be described as having moderate learning difficulties.

The developmental curriculum is defined as:

> a curriculum covering sharply focussed educational, social and other experiences with precisely defined objectives and designed to encourage a measure of personal autonomy. Children needing such a curriculum may be described as having severe learning difficulties.
>
> (As quoted by Brennan, 1987, p. 37)

These definitions are coded: modified curriculum equals moderate learning difficulties, developmental curriculum equals severe learning difficulties. They are also vague in not specifying appropriate levels of objectives in the modified curriculum, the appropriate range of knowledge and experience, or what 'restricted in its expectations' means in the context of 'appropriate objectives'. The definition of the developmental curriculum is so general that it could apply to the modified curriculum if the reference to severe learning difficulties were removed.

The Warnock Report used a three-way classification of the forms of special educational need which are not exclusive of each other (section 3.19):

- special means of access to the curriculum through special equipment, facilities or resources, modification of the physical environment or specialist teaching techniques;
- special or modified curriculum;
- changes in the social structure and emotional climate in which education takes place.

These three forms correspond to modifications required for different impairments or deficits:

- access for sensory/motor difficulties;
- curriculum level for intellectual difficulties;
- social/emotional climate for emotional and behaviour difficulties.

This general three-way classification is very useful for analysing the variety of changes required to a common curriculum. It will be included in a model to be described in a later section of this chapter.

THE 'SPECIAL' IN SPECIAL EDUCATIONAL PROVISION

Swann (1983) has asserted that only a small proportion of the teaching in special needs education is out of the ordinary. This position expresses an integrationist emphasis on the similarities between ordinary and specialist teaching, the differences being considered relatively minor. By referring to the organisational aspects of special schools and units, such as the age grouping and the teacher–pupil ratios, and to the levels of complexity of the learning activities, this position considers only certain forms of modification, ignoring modifications of access and of social/emotional climate. Some of the additional financial resources and special needs modifications could, without doubt, be available in ordinary schools, but this is no substitute for a more thorough analysis of what is special about special needs education. The following analysis is based on Figure 5.1 and on the Warnock forms of modification. Several examples of modifications in different areas of special needs education are used to illustrate the analysis.

As a general principle, it is assumed that the greater the degree of functional impairment, the greater the degree of modification or differentiation that is needed in the curriculum. It is also assumed that differentiation takes place within a broad and flexible common curriculum framework. It is clear from Figure 5.1 that there are different levels at which modifications can be made, at goals, objectives and methods, at objectives and methods, and at methods only. In view of these possibilities one would expect that special needs teaching would be heterogeneous and show different degrees of being different from mainstream teaching. As special education has been available historically in separate schools and units, one would expect that the legitimacy for such specialisation would depend on developing teaching which is very different from ordinary schools. Curricula would therefore be of a kind which showed changes not only in methods and objectives but also in goals. Traditionally this has taken a different form in the different areas of special education. In the field of emotional and behavioural difficulties, it has in some cases taken the form of an emphasis on psycho-therapeutic interventions focused on the area of deficit. In other fields, such as moderate conceptual/intellectual difficulties, it has also focused on the area of deficit, not with therapeutic or corrective goals, but with adaptive goals emphasising basic scholastic skills. Most of the recent criticisms of special schooling have been of just this excessive focus on the area of deficit at the expense of a broad, more balanced curriculum (Swann, 1983; Hegarty, 1987).

However, a broadly balanced common curriculum, as I have

argued above, can accommodate additional goals and objectives which take account of individual needs. This has been the case in many areas of special needs practice. In the field of severe visual impairment, for example, the special curriculum elements of learning braille and mobility are not additional but central learning goals (Chapman and Stone, 1988). Not only are changes required in the methods used in the curricular areas common to all children, but there are additional goals which are relevant only to this particular group of children. Time is needed for learners to use these alternative forms of accessing the common curricular areas, which puts the practical timetabling under pressure. This can lead people to reconsider the balance of different elements of the curriculum for different groups and individuals and even to extend the schooling period.

The field of severe and profound intellectual difficulty illustrates that additional goals are focused not only on learning to make use of access means, but sometimes on correcting or rehabilitating aspects of the main area of deficit. In the curriculum produced by Rectory Paddock School (1981), for example, there are goals concerned with enhancing cognitive strategies in the field of memory, which is a major area of deficit for the children involved. There are similarities between these kinds of additional corrective goal and those of the currently popular programme of Instrumental Enrichment (IE), for children with intellectual difficulties (Feuerstein et al., 1979). In the present discussion I am concerned less with the validity of the causal theory of low intellectual functioning in terms of mediated learning experience than with the nature of the goals of the IE programme. The goals of IE are to restore a normal pattern of intellectual development by changing cognitive structures. This approach advocates special or additional goals which are focused not just on environmental adaptations for the child, i.e. instructional conditions, presentation and response modes, but on the adaptation of the child to the environment, i.e. are restorative or corrective of deficits.

THE EFFECTIVENESS OF DEFICIT-FOCUSED PROGRAMMES

A detailed evaluation of the effectiveness of programmes with the goal of restoring cognitive or other deficits is not appropriate for this chapter. However, as any judgement about whether additional restorative goals are worth pursuing depends on such evaluation, some of the issues which arise will be discussed. Programmes like IE may result in some enhanced cognitive functioning (Shayer and Beasley, 1987) but may not affect the child's attainments in other fields. If the assumption is that IE restores or corrects cognitive functioning, which is the deficit underlying school learning problems in traditional areas of the curriculum, then an evaluation of such a programme would show some effect outside the area of deficit. Even if no positive evidence has been found for a particular programme with corrective goals, there is still the prospect that in future a new programme or method could be designed to be effective. The example of training of psycholinguistic and perceptual abilities as underlying factors in school learning illustrates this point. Arter and Jenkins (1979) have argued in an influential review that deficits in school learning were largely resistant to training by existing procedures, and that ability training did not improve academic performance. However, more recent work in the specific field of auditory perceptual skill deficits and reading indicates that training in such skills does transfer to the area of reading (Bradley and Bryant, 1985).

Another area where there has been considerable interest in an intervention programme with rehabilitative goals is the use of conductive education for children with motor disorders (Cottam and Sutton, 1985). As with IE, the conductive education programme is directed at the deficit but with the goal of enabling children with cerebral palsy and spina bifida to participate in normal schooling without using wheelchairs, ramps, special toileting and modified instruments for eating and writing. It has been said that conductive education is not a therapy in the traditional sense, because the intervention is not given to prevent or lessen spasticity. The child is taught to use movement in order to perform certain functions: for example, to hold on in order to be able to sit. Though there is some dispute about how it relates to the professional field of physiotherapy and specialist teaching, this is a programme with goals which are clearly additional to those of an ordinary school curriculum. As with other deficit-focused programmes, its adoption depends on positive evaluations of its effectiveness.

A MODEL OF COMMON AND SPECIALISED GOALS

The model in Figure 5.2 represents how a common curricular framework for all children can include differences in goals, objectives and methods for some children.

This model follows the Warnock three-way breakdown of modifications or adaptations in which the ordinary teaching environment is adapted to the child's characteristics to enable the child to participate in a common curriculum framework. Drawing on the above discussion, the model also includes features which are intended to adapt the child to the ordinary teaching environment.

FOCUS OF ADAPTATIONS

	Adapting environment to child	Adapting child to environment
CURRICULUM Common goals	• Modes of instructional presentation and learner response • Level of objectives • Social structure/ emotional climate	X
Specialised additional goals	X	• Alternative access • Restore function/lessen deficit

Figure 5.2 *Relationship between curricular goals and adaptations for disability and difficulties*

The examples discussed in the last section illustrate two broad types of specialised additional goal which are compatible with a flexible common curriculum framework. The first type can be called alternative access programmes, which have as their goals the learning of different means of communication and movement, as found, for example, in the education of children with sensory impairments. Learning to use braille or to lipread, for instance, are for some children necessary conditions for access to a common curriculum. The second type of specialised additional goal can be called restorative or rehabilitative programmes, such as IE and conductive education, which are directed at restoring some function in the main area of deficit, whether it be emotional, intellectual or motor.

One problem with this model is that it is based on assumptions that adaptations, particularly of a restorative type, are effective and that we have a clear notion of what effectiveness means in this field. There is another problem about terminology which is important to discuss. The term 'remedial' has been deliberately avoided as it has been subjected to considerable criticism in its reference to remedial education (Golby and Gulliver, 1979). As applied to special programmes the term has been taken to imply that the child is the source of the difficulties even when there is inadequate and inappropriate ordinary teaching. Secondly, remedial implies that the child has a deficit which can be remedied in some way, an assumption which is rarely substantiated. The position taken in here is that (a) programmes with restorative or remedial goals are inappropriate when ordinary teaching is deficient, (b) programmes are not remedial or restorative unless they are known to be effective and (c) attributing a deficit or ability to a child is not to attribute an inherent and unalterable characteristic.

These additional programmes fall into an area which is on the borders of education and therapy. To help to clarify the nature of these deficit-focused interventions, some general working conception about what is involved in education and health interventions is needed. Education interventions will be taken to concern promoting all-round worthwhile human development in relation to the available resources. Health interventions are about maintaining and restoring order to all-round human functioning. When order cannot be fully restored, i.e. when there is no cure, there is still the possibility of correcting the condition to a limited extent, reducing its impact on the person's life or preventing it from getting worse.

Those interventions aimed at correcting, reducing or preventing are usually the responsibility of the therapeutic professions, such as physiotherapy and occupational, speech and psychotherapy. Internal bodily and physio-chemical interventions are not used by these professions as they are the preserve of the medical profession. Interventions by the therapeutic professions are similar to those used in teaching, being based on learning processes, but they have different goals. However, in the case of children with difficulties and disabilities there is an overlap between the goals of non-curative, rehabilitative therapies and those of restorative specialist teaching. Examples of this can be found in several areas of special needs education which were discussed earlier in this chapter. The overlap implies that there is no definitive boundary between special needs teaching and various therapeutic interventions, although there are differences in the core activities of the different professional groups. These issues, particularly how they bear on the organisation of services, the professions and inter-professional relationships, will be discussed in Chapter 7.

The reason for raising these issues here is to consider what can be meant by restorative goals if a cure or prevention is not possible given current knowledge and know-how. In the discussion about a general systems approach in Chapter 2, some mention was made of the uncertainties about the appropriate level and nature of intervention for certain conditions. These centred on the preferred level of causal analysis and on the effectiveness of interventions. With such uncertainty there are likely to be different opinions about the potential and limits of restorative programmes for non-preventable or non-curable conditions. This is one of the main reasons why remedial, corrective or rehabilitative programmes can raise false hopes or elicit false dismissals.

CONCLUSION

I have argued in this chapter that the search for a common curriculum for all which is sufficiently general and flexible to incorporate programmes with specialised additional goals for some is a continuing challenge for educators. Even if curricular modification or adaptation is seen mainly in terms of adapting the environment to fit the child, as the Warnock Report viewed it, there is still the need for additional specialised programmes to enable children to learn to use alternative ways of accessing the common curriculum. Programmes with the goals of restoring functions or lessening deficits similarly involve additional goals. With more time spent on these additional programmes there is less time for the common curricular goals. There are no simple definitive solutions to this issue, but they underlie the major administrative, organisational and service problems in this field and they require practical consideration.

—6—
Designing the curriculum: teaching and assessing

INTRODUCTION

In this chapter I will discuss some of the central questions about designing and implementing the curriculum as these relate to special needs teaching. These questions have a long history in the general field of curriculum, but it is only recently that they have become central in special needs education. One view is that this could be a mark of the isolation of the field from general education thinking and practice. Another view is that curriculum implementation became a central issue with the promotion of the objectives approach and that the objectives approach arose for reasons specific to the special needs. Whatever the case, the place of objectives approaches in teaching children with special educational needs is well established, almost an orthodoxy (Ainscow and Tweddle, 1979; Westmacott and Cameron, 1981). This is in the context of some well-established opposition in this country to objectives-based approaches among liberal and progressive mainstream curriculum writers (Kelly, 1982).

My intention in this chapter is to discuss the origins, characteristics and development of objectives approaches within special needs education in relation to the wider mainstream criticisms of objectives in education. This will lead to the proposal that, although there are underlying contradictions between objectives and alternative approaches, such as process approaches, there is basic interlinking between them. The chapter continues with a discussion of the relationship of objectives to assessment in this field, of what is called curriculum-based assessment. Out of this emerges a discussion of the functions of assessment in identifying and meeting children's special educational needs. One of the main themes of the chapter is a critique of an overly simplistic behavioural objectives approach which has been influential in this field. The chapter presents an outline of a pluralistic approach to the place of objectives and assessment in the education of children with special needs.

BACKGROUND TO OBJECTIVES FOR SPECIAL NEEDS

Not only did the objectives approach become established in special needs education much later than in mainstream education, it was also introduced with a focus on individual children rather than on general planning for groups of children. One explanation of this difference is that special education has a particular focus on the individual child in contrast to mainstream education. That, however, does not take into account the fact that special schooling and teaching is also about group-based teaching. Another explanation is that objectives approaches were introduced mainly by educational psychologists as a way of applying behavioural approaches to special education, hence the term 'behavioural objectives'. This interpretation fits with the applied psychology origins of objectives approaches (Solity and Bull, 1987; Wheldall and Merrett, 1984) and the lack of reference in Ainscow and Tweddle's 1979 book on the topic to the work of mainstream objectives theorists, such as Tyler, Charters and Davie.

The significance of this is that psychologists have had their own agendas for introducing objectives approaches which derived from their professional role in the education service. Professional educational psychologists began to develop an interest in behavioural approaches or applied behaviour analysis at the time of the peak of dissatisfaction with the use of traditional psychological assessment techniques. This dissatisfaction was related partly to the growing lack of confidence in psychometric tests of ability and other traits and partly to the problems associated with intervening effectively to alter these identified deficits. All of this was in the educational and social context of a basic questioning of the fairness of selection for placement at different kinds of school.

The behavioural approach provided a positive alternative to 'ability' approaches in two respects. Firstly, by discounting states or processes which were not directly observable, the problems of identifying more general psychological characteristics were eliminated at a stroke. Secondly, by adopting the principle of the functional relationship between observable environment and behaviour factors, a belief in altering behaviour was renewed. It is clear that such a scheme would be very useful to applied psychologists in education. My argument is not that this movement arose without any empirical support, but that professional demands were as influential as any empirically based evaluations in the introduction of behavioural approaches. This movement in professional educational psychology has also to be seen in the context of the contemporary criticisms of behaviour analysis within the academic field of psychology and the growth of cognitive and developmental psychology.

Although the use of objectives has been widely promoted by educational psychological services around the country, the value of an objectives approach has also been recognised as a way of introducing greater curricular purpose into special schools, particularly for children with moderate and severe learning difficulties. This move has been interpreted more critically by Swann (1983) as a self-protective strategy by special schools. With pressures for integration, special schools have had to identify their special contribution. The objectives approach has been promoted, according to Swann, as one way to create a specialist contribution.

OBJECTIVES APPROACHES

The major case for using objectives in teaching usually rests on the effectiveness of teaching and learning. Objectives are concerned with the intended outcomes for learners as opposed to what the teacher intends to do with or present to the learner. Specifying objectives enables the 'targeting' of learning. In the usual justification for the primacy of learner outcomes it is asserted that the purpose of teaching is to bring about learning, and finding out whether it has occurred depends on specifying an outcome. The emphasis is clearly on predetermining outcomes as a basis both for identifying ways of attaining the outcomes and for evaluating whether the outcomes have been attained. The approach is an example of a rational planning model used in many other areas of social action and management.

In its individualised use in special needs education it has enabled teachers to develop teaching programmes for children with learning difficulties which pinpoint particular personalised learning outcomes as the basis for teaching. One feature of formulating learner outcomes in specific observable terms, as suggested by Mager (1962), is that the steps towards attaining the intended outcome can themselves be set in observable terms, which enables the sequencing of steps towards the intended learning outcome or task, and the sequencing of these elements or steps into a programme is called task analysis. Task analysis is one of the main techniques associated with objectives approaches. From one point of view all curriculum sequencing involves identifying elements of the intended learning and setting them in a sequence for teaching and learning. However, task analysis refers to a particular kind of curriculum sequencing as it uses behavioural definition of learning outcomes as the elements.

PROBLEMS WITH BEHAVIOURAL OBJECTIVES

There have been many criticisms of objectives approaches from within mainstream curriculum thinking and within the special needs field. It is not my intention to discuss these in any detail but to identify some of the main issues which arise in the field as regards children with special educational needs. Much of the general criticism derives from antagonism towards what is seen as the mechanistic and technological nature of this approach to teaching. MacDonald Ross (1975) summarises these points and illustrates the liberal humanistic aversion to what appears to be an excessively time-consuming and precision-oriented approach which runs contrary to cherished educational ideals. From one point of view, the technical nature of the objectives approach is portrayed as an advantage. It can provide curriculum designers/and teachers with clear procedures for planning. The problem here is the time required to formulate behavioural or specific performance objectives. Class teachers often feel that this is an excessively time-consuming operation which would interfere with their other responsibilities even if they were proficient in formulating such objectives. Proponents often respond to sceptics either with recommendations to try the approach and then judge or with schemes of preformulated objectives for teachers to use, as in DATA PAC (Mawer et al., 1983). This, however, gives rise to claims that the class teacher is being cast in the role of technician and not as a professional. This criticism is also linked to the one which represents the objectives approach as constraining the freedom and creativity of the teacher to take advantage of unforeseen learning opportunities in the classroom. The use of DISTAR (Engelman and Carnine, 1982) as a comprehensive scripted approach to teaching is often quoted as an example of such a programme.

A significant aspect of these debates is that the elements of a criticism from one position can be turned round into a positive feature from another position. An objectives approach is for some proponents a general strategy for planning and evaluating what is to be taught, the content; it is not concerned with what should be taught. What matters here are the means, not the ends to which they are used. For others this is one of the major weaknesses of the objectives approach (MacDonald Ross, 1975; Whitaker, 1988). The preoccupation with teaching strategies which do not involve some consideration of the selection of the ends poses serious questions about the value-free claims for the objectives approaches.

In the objectives approach there is the basic assumption that the matter or content of teaching is distinct from the manner or

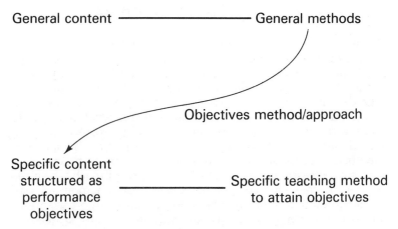

Figure 6.1 *Teaching methods and structured content in the objectives approach*

method of teaching. The ends and means of teaching can be conceptualised as separate. This is expressed in two ways: firstly, what to teach is separated from how to teach; and secondly, how to teach is seen in terms of how to structure the content, i.e. formulating sequences of intended performance outcomes, and not what specific methods are used to help the learner attain the objective. There is a critical distinction here between the general objectives method of structuring content and the specific methods used in classroom teaching to attain the objective (the structured content). This is represented in Figure 6.1.

Proponents of the objectives approach usually conflate these two senses of 'method', which enables them to claim that the objectives approach does not prescribe teaching methods (Raybould, 1984). This is correct in relation to the selection of specific methods for the structured objective. However, the very process of structuring the content or matter of teaching in performance outcomes for learners is itself a prescribed method — a higher-level general method. A major point of contention is just this way of conceptualising and translating content into the practice of teaching. In the process approach there is a basic rejection of the assumption that the ends and means, the content and methods of teaching can be separated (Kelly, 1982). The general and specific methods or processes of teaching are taken to affect what is learned. It is the manner, the principles of procedure, rather than the matter of learning which is primary in the process approach to curriculum design.

VARIATIONS WITHIN OBJECTIVES AND PROCESS APPROACHES

It is interesting to note that recent developments and variations within the approaches show some possible convergence between objectives and process approaches. A move within the process approach which is best represented by Stenhouse (1975) is to divide curricular activities into those which are instrumental, for which objectives are necessary, and those which are developmental and concerned with initiation into intrinsically worthwhile activities. The former involves training, the latter education, according to some process theorists. This does not imply that instructional, training or objectives approaches are not an important part of the curriculum, it has been argued, but they do not represent the only approach let alone the most significant one.

Within the objectives approach there are similar variations which indicate some recognition of the limited applicability of this design approach. Objectives approaches are sometimes thought not to require a behavioural definition of objectives; more general and less observable learner outcomes are acceptable. Another variation is that objectives are more relevant to the mathematics/science areas of the curriculum than to the humanities. This variation can be linked to the distinction between two kinds of objective. Eisner (1969) has distinguished between instructional and expressive objectives, instructional being learner outcome objectives, while expressive objectives describe educational encounters. Expressive objectives focus on what the learner will encounter or experience, they do not specify in advance what will be learned. They are evocative and not prescriptive for the learner. Teachers are said to have recourse to these objectives rather than to learner outcome ones for more sophisticated and complex areas of learning. This distinction is a very useful one but it is unfortunate that the word 'objectives' is used in both cases. The difference between instructional and expressive objectives corresponds to crucial differences between objectives/product and process approaches.

Within special educational needs, there have also been variations and interpretations which have softened the objectives approach. The Ainscow and Tweddle (1979) version was introduced in a plausible and flexible way with no reference to behavioural psychology, in contrast to the Solity and Bull (1987) and Wheldall and Merrett (1984) versions. That objectives specification is time-consuming was recognised and its use throughout the curriculum for children with learning difficulties was not advocated. Ainscow and Tweddle's distinction between the closed and open curriculum marked the boundary between where mastery of objectives and more general familiarity was expected. The version of objectives developed by Wedell (1987) also represents a flexible general strategy which can accommodate the negotiation of objectives with the learner and the use of information about the learner characteristics to select appropriate methods of instruction.

The more recent version by Ainscow and Tweddle (1988) represents an apparently basic revision of their 1979 version. There is a recognition of the limitation of using performance objectives because they can: (a) lead to a narrowing of the curriculum with a focus only on those areas which can be set into a specific objectives format; (b) promote a static and inflexible approach to the curriculum; (c) encourage teachers to see learners as passive; (d) lead to isolation of children on individual programmes; and (e) make teachers feel inadequate and anxious about achieving targets. This version rejects the use of objectives as a science of instruction in favour of objectives as 'a language to aid planning and communication of educational purposes' (p. 32).

The new Ainscow and Tweddle version is presented in the same terms which are used by process theorists to criticise and reject objectives approaches and yet the value of objectives is still maintained. What characterises this development is the adoption of elements of the design language of both objectives and process approaches without any explicit reference to what is being done. It seems to imply a retreat from the specific applications and developments which derived from their 1979 position. It could represent a defensive move to forestall criticism by using less product-oriented language while in practice still operating mainly in a product- or objectives-oriented way.

FUNDAMENTAL CONCEPTUAL DIFFERENCES IN APPROACH

Table 6.1 summarises some of the key points which divide the two broad approaches. As the table illustrates, there are some fundamental differences between the approaches in terms of assumptions about the nature of what is to be learned and about the process of learning. Any approach to teaching makes some assumptions about the content and process of learning. In terms of the nature of what is learned, the objectives approach assumes an objectivist theory of knowledge: that it is established 'out there' and that it can be analysed into different forms and elements. The process approach assumes a more subjective or constructivist theory in which humans actively construct and revise knowledge (Kelly, 1982).

Table 6.1 *Conceptual differences between product/objectives and process approaches*

Product/objectives	Process
Focus on ends	Focus on means
Ends distinct from means	Ends and means interrelated
Objectivist assumptions about knowledge	Constructivist assumptions about knowledge
Psychological assumptions: mechanistic, atomistic	Psychological assumptions: organismic, holistic
Outcomes can be planned, predetermined	Some outcomes are not intended
Focus on what education *is for*	Focus on what education *is*
Content and structuring of content are primary: setting objectives	Methods and processes are primary: establishing principles of procedure
Sequencing: linear sequence of units of learning	Sequencing: models the processes of enquiry/design
Training, instructional orientation	Facilitation, guidance orientation

Associated with these assumptions about what is learned are different psychological assumptions about the process of learning. The objectives approach is based on a mechanistic model of the psychology of learning (Overton, 1984). Learning is seen as the gradual accumulation of units, whether they be overt responses or cognitive units. Both radical behaviourism and information-processing theories are mechanistic in this sense. Causation is in terms of contingent prior and subsequent factors which determine learning. In the process approach there are organismic assumptions about learning. Learning involves the developmental restructuring of underlying structures as opposed to the accumulation of separate units. These structures have a pervasive effect across a range of behaviours in different situations. Causation is seen in terms of identifying those structures which enable certain functions to be fulfilled. An example of an organismic psychological theory is Kelly's Personal Construct Theory (Kelly, 1955). Change arises from external conditions and actions, according to mechanistic assumptions. Therefore, optimal learning requires outside planning and intervention to control the conditions which influence learning. Change, according to organismic assumptions, is given and needs no explanation. It is only the form and direction of change and the constraints upon it which are of interest. The learner is inherently active, and learning requires facilitation or guidance rather than intervention or control.

From these different orientations to the learning process and what is learned, there follow certain differences in the teaching process. Given mechanistic learning assumptions and an objectivist theory of knowledge, teaching is concerned with the structuring and sequencing of the units to be learned. The notions of teaching as instruction and of the transmission–reception metaphor are appropriate here. With a constructivist theory of knowledge and organismic learning assumptions, teaching is concerned with establishing principles of teaching procedure which take account of what is learned and how teaching occurs. The sequencing of teaching is based on the processes of enquiry and design; it is a question of sequencing the processes of learning rather than the units of what is learned (Posner and Strike, 1976). The notions of teaching as facilitation or guidance are appropriate here.

INTERLINKING PROCESS AND OBJECTIVES APPROACHES

What I have represented above is a basic opposition between process and objectives approaches. Some curriculum theorists have acknowledged these philosophical differences but reject the popular idea that they imply that design is strictly of one or other approach (Skilbeck, 1984). Part of the opposition can be attributed less to the philosophical differences than to socio-political expressions of these differences for the role of teachers in curriculum design and for learners in the learning process. The objectives approach has associations with the curriculum being outside the control of classroom teachers and learning outside the control of learners. The process approach has strong links to the idea of the class teacher having a central role in planning the curriculum and learners constructing their learning.

However, as Skilbeck argues, there are no grounds for separating 'objectives' from 'processes'. Figure 6.2 is one way of representing the inextricable link between processes and products/outcomes. The model assumes that there are three main elements to consider: (a) the outcome for the learner; (b) the process of learning and (c) the process of teaching. Two of these aspects are represented in the figure.

According to this model, teaching always involves a teaching process and learner outcome aspect. Specific instances can vary depending on the relative emphasis placed on the teaching process and learner outcomes. The objectives approach, for example, places major emphasis on specifying learner outcomes, but has implications of a general kind for the teaching process. Similarly, the process approach places most emphasis on specifying principles for teaching procedures, but in so doing necessarily uses some general notions about learner outcomes to select these procedures. The possibility of high process and product specification is not found in practice as it would involve an uneconomic use of time. Low process and product specification represents an ineffective design orientation.

Although purist exponents of the two broad approaches may

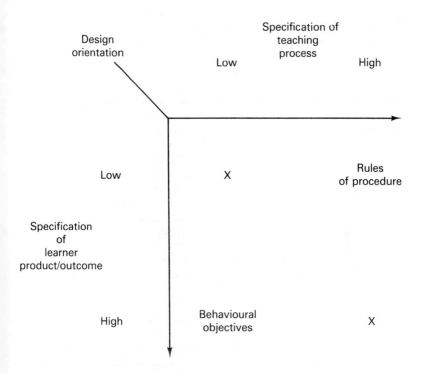

Figure 6.2 *Interlinking process and objectives approaches*

resist this interlinking, there is clear evidence that they do make use of both process and product notions. Kelly (1982), for instance, in arguing for principles of procedure maintains that some teaching approaches are 'counterproductive'. This can be interpreted as the use of a general product orientation to inform the selection of a teaching process or method. Attempts by process and objectives theorists to choose between processes and products are fundamentally flawed.

A PLURALISTIC APPROACH TO OBJECTIVES

In this section I will draw out some implications of the above position for teaching children with special educational needs. I have listed below some of the key areas in which there have been disagreements about the concept of objectives or intended learner outcomes:

Outcomes:

- as the behaviour/action   *or*   are indicated by behaviour/action
- one kind of outcome   *or*   various kinds of outcomes
- one level of specificity   *or*   different kinds of specificity
- same specificity for all   *or*   different specificity for areas of curriculum different areas of curriculum
- single, isolated outcomes   *or*   multiple, related outcomes
- as intended/planned   *or*   unintended outcomes
- purpose in teaching   *or*   successful encounters are implies predictable unpredictable learner outcomes
- set by designer/teacher   *or*   negotiated with learner
- same for all learners   *or*   dependent on learner characteristics

The position on the left of the above list represents a purist unitary behavioural approach to learner outcomes. The pluralistic position to the right, which is advocated here, is more purpose, context and content specific though it does not have the simple appeal of a unitary view. Behavioural descriptions indicate learning outcomes but there is no simple clear-cut relationship between outcome and behaviour. Learning may occur but not be expressed behaviourally under certain conditions.

This pluralistic position also rejects the radical behavioural reduction of all learning to one kind. Learning can be of various kinds, a view expressed by the objectives-oriented cognitive theorist Gagné (1985). General rule or strategy learning, for example, is such that it is evident in many different tasks and contexts and could not be reduced to a single sequence of responses. This implies that outcomes can be described at various levels of specificity/generality. There is not only one level of specificity, that of behavioural performances; to rule out 'fuzzy' outcomes is to rule out higher-order learning outcomes.

Another feature of a pluralistic approach to learning outcomes is the recognition that objectives are not single, isolated outcomes. Teaching procedures and learning activities are associated with a set of possible outcomes. In planning a teaching programme, account needs to be taken of the relationship between different kinds of outcome, cognitive and social/emotional, short and longer term. The tendency to focus on the cognitive/intellectual and to

ignore how the manner of teaching can bring about possibly undesirable outcomes has to be avoided by bringing a wider set of
objectives into the initial planning. Some outcomes, however
much advanced planning has taken place, are not predictable and
are therefore unintended. By contrast, in some very significant
areas of learning, purpose in teaching does not require predictable
outcomes but expects and welcomes the unpredictable. In these
cases, the measure of successful teaching may be a novel and
unpredicted outcome. The balance between predictable, planned
outcomes and unpredictable, novel outcomes has to be struck
within education. Either principle cannot be supported in isolation
of the other: the principles of imparting and those of guiding are
mutually interdependent.

IMPLICATIONS FOR SPECIAL EDUCATIONAL NEEDS

The pluralistic approach to objectives has implications for special
needs teaching in several respects. Firstly, there are no grounds
for considering a behavioural objectives approach as having special
relevance to this field. This follows from the diverse nature of
special educational needs. Secondly, it is important to be careful
about how the term 'structure' is used. Children with severe and
moderate learning difficulties are thought to require a structured
objectives approach on account of their slow rate and narrow
transfer of learning (Faupel, 1986). This is a limited use of the term
'structure' as it refers only to sequences of small steps of specific
learning outcomes (Swann, 1983). Another example of where the
term refers only to specifying learner outcomes is in some recent
curriculum research for pupils with moderate learning difficulties
(Redmond et al., 1988). Both these examples overlook the possibility of specifying mainly the teaching procedures rather than the
learner outcomes. This emphasis can be attributed to a behavioural
influence in curriculum design. Thirdly, there is a need to guard
against over-identifying a behavioural objectives approach with
learning difficulties. What a behavioural objectives approach has
offered is the opportunity for children with learning difficulties to
work at their own level, to progress at their own pace to levels
they can manage. These features are also applicable to a design
where the emphasis is on teaching procedures. The level at which,
for instance, an enquiry or design project is introduced, the specification of how the learner is guided and at what pace could also
be adapted to take account of the learning characteristics of the
child without a primary focus on specific performance outcomes.
This is one of the challenges presented by adopting a more pluralistic approach to teaching.

CURRICULUM-BASED ASSESSMENT

As I have mentioned before, one of the apparent advantages of a behavioural conception of learning is that it redirects attention away from general learner characteristics towards specific observable behaviours. This means that learner deficits which are expressed across learning situations and over time can be reduced to the absence of learner behaviours. This position, coupled with the assumption that these behaviours can be learned, is consistent with maintaining a positive conception about the prospects for learning, whatever the severity of learning difficulties. The usual line of argument is to concentrate on what can be altered (Ainscow and Tweddle, 1979). It is assumed that deficits as characteristics cannot be assessed validly or altered, and therefore can be ignored (Ysseldyke and Salvia, 1978) from a teaching viewpoint. From these assumptions the argument switches the conceptual framework to identifying those 'skills children must learn to realise the aims we set for their education' (Solity and Bull, 1987, p. 34). Assessment is viewed as a continuous process over time which starts with the child learning in the classroom and involves assessment in response to teaching. Howell et al. (1979) distinguished between this approach to assessment – task analysis – and the traditional approach of identifying learner deficits or difficulties — learner analysis. The learner analysis approach is sometimes referred to pejoratively as a medical or a within-child deficit approach.

The task analysis approach represents an approach to assessment in which learner performance is assessed against a clearly defined criterion or domain — criterion-referenced assessment. The learner analysis approach is usually associated with assessment which compares learner performance against a standard set by other learners — norm-referenced assessment. Curriculum-based assessment usually refers to the process of assessment involving task analysis, objectives setting and criterion referencing. This assessment requires that the curriculum be defined as a series of tasks which are sequenced and expressed in a behavioural objective form. There is an initial assessment of the learner's starting skills to enable placement on the sequence of objectives — placement assessment. Suitable methods, materials and classroom arrangements are selected to enable the learner to achieve the next step on the sequence. Progress is monitored and the assessment can be used as feedback to make changes to objectives or methods — formative assessment. These stages are represented in Figure 6.3.

Consider the example of a learner who is having difficulties with the next step in a sequence after changes in teaching methods and

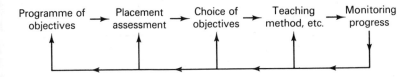

Figure 6.3 *Curriculum-based assessment*

arrangements have been tried. The next objective can be task analysed into a sequence of sub-steps as a way of bridging the gap between the current level and the next step. This powerful scheme presents a complete instructional system in which progress, however small and at whatever level, can be planned and monitored. The central function of assessment in this scheme is as a feedback system, as formative of the teaching and learning process. Although the scheme requires an initial assessment to identify the next learning step, this is seen as derivative of the initial programming and sequencing of the curriculum.

FALSE OPPOSITION OF CRITERION AND NORM REFERENCING

The opposition of criterion- and norm-referenced assessment orientations is exaggerated and over-polarised. Criterion referencing has strong support because of its links to formative assessment. It enables assessment of proficiency in relation to teaching and learning intentions and is not based on comparison with others. It has been described as providing an instructional improvement orientation rather than the status determination orientation of the norm-referenced assessment. It forms the basis of what is considered to be a non-competitive form of educational assessment. However, there are certain critical misconceptions about the nature of norm-referenced assessment and its relationship to criterion-referenced assessment. Norm referencing and criterion referencing are of a learner's performances not of the person her/himself. Norm referencing is not necessarily of learner

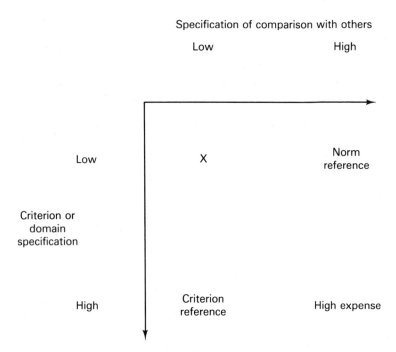

Figure 6.4 *Criterion- and norm-referenced assessment*

abilities but can also be used for assessing learner attainments. It is also false to presume that the distribution of performances which arise from norm-referenced assessment represents some biologically given distribution of abilities.

Figure 6.4 indicates a clear link between the two orientations to assessment. Norm and criterion referencing involve elements of domain specificity and interpersonal comparisons, but they differ in the relative balance placed on each. In criterion-referenced assessment, the learner's performance is referenced mainly against a well-defined criterion or domain. However, the domains or criteria are selected by reference to the performance of significant others. This comparative or normative aspect is weakly represented in criterion referencing where the focus is on specific characteristics. Specifically defined criteria are needed to establish the degree of mastery. In norm-referenced assessment, performance is referenced against the average level of a representative sample of some group. Here the setting of a norm depends on a general domain from which items are derived to differentiate between people. The underlying domains in norm-referenced assessment are often overlooked in the technical concerns about item selection and scaling. The domains in norm referencing are broad and at a general level of description.

Using this analysis one can envisage an orientation with high degrees of both kinds of referencing. This combination is rare because such an assessment procedure would involve considerable expense in terms of specifying multiple specific domains and establishing norms of performance for these domains. There is a trade-off between breadth and specificity of assessment. As assessment becomes focused on broader, more general characteristics, there are economic reasons for referencing against group norms.

MISCONCEPTIONS ABOUT NORM REFERENCING

Norm-referenced assessment has been associated historically with selection decisions: for example, into grammar schools and special schools. Selection decisions are required when there is limited availability of certain educational provision compared to the demand. Norm-referenced assessment, particularly in the form of ability and aptitude tests, has been used in these competitive situations partly because it has the general scope required for decision-making over longer time periods. The effect has been to bring norm-referenced assessments into disrepute because of the false implication that those not selected do not have the required competence. This implication misrepresents the nature of norm referencing, which indicates a person's relative standing on some characteristic in comparison with others. It does not indicate whether the person has sufficient competence for the activity in question. This requires setting a cut-off point based on evidence about the degree of competence that is required for the performance in question.

When there is limited availability of particular kinds of schooling this leads to a competitive situation in which the selection decision is 'how capable is the person relative to others to . . .?', rather than 'does the person have the required capabilities to . . .?'. Differential performance between people is a requirement for constructing a norm-referenced procedure. But once the procedure is standardised there is no inherent reason why assessed characteristics cannot change, as can the proportion of people attaining a particular level. When norm-referenced tests gauge change they do so at a general level in terms of broad domains. Criterion-referenced tests are more relevant to gauging change at the more specific levels of classroom learning.

As mentioned above, norm referencing is often associated with the assessment of abilities. Typical of such assessment are IQ tests, which have often been interpreted as a measure of fixed general learning ability or potential. These assessments have been conducted traditionally on a single occasion outside the contexts of teaching and learning. They have been contrasted with achievement tests which are designed to assess attainment in response to teaching. As I argued in Chapter 2, the traditional distinction between ability and achievement assessment is untenable. Ability tests are based on attainment information which is used for predicting or anticipating future learning outcomes.

AN ALTERNATIVE TO THE FORMATIVE–SUMMATIVE DISTINCTION

Rather than distinguish between two kinds of assessment it is preferable to consider all assessment as summarising learning progress and having predictive purposes. Assessment can then be used for two broad purposes: (a) correcting or altering teaching approaches, and/or (b) moving on to another stage of learning. This is a different conception from the currently popular distinction between formative and summative assessment. Assessment is separated in the formative–summative distinction into ongoing assessment which is used to inform the teaching–learning process and summative assessment which summarises overall progress made. Summative assessment is then typically used to anticipate or predict performance in another cycle of learning or some other activity. However, it is rare for the predictive use of all assessment to be considered explicitly. Formative assessment is what counts in this conception of assessment purposes. In the alternative conception presented here, all assessment involves some prediction and the formative–summative aspects are treated as related.

The main difficulty with the formative–summative distinction is the assumption that formative and summative assessment are distinct kinds of assessment. The presumed distinction is really about the different levels of assessment, specific small scale or general broad scale. Formative assessment usually refers to short period assessments at a specific level during a course of learning. Summative assessment usually refers to overall general assessments over a longer period at the end of a course of learning. Yet formative assessments depend on small-scale summative assessment as they summarise attainment at some step in the sequence of learning. Because of the small scale of this summative assessment it can be used as feedback for altering the teaching approach. Whether the assessment information is used to alter the teaching or to move on to another stage of learning, this is based on a small-scale prediction about the learner. Errors in prediction at this level can be easily corrected by altering objectives or teaching methods without adverse consequences. This is not so for general end of course summative assessments. Changing whole courses of objectives and methods involves major teaching investments.

The proposed alternative to the formative–summative distinction therefore involves the following assumptions:

- the distinction between general large-scale units of learning, e.g. modules, and specific smaller-scale units, e.g. steps within a module;
- all assessment involves description of attainment at some level of generality/specificity;
- using assessment information depends on some specific short-term or more general longer-term prediction about learning;
- the predictive use of assessment information is used formatively to alter teaching approaches and/or to move to another stage in learning.

TASK AND LEARNER ANALYSES

Behaviourally oriented assessment in special needs education has led to an excessive focus on learning outcomes with relatively little interest in the learning structures and processes — the cognitive, motivational and emotional processes which lead to learning outcomes. Cognitive approaches in psychology have tended towards the view that assessment also focuses on learner's perceptions, strategies and interests in relation to the task (Case and Bereiter, 1984). Assessing learner processes, such as strategies, is important as it can inform decisions about learning steps and teaching procedures which are relevant to attaining certain learning outcomes. In the light of this discussion, it is difficult to justify the polarisation in the special needs field between a task analysis and learner analysis orientation to assessment (e.g. Solity and Bull, 1987). It is evident that comprehensive assessment would involve both task and learner analysis.

In the revised approach presented by Ainscow and Tweddle (1988), their proposal for a third way, an analysis of the learning environment, still does not include explicit reference to the learner. In the learning environment they include objectives, tasks, activities and classroom arrangement, and state that these 'should be reviewed in terms of pupils' knowledge, skills, interests and previous experience' (p. 18). It is odd that they do not consider this

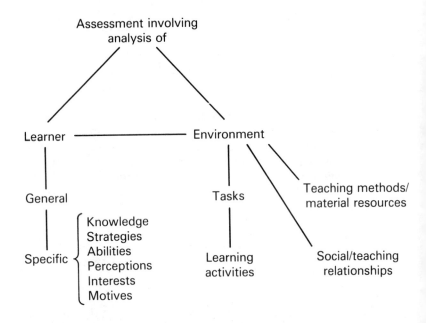

Figure 6.5 *A redefined interactionist perspective on assessment*

review to involve a learner analysis. Figure 6.5 represents a redefined interactionist perspective on assessment which focuses on both learner and learning environment.

A TEACHING ASSESSMENT OF LEARNER CHARACTERISTICS

The above perspective differs from other interactionist approaches to assessment in recognising the characteristics of the learner as a major influence on the level and rate of learning. The reluctance to acknowledge the influence of learner characteristics can be attributed to particular assumptions about traits and abilities and to problems in assessing them.

There are alternatives to the traditional one-off assessment procedures which are conducted outside a teaching context and then interpreted as measures of stable general learner characteristics. Following the redefined interactionist perspective outlined above, learner characteristics would be assumed to interact with the context of learning and to be specific to the fields of learning. As outcomes of learning and development, learner characteristics may also be alterable. This denies the criticism that identifying learner characteristics involves the attribution of inherent and unalterable characteristics.

This model of learner characteristics is a more dynamic one in which a distinction is made between what has been learned independently till the present and what could be achieved in the future in a specific context and field with environmental assistance and facilitation (Vygotsky, 1978; Feuerstein et al., 1979). It is crucial to distinguish this model from the behavioural and the classical abilities models. It is similar to the behavioural model in implying assessment by teaching, but it differs from it in acknowledging the significant role of learner characteristics. It is similar to the classical abilities model in recognising the role of learner abilities and resources, but it differs from it in integrating abilities into the teaching–learning context.

In proposing this orientation, I am aware of the relatively underdeveloped and uncertain state of the existing assessment procedures (Haynes, 1971). This situation presents a challenge to educational assessors, particularly in the special needs area, to develop and test these procedures further. The basic principle of assessing learning abilities in a particular field is to identify the highest level at which the learner can perform the task independently. The next stage involves a form of assessing to the limits, in which various kinds and styles of teaching assistance are offered to see how much further the learner can attain. This gap between independent and assisted attainment is sometimes referred to as the zone of next development (Vygotsky, 1978).

It is important that what the learner can do with assistance on a particular task item is then done independently on a parallel task item. Learning ability is then gauged in terms of (a) the level attained by the learner independently; (b) the extent of gain derived from assistance; and (c) the degree of help required to achieve the gain. It should be apparent that in introducing the last two factors assessment becomes more complex than the traditional ability assessment model which is based only on the first factor. There are, however, many questions to consider: whether this complex model can be standardised to provide quantitative indices, whether it requires a systematic qualitative procedure or just a 'clinical' format, and whether these actual procedures for assessing learning abilities turn out to reduce the biases and abuses of traditional ability testing.

CONCLUSION

To conclude I have outlined a model of the different functions of assessment with reference to special educational needs in Figure 6.6.

Following the discussion in Chapter 5, the model assumes common curricular aims for virtually all children (1). At the level of curriculum planning, the possibility of additional or different curricular elements is accommodated within a common framework (2). Following the discussion earlier in this chapter, the design of curricula involves specifying both learner outcomes and teaching procedures (3). Assessment is used predictively to alter teaching methods and/or to move to different objectives. Though it is possible to consider the model by starting at several points, let us assume that a child is in an ordinary school class. The child's progress is monitored and, if adequate (4), continues to the next stage of learning in the progression. If progress, however, is assessed as inadequate (5), by criteria which can vary but are usually in terms of age-appropriate attainment level and rate of learning, then adaptations can be made to objectives and/or teaching procedures. Adaptations at this stage are frequent and common and can be considered routine and ordinary (6). At some point such adaptations may come to be considered exceptional (7), by criteria which again can vary, but depend on the frequency and degree of changes to objectives and procedures required to enable some learning. Having to make exceptional adaptations implies that the child's learning characteristics, resources and deficits have been reassessed (8). This reassessment is the outcome of a teaching-based assessment and may need to be confirmed by an independent predictive assessment. Once the learner's characteristics are judged as exceptional then this would have implications for the age-related objectives and teaching procedures to be used (9). It could also have implications for the use of schemes of additional or different objectives/procedures (10). Whether schemes of additional or different objectives/procedures are used depends itself on what is already included in the schemes of common progression (11). Using additional schemes would also have implications for the balanced relationship between the common and additional/different objectives and teaching procedures, discussed in Chapter 5.

The model could also be entered at the point of assessing the child's learning characteristics. This is usually done prior to the

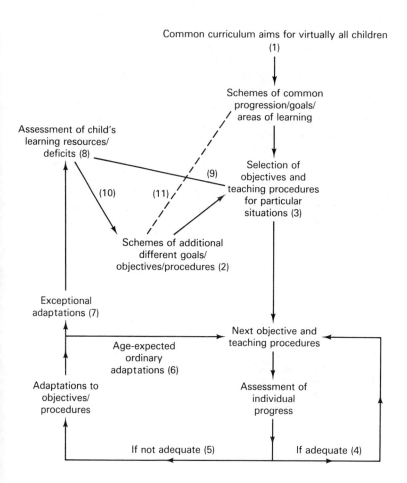

Note: Numbers in brackets refer to those parts of the
      model discussed in the text.

Figure 6.6 *A model of the functions of assessment*

child entering a formal course of learning, when there are clear grounds for expecting exceptional learning characteristics, such as in severe disability and impairment. The assessment of the child at this stage still requires a teaching-based assessment even though it is not based on previous assessments in school.

The above model is presented in general terms and does not include the whole range of key assessments which are needed at every stage of the school career of a child with special educational needs. Nor does it relate to decision making about special educational needs in terms of the organisation of the education service. What the model represents is a clear acknowledgement of the challenge of providing for individual differences within a common curriculum framework. It recognises that the dilemmas posed are not best dealt with by ignoring individual learning characteristics. The behavioural strategy of focusing only on what can be altered leads to a narrow view about what is worth altering and gives a partial view of learning, teaching and assessing. Nevertheless, this model does learn from the behavioural approach in attaching importance to specifying learning outcomes and to assessing in relation to educationally defined goals within the context of teaching.

—7

Professional issues

INTRODUCTION

As in other areas of service provision, issues relating to profession-alism are among the most important in special needs education. There has been a growth of interest in parent–professional relationships and in the role of parents in the education of children with special educational needs. Yet there has been no similar analysis of the role and contribution of professionals to services for children with special needs. Where there has been any con-sideration of the issue, it has been to reveal professional self-seeking in the expansion of services in this field (Tomlinson, 1985). My aim in this chapter is to consider some of the professional issues in the field of special needs education from a perspective which confronts the conflicts and dilemmas of professionalism. This involves considering the different professional groups involved in the field and focusing on internal and inter-pro-fessional issues. This will inevitably lead to a discussion of the service context and the relationships between professionals and those they serve.

THE PROFESSIONALS

Special needs education occupies a significant position at the inter-section between the three major statutory services — health, edu-cation and social services. Although special needs education is clearly placed administratively within the education service, it has strong historical links to health services and is still dependent on contributions from health and social services. There are many different professional groups from these services which contribute to special needs education, some playing a greater role in the statutory procedures than others. This particular discussion will concentrate on teachers, special needs teachers, educational psy-chologists and certain therapeutic professions, such as speech and physiotherapists. There is no implication in this that the contri-butions of medical officers, social workers and others are insignifi-cant (Madden, 1987).

What complicates the matter is that the contributions of different professions are described under different conceptual and service frameworks. Advice and provision given by therapists, for example, can often be seen as therapy and not as education. Special needs education is what educators or teachers provide. Not only can a professional service be described in different terms but the same person receiving a service can be referred to as either a patient, a client or a pupil. There are different assumptions and norms involved here which relate to different professional cultures. These professional groups have different histories, have been established for different lengths of time and have different training and education — and with this go differences in social status and income.

It is also very important in this discussion to distinguish between individual professionals and professional institutions. The actions of both are relevant, but it is the influence of professional institutions which is often overlooked, particularly by individual professionals themselves. Professional institutions are the systems by which individuals are selected, prepared and given credentials to practise as professionals. This involves the working of professional associations or trade unions to promote professional interests and their conceptions of the clients' or consumers' interests, and to negotiate working conditions and salaries.

PROFESSIONALISM

School teaching, professional educational psychology and therapy are relatively new professions compared to law and medicine. Even those medical practitioners who have most contact with special needs education belong to the relatively new field of community medicine. What characterises these relatively new semi-professions (Etzioni, 1969) compared to law and medicine is their shorter training, lower public status, less specialised bodies of knowledge and relative lack of autonomy from supervision and control. As some commentators have noted, these newer professions have aspired to fully fledged professional status.

The key to full professional status in this analysis is professional autonomy — having occupational behaviour judged by colleagues and not by outsiders. Professional autonomy is seen to be based on the mastery of a field of specialised knowledge and on a commitment to the ideal of serving the client. It is granted to the members of an occupational group which agrees to exercise some control of members because effective service depends on the application of specialised knowledge and techniques and the use of individual judgement. Professional autonomy is therefore based on the authority of knowledge, authority based on technical expertise. This form of authority is seen to be incompatible with authority based on administrative hierarchies where controls are exerted from higher positions outside the occupational group. When the substance of an occupation's work requires little autonomy it can be argued that the group can be supervised by a bureaucratic organisation (Goode, 1969). The professions concerned with children with special educational needs can be seen in these terms. This analysis is useful in gaining some understanding of why professional groups attach particular importance to their technical expertise and of how potential tensions can arise between professional groups and administrators of services.

The history of teaching as a profession is characterised by divisions which correspond to the different phases and kinds of school. This is reflected in the separate existence of professional associations for special school teachers, traditional remedial teachers and ordinary classroom teachers. Reference to a teaching profession can therefore ignore the historical differences in training, status and professional culture which exist within the large group of school teachers. This is bound to affect the coherence of the education provision for the range of children with special educational needs. Not only have there been differences between special schools and between remedial and ordinary teachers, but within special school teaching there have been divisions between professional groups concerned with the variety of handicaps or areas of difficulty. Teachers of children with sensory disabilities have formal requirements for extra training, while those for other groups in special schools have not. The overall extent of specialist training for teachers of children with the more severe degrees of special educational needs (2 per cent) has also been historically low, as it has for those teaching special needs in ordinary schools. This is reflected in the relatively low status of these teachers within the teaching profession, despite the extra salary allowances for special school teachers.

When an occupational group lays exclusive claim to providing a service to meet certain client needs, the justification offered is in terms of protecting client interests. This protection takes the form of ensuring the quality and the effectiveness of the service. What becomes an issue is how the effectiveness of the service is judged, who judges it and whose interests are being protected. Claims to specialist expertise which is allegedly not available from other potential service providers imply that individual professionals have valid knowledge and effective techniques at their disposal. This is where tensions between providers and clients can arise. The means and the authority to judge effectiveness is not always available to clients, and professionals can claim that evaluating effectiveness is beyond client capability. One of the key questions is therefore whether clients are enabled to participate in a genuine evaluation which makes it possible for them to exercise some influence on the services they receive. Although there are crucial policy issues involved in how clients or consumers participate, including the degree of choice available to them, it is clear that professionals have a considerable interest in these issues. It is in this sense that professionals in this field could come to realise that much of what they do, despite their genuine concern for children with special educational needs, has much to do with their own professional interests (Tomlinson, 1982).

Though this perspective applies to the major professional actors in the field of special needs education, there are specific contexts and aspects which relate to different professional groups. Educational psychologists, for instance, form a much smaller group than special needs teachers, i.e. those teachers whose main responsibilities are for children with special educational needs. They have modelled themselves more on medical officers and have made claims to scientific and technical knowledge as the basis for their contribution. The main feature of the educational psychologist's work that distinguishes it from that of the teacher is that there is no intensive direct work with a client. Educational psychologists act mainly in an advisory and consultative role. Like other advisory work it is complicated by the question of who is the client. Teachers and psychologists are both in the situation where there is uncertainty about whether they are accountable to the LEA or to the parent and child or both. In some circumstances they may be under pressures to conform with LEA practices which they could see as conflicting with the parent's and child's interests. However, educational psychologists can have the added complication of being accountable to teachers who might request their advice and support. The way in which this is managed can influence their relationships with teachers.

INTER-PROFESSIONAL RELATIONSHIPS

Within the special needs field many professional difficulties arise not only in relation to parents and children and the employing service but in inter-professional relationships. Although there are issues which are internal to the different professions, these are not distinct from the inter-professional ones. The different professions and sub-professions arise and maintain and develop themselves in relation to changing client needs. This is conditioned, however, by what other professional groups can offer clients. Rivalry and suspicion between professional groups can be understood in terms of their being eager to maintain separate occupational positions and identities, despite genuine concerns to help the client. Some of the difficulties in the relationships between parents and professionals can be seen to originate in these inter-professional differences. Often this is not apparent to clients who may be given conflicting advice and/or have certain of their needs overlooked. Parents have also reported being over- whelmed by the number of different professionals with whom they have had contact. The proposal for a 'named person' in the Warnock Report, like that of the 'befriender' in the Fish Report, arises out of the need for parents to relate to a single person who can co-ordinate information and services.

There has been some recent evidence of the difficulties in inter- professional relationships (Goacher et al., 1988; Tomlinson, 1982). These can arise at the professional institutional level, with pro- fessional associations and professional training, at the local service level and at the level of individual professionals. Consideration of these levels is important in understanding the difficulties. For instance, certain individual professionals can form effective work- ing relationships without there being parallel links at the insti- tutional level.

The history of special needs education involves a continuing pattern of tensions between professional groups. These tensions arise in relation to key decisions and responsibilities in the wider network of service. A dominant position in this network involves the identification of children for special schooling or services. By around the mid-1970s educational psychologists had managed to attain a central role, replacing the initial medical pre-eminence in this decision making. The 1981 Education Act has been interpreted as increasing the influence of administrative officers in this decision making. However, it has also involved parents in the decision making and in so doing has opened up the identification and placement process to more scrutiny. The effect could be seen as reducing the traditional influence of educational psychologists by requiring that the LEA, as represented by an education officer or a panel including an officer and professionals, determines the special education provision. However, practice varies between LEAs with some principal educational psychologists still being involved in decisions about provision but often as part of the panel (Goacher et al., 1988). As part of the developments under the 1981 Act, the influence of the group of special needs teachers and advisors has also increased with the growing awareness of special educational needs and the integration of children with more severe needs.

Some commentators identify a considerable investment by pro- fessionals in the system of special schooling which works against the principle of integration (Potts, 1983). This investment involves a dynamic conservatism by sub-professional groups, such as special school teachers, who would see the conditions of their work change in a way that would require retraining or at least relocation to ordinary-school-based work. Change would also involve different styles of teaching in which specialist teachers would need to collaborate with teachers in ordinary schools. This could represent not only a challenge to the traditional experience and skills of special needs teachers, but exposure to a situation where control and responsibility has to be shared.

The sharing of control and responsibility is a necessary part of the multi-professional work required by statutory assessment procedures in the 1981 Education Act. The difficulties of teamwork in this process of formal assessment and decision making about additional provision have a long history. Circular 1/83 recognised these and recommended that effective collaboration required different professionals to seek agreement with each other about role and function.

This was taken to imply that advice should relate to the particular professional's field of specialism, leaving others to concentrate on their field of specialism. This would be a fine principle if there could be mutual agreement about what constituted each area of expertise. At one level different areas of expertise can be identified, but at a more detailed level there are possible areas of overlap, say, between educational psychologists and specialist teachers. When this occurs there may be a need to resolve the divergent advice. The system for summarising all the advice can be devised to iron out some of these possible differences. Circular 1/83 recommended that advice be collected in a particular sequence with each professional providing advice to the next advice giver. In this way, differences which could occur with simultaneous independent advice are avoided. However, this sequence does place educational psychologists in a dominant position and this can be seen to work against effective co-operation. There have also been criticisms of the relatively low status attached to educational advice provided by class or specialist needs teachers. Some specialist teachers, in the sensory disability field, for instance, question the relevance and validity of the educational psychologist's advice when the psychologist has had little direct contact with the child or has little particular knowledge and experience in the area of impairment.

The problems of achieving effective multi-professional assessment extend to health service contributions. There are different practices about collating advice from speech and physiotherapists. Some therapists prefer not to have their advice summarised by the medical officer and incorporated in the medical advice. In other

LEAs advice from different health professionals is sent directly to the LEA. This illustrates the sensitivities that can exist between professionals with respect to the power to interpret, collate and summarise. One possible resolution is for LEAs to have a multi-professional panel which collates advice from all sources and then makes decisions about statementing. However, these panels can become very large with full professional representation and slow in reaching decisions about advice on special educational needs. The delays in receiving professional advice are also well documented. The administrative pressures to reduce the number of participating professionals can therefore be understood as a way of speeding up the decision-making process. Yet this can lead to some professional groups having more influence in the decision making than others, something which can be a source of discontent.

INTER-PROFESSIONAL PROBLEMS: EXAMPLES

Effective inter-professional co-operation requires more than mutual agreement about respective roles. It also requires mutual understanding and appreciation of the value of other professional contributions to assessment and intervention or provision. In this section I will discuss three instances of inter-professional difficulties. These have been selected to illustrate the kinds of issue which arise in this field.

Teachers and therapists

The first example is about the relationship of teachers, both ordinary and educational needs specialist, with speech and physiotherapists. With the increase in special educational provision for children with language and communication difficulties, speech therapists have had more involvement in school- or unit-based provision for such children. This has brought teachers and speech therapists into closer working contact. Some of the difficulties involved can be attributed to the shortage of therapists and the fact that therapists have been employed by health services; with stringent financial controls on health service funding, speech therapy services for children have not always been a high spending priority. This is aggravated by the scepticism of some medical professionals about the value of such rehabilitative services. These professionals can influence health service funding decisions.

Speech therapists are aware of the need to document the effectiveness of their services as part of their effort to improve their professional standing (College of Speech Therapists, 1988). Even with the powers given to LEAs in the Education Reform Act 1988 to employ speech therapists, it is uncertain whether LEAs will find the extra finance necessary. LEAs could argue that speech therapy has been a health-funded service and that there is no reason for them to fund therapists fully. Though there are examples of LEAs working successfully with Social Services and the District Health Authorities to joint fund special provision for children, this is not very common and is well known as an area of administrative difficulty.

Not all difficulties can be attributed to the different administrative and funding structures of the statutory services which employ speech therapists and teachers. The two professional groups have limited knowledge of each other's specific skills, knowledge base and intervention assumptions. The professional cultures of the two groups are quite distinct. Speech therapy has recently withdrawn from LEAs to become part of the health service. It has a strong therapeutic or rehabilitative orientation with its immediate allied professions being medicine and other health service professions. The question of how speech therapy and education goals can be co-ordinated is a crucial issue. It depends on the extent to which teachers adopt a curricular conception that includes restorative or rehabilitative as well as developmental goals. This issue was discussed at some length in Chapter 5. The question is also complicated by differences in framework and methods between teachers and therapists which can be reinforced by the professional need to have a distinctive approach.

There are undoubtedly examples of effective inter-professional teamwork between speech therapists and teachers. Where there is not, there can be a tendency to overlook obstacles which exist within the employing services and the professions themselves. There are other additional difficulties which arise from therapists working in schools and units. The supervision of therapy can raise questions of whether therapists report to teachers and/or to therapists not working in a school base. The basis of supervision is different in health and education services and there can also be tension between therapists and teachers over differences in contact time, holidays and school duties. Another issue which emerges from the relative scarcity of therapists is whether therapists work with teachers on a consultative/advisory basis. If therapists see themselves as doing therapy indirectly, with teachers or assistants doing the direct work with children, this can put teachers in a subordinate position of working to therapists' goals. This approach lends itself to seeing teaching as concerned with basic skills in number work and handwriting, for example, with therapists focusing on language and communication. Some teachers with a broad approach to the curriculum would question the idea that they did not plan language development work.

The problems can be more pronounced for specialist educational needs teachers than for ordinary class teachers. Ordinary teachers do not necessarily see themselves as having special competence to work effectively in the area of language and communication difficulties. The speech therapist can be seen as having quite distinct skills and knowledge in the language field. The boundary between these groups can be managed more easily than that between specialist educational needs teachers and therapists. Specialist teachers are more likely to see themselves as having some specialist knowledge and skills in the same field as therapists. One way of managing and integrating different conceptions about and methods for language development is for the two groups to have some shared skills and knowledge. A recent development has been to encourage speech therapists to do a one-year postgraduate teacher training course. It is interesting that this was prompted by the need to secure more speech therapy in LEAs rather than to equip speech therapists with educational knowledge and experience.

Physiotherapists are another therapeutic group which has a sensitive relationship with specialist educational needs teachers. This will be discussed in relation to conductive education, which was also referred to in Chapter 5. Though the initial interest and use of conductive education was among a few physiotherapists in special schools (Cottam, 1985), the current developments in training involve the training of teachers to be conductors. Physiotherapists, as represented by the Association of Paediatric Chartered Physiotherapists, are not opposed to conductive education. The physiotherapist's position is that conductive education has been adopted and used for many years in this country with excellent results (*Therapy Weekly*, 6 June 1988).

It is notable from the professional viewpoint of this chapter that the use of these methods over the last twenty years is not counted as 'true' conductive education. Sutton (1986) claimed that there have not yet been any cases of children achieving orthofunction in this country — i.e. mastering the effects of motor disorder sufficiently to function independently. He attributed this to practices with only the barest link to the Peto knowledge base and pedagogy being called conductive education. This argument leads to the conclusion that conductive education requires specialist training in the knowledge and methods shown to be effective in the Peto Institute, Hungary. This is an illustration of the way in which professional claims to serving clients depend on the effectiveness of the service. Where there are difficulties in establishing clear-cut evaluations of interventions, this makes it difficult to identify effective methods and therefore effective knowledge and skills. Without these, the claims of different professional groups remain uncertain and difficult to resolve. However, evaluation is itself open to the influence of different theoretical persuasions and professional interests, which makes it difficult to mount, let alone to establish, decisive outcomes. There seems to be no easy way out of these inherent complexities.

Educational psychologists and advisory teachers

The second example of inter-professional difficulties is about the role of educational psychologists in relation to teachers, especially advisory and support teachers. The historical origins of professional educational psychology go back to the early part of this century, when psychologists were employed in the education service to advise on the identification of children who could not benefit from ordinary schooling. Education was the first area in which the developing discipline of psychology was applied. With the growth of psychology in the education service, educational psychologists became increasingly central to the process of ascertaining children for special schooling. Educational psychologists are currently required to have professional training and experience in teaching as well as a first degree or equivalent in psychology and one year's postgraduate training as an educational psychologist. Educational psychologists differ from other professional psychologists in this country, and from education-based psychologists in some other countries, in being required to have dual professional training. Clinical psychologists are often required to have experience in the mental health field but not to be professionally trained in some other established field.

From one perspective the dual training and experience gives educational psychologists a strong background, but it also creates uncertainty about whether they are mainly educationalists or psychologists. For some purposes this does not matter as they can act in both capacities, but with the increasing pressures from other branches of professional psychology for integrating and unifying applied psychology it can pose a dilemma. Criticisms over the last twenty years about the use of traditional individual psychological assessments in the education service have also posed dilemmas for educational psychologists. One response was to seek a different theoretical model which did not assume fixed general characteristics and which could be used in school and classroom contexts. As explained in Chapter 6, this response has represented a major change in professional educational psychology practice, but it has also had implications for the relationship of educational psychologists with teachers. Much of the educational use of behavioural methods requires direct teacher involvement. The educational psychologist's role becomes one of preparing, advising and supporting teachers, rather than having a separate and relatively self-contained independent assessment role. Although many educational psychologists in practice combine traditional with more recent approaches, there has been a move to collaborating with teachers which challenges the educational psychologist's separate professional identity. This challenge has also come from the growing group of special educational needs advisory and support teachers who work in LEA-based special needs services. With the 1981 Act there has also been an increase in the number of inspectors and advisers specialising in special educational needs. Part of their responsibility has been the management of support services, which might have previously been managed by educational psychologists under the School Psychological Services.

The main challenge to educational psychologists is to their advisory role with respect to individual children. This is in relation to the support and help offered directly to teachers and to the advice required for the 1981 Act statutory assessment procedures. As regards support for ordinary teachers, educational psychologists may find that this conflicts with advice given by educational needs, subject or phase specialist advisory teachers and advisers. Educational psychologists' advice, if based on behavioural objectives approaches, can conflict with the process-oriented advice more often provided by advisers and advisory teachers. As regards advice for statutory assessment, specialist educational needs teachers, if they are contributors, and class teachers who have most experience of the child, often question the relevance and validity of psychological assessment and advice.

These criticisms do not necessarily undermine the crucial role of educational psychologists in the statutory advice-giving process. On the contrary, educational psychologists have traditionally had an important role in providing assessment and advice which was independent of the ordinary school teachers who were having teaching difficulties with individual children. The importance of having an independent assessment of a child's educational needs can be easily overlooked especially by school teachers, as can the wide-ranging experience of educational psychologists in relation to the variety of special needs in the education service. Educational psychologists can be seen therefore as generalist and school-independent assessors and advice givers. However, as argued elsewhere (Norwich, 1988), whether this function is essentially a psychological one is open to question. It is conceivable that such a function can be maintained within a different organisation of special educational needs advisory and support services. These relationships between educational psychology services and special educational needs and advisory and support services are a persistent source of disagreement and difficulty.

What is at issue is whether the independent assessment function could be incorporated into an integrated special educational needs advisory and support service or should remain with a separate psychological service. There is no easy resolution to this, short of a major reorganisation of support services, which might be resisted by educational psychologists. An independent assessment function would still require considerable advanced preparation not dissimilar in several respects to the preparation required for educational psychologists. Entry to the professional positions in which the function was carried out could, however, include teachers without the equivalent of first degrees in psychology. This does not imply that psychology would be removed from the preparation, but the orientation would shift to a more broadly based educational one. Though this could be interpreted as a threat to educational psychologists' job security and to the future contribution of psychology to education, this need not be the case. Educational psychologists could be re-employed within the reorganised special educational needs advisory service, at the same salary and status level. Some educational psychologists may see this kind of reorganisation as a restriction on their broader roles as applied psychologists in education. Another possibility would be for them to consider setting up or joining an LEA human resources and development service. This service could include other social scientists who also have an interest in the contribution and use of the social and human sciences in education generally.

Although these ideas may seem speculative, they do highlight the extent to which professional perceptions of what is possible can become restricted. Occupational and industrial psychologists, for example, do not necessarily form occupational and industrial psychology services, yet they still maintain a professional identity and interest in psychology. Whether these possibilities are worth pursuing depends on conditions being favourable within LEAs for this kind of reorganisation, with the necessary financial resources available for preparation and implementation. However, the main point of this discussion is to illustrate how the service context and the historical development of a professional group in relation to other groups pose dilemmas about future roles and functions.

Special needs and ordinary teachers

The third example is about the relationship between special educational needs teachers and ordinary school teachers. Though this does not concern a relationship between distinct professional groups, it involves similar issues. In particular, this example illustrates one strand of the professional culture of teachers, which is a sensitivity about occupational specialism. This is most clearly represented by the notion that all teachers are teachers of children with special educational needs. What underlies this notion is the intention to promote greater interest and responsibility for children with special needs. However, the argument goes further than this in doubting that there is much expertise involved in special needs teaching (Dessent, 1987). It takes the form of asserting that the skills and qualities for ordinary and special schools, and those required to meet special educational needs, are desirable in any good teacher (Sayer, 1985).

These professional integrationist views are aiming to counter the excessive claims to expertise which can arise when special needs education is provided in separate schools and units. There are obvious benefits for ordinary teachers in attributing expertise to others for working with children with special educational needs, as it can justify relinquishing responsibility for them in ordinary schools. As Dessent (1987) argues, the belief that someone with more expertise exists justifies the continued exclusion of pupils from mainstream schools. The argument that the skills and experience required for children with special needs, e.g. the ability to individualise teaching, are desirable for all teachers is valid in many cases. However, it reveals an excessive focus on what is common to all areas of special needs teaching. It concentrates only on what should be rather than also acknowledging what is and can be offered. Firstly, there are no easy valid generalities about the skills, knowledge and attitudes for different areas of special educational needs. It is clear that not all teachers have the knowledge, interest or skills to teach alternative means of accessing the curriculum, such as braille. There are certainly specific skills and knowledge required to teach specialist programmes concerned with alternative communication systems or with the goals of cognitive enrichment as in Instrumental Enrichment. To assert this is not to imply that these specialist skills cannot be learned by all teachers; it is to recognise that different teachers have opted to work with different age groups, perhaps with different areas of the curriculum and/or with children with exceptional learning characteristics. By so doing they learn specific skills either at a preparation stage or while on the job, skills which are not immediately transferable without relevant training experience.

The recognition of specialist skills, knowledge and attitudes does not deny that there are elements which are common to all forms of teaching. All teaching involves skills in assessment, goal planning and the use of appropriate methods and materials. However, the differences which arise for different ages, areas of the curriculum and learner characteristics are of some significance.

With moderate to mild special educational needs, the relevant knowledge and skills are less distinct from those required for ordinary teaching. What differs is the relative emphasis placed on these common elements of teaching. Much of this depends on the group context of teaching, the group size and number of teachers associated with a group. For instance, the work of support teaching in an ordinary classroom is in many respects different from class teaching in both a special and an ordinary school. For children with moderate special educational needs, the skills, knowledge and attitudes required can be seen as extensions of those required for ordinary teaching. Yet prescriptions that ordinary teachers ought to have such characteristics do not remove the degree of difference. Recommendations that ordinary teachers should have increased opportunities to individualise their approaches to children with special needs can be supported. However, this depends on the curricular orientation and resourcing of the ordinary schools. With the move to making curricula more relevant to the variety of individual children, there may be less demand for certain forms of special needs teaching. But it is doubtful whether this can reduce the demand for educational needs specialists in view of the complex expectations on teachers to maintain and improve educational achievement for all children.

STRATEGIES FOR INTER-PROFESSIONAL COLLABORATION

As we have seen, inter-professional difficulties are partly attributable to the separation of services which are administered by separate statutory agencies (Welton, 1983). This is complicated by the changing basis of the relationship between central and local government, particularly in the education service. There is usually some agreement that integrated services require integrated planning, implementation and review at all levels. There are different views, however, about the best way of achieving this kind of service integration and collaboration. One approach has considered the establishment of a unified agency for children that includes health, social services and education to promote better service co-ordination and enhanced professional relationships. One reason why this is not likely to work any better is that differences between professionals occur not only between employing services but within a single service. Organising services around children would also bring out different boundary issues in relation to responsibility for adolescents and young adults. It seems difficult to conceive of a system of service delivery for education, social services and health which does not also have distinct occupational bases. Given the differences in the nature of the services, in the degree of preparation required, and in the degree of supervision of the different groups, it is hard to conceive of situations where there would be no inter-professional boundaries.

What is needed, given such boundaries, is more central and local government interest in professional and inter-professional matters as regards services for children. This has been underlined by recent reports on the breakdown in inter-service collaboration over child abuse cases. In this context, there is a delicate balance to be struck between government direction and government facilitation of inter-professional collaboration which is based on a respect for professional autonomy. Government has an interest in the qualifications and training of professionals and can promote schemes for more joint training. One recent example of a government initiative in the field of special educational needs is the two-year cross-service project on management and organisation development for special needs services (Evans et al., 1989). This joint DES- and DHSS-funded project has designed resources for promoting improved services based on an inter-service and inter-professional development model.

Not all inter-professional difficulties can be approached, however, through organisation and management development strategies. As the examples discussed in the last section indicated, there are important roles for professional associations, local professional services and individual professionals. If it is assumed that there will continue to be some degree of specialism between and within professional groups, then there are several broad strategies which are relevant to improved professional relationships. These strategies would aim to promote a professional maturity in which different groups have a commitment to communicate and co-ordinate with allied groups. This needs to be based on thorough and regular self-evaluations of professional services which may necessitate genuine internal changes. This might lead to a group relinquishing certain key functions, developing new ones, understanding areas of overlap with other groups and maintaining a professional identity based on functions which do not overlap substantially with those of other professional groups. Mergers or amalgamation of professional groups may also be appropriate, though not only when groups are under outside threats. With professional maturity the sharing of skills and knowledge between different professionals will be possible in a way that copes with threats to professional identities. Joint training, particularly at in-service level, could be one way to increase mutual understanding and appreciation and to help resolve difficulties which exist.

Examples of effective collaboration between professionals can be found in the inter-service and inter-professional participation in the pre-school Portage programme for children with learning difficulties, and in the use of family therapy approaches in child guidance teams. In both examples individual professionals with different backgrounds have a common preparation in knowledge and skills and there is some system for managing and reviewing work. This provides a common conceptual framework which enables collaboration, some degree of flexibility about who does what and an explicit system for service evaluation. These schemes are, nevertheless, based on the further preparation of individuals for whom Portage work or family therapy is usually not their sole professional function. They depend on the contribution of individual professionals with some prior allied experience and skills who have different professional identities. The relative success of these schemes in inter-professional terms illustrates the importance of finding common professional skills and understanding without encroaching on the core functions of different professional groups. Systems for identifying, developing and maintaining such links between groups are central to the improvement of co-ordinated services for children generally, including those with special educational needs.

PROFESSIONAL AND CLIENT

As the previous discussion in this chapter indicated, professional and inter-professional issues are in the final analysis concerned with the relationships between provider and client; in this field, between the range of professionals and parents on behalf of their children. The pressure for co-ordinated and effective cross-service collaboration derives from the obvious fact that it is one and the same child who receives the range of professional services. Yet the picture is more complex as parents make decisions on behalf of their children. Professional–client relationships in this field are therefore three-way and also involve a complex organisational network within which professionals work. In the public services, such as the education service, the individual professional has to manage relationships not only with clients but with his or her employing authority, a large organisation with its own policy and practices.

Much has been written recently about the changing pattern of relationships between parents and professionals in education generally and in special needs education (Sandow and Stafford, 1987; McConkey, 1985; Lunt and Sheppard, 1986; Wolfendale, 1983). It is not my intention to cover this ground in any detail. My interest is in discussing some of the underlying issues and assumptions. The role of parents in the statutory assessment and statementing procedures has been referred to in Chapter 3. Parents were given clear rights to participate in decision making, and Circular 1/83 spelled out what was involved in partnership with regard to cultivating a good working relationship. However, as some commentators have noticed, there were limits to parental rights (Potts, 1983) with regard to parental requests for assessment (section 9 of the 1981 Act) and to the outcomes of appeals not being binding on LEAs (section 8).

Research on parent–professional relationships has revealed that some LEAs have had difficulties in keeping to the recommended guidelines. Goacher et al. (1988) found that parents in their sample welcomed the statutory assessment as a way of gaining extra resources, though there were difficulties in communication which reveal unease on the part of some professionals about being frank and open. There was also evidence of parents not being fully informed by LEAs about the special educational needs system. Although the incidence of parental appeal against LEA decisions is low, this conceals a higher incidence of dissatisfaction. Many parents believed that they were unable to influence the outcome of the procedures in any substantial way. From this study it was concluded that the full involvement of parents as partners in decisions about their children's education was far from being realised.

A recent study of relationships and perceptions in one LEA has also indicated problems in partnership (Sandow and Stafford, 1987). Parents were found to value professionals who knew their child well, and frequent contact was preferred to occasional expertise. A common parental concern was whether professionals could contribute to their child's education. By contrast, professionals valued offering specialist help, information and advice, and not the regular contact sought by parents. Partnership was not high on the list of parental or professional priorities. These findings reveal that partnership is a complex process, often more an aspiration than a reality, and involves considerable ambivalence. As Potts (1983) has noted, partnership in terms of its origins and covert aims can reinforce professional influence. It is also unwise to generalise about parent–professional relationships as these vary considerably across different special educational needs, and depend on social class and other social and personal factors. However, the current ideals are worth examining.

The ideals of partnership

Much of the move to involve parents in the education of children with special educational needs, by home- and school-based programmes, can be seen as providing more effective ways for professionals to extend and enhance their services. Such involvement is often directed by professionals to ends which they select. That parents may want to have less involvement in these programmes, as they have other demands on their time and energy, can be easily ignored. It is important to note that partnership implies that the different parties have some influence on the process in which they are participating. This idea has been taken further in the notion of the 'equivalent expertise' of parents and professionals (Wolfendale, 1986), an idea which expresses the principle of working together on the basis of equality.

Although there are some examples of parents being involved in decision making in relation to their own children and at school and management levels, the extent to which this can be fully effected in practice is open to question. The history of public services in this country is one of professional or provider dominance. This applies particularly to the field of special needs education, where the client has been seen as disadvantaged and vulnerable. There can be no doubt about the compassion and concern expressed for parents and their children with special educational needs, but these attitudes have to be seen within the context of the competition for finite finance and the complexities of service delivery. Within the current socio-economic context, it would be more accurate to consider the goals of partnership as difficult to attain and to recognise that partnership also serves the professional interests of developing services.

There is nothing morally reprehensible about serving professional interests so long as client interests are also served well. This is where a very delicate balance has to be struck. Many parents can feel confused and lacking in confidence when faced with professionals. There is also a high risk of reinforcing unwittingly these parental responses. The view that professions can have a 'disabling effect' (Illich, 1977) is relevant to these problems. Although not without its weaknesses, the concept of parents as consumers captures some of the notion that parents should be enabled to become more independent and to make informed choices about their own and their children's needs (Cunningham, 1983).

One of the main difficulties that arises in professional–client relationships in the special needs field is that there is insufficient analysis of the underlying financial, administrative and political factors and processes. Notions like partnership and equivalent expertise are useful to the limited extent of promoting the principles of participation and client self-determination. However, they can operate as a substitute for reflecting on the difficulties of attempting to satisfy several principles. For example, participation is not always compatible with the consumerist principle of informed choice. Parents can be expected if offered genuine choice to opt for alternatives which do not fit with prearranged schemes or programmes. If parents are encouraged to believe they can influence the outcome of the 1981 Act procedures, then they can be expected sometimes to feel manipulated into accepting certain provision when genuine alternatives to special school are unavailable.

CONCLUSION

I would like to draw attention here to the discussion in Chapter 5 about the curriculum for children with special educational needs, its differentiation and organisation. Without some clarity about what needs to be done for children with special needs there is likely to be some uncertainty about who does what. Some of the professional issues discussed in this chapter are therefore strongly associated with the issues of curriculum and the overlap of education and therapy. Co-ordinating what needs to be done for children with special needs also depends on co-ordinating the different theories about the difficulties and development of children. As discussed in Chapter 2, this depends on constructing an integrated theoretical framework, such as the general systems approach. Given the present context of theoretical uncertainty, we would therefore expect some professional identity and boundary uncertainties. Finally, problems of professional relationships are linked to client–professional ones. These pervasive problems are concerned with attaining the egalitarian ideals of partnership and equivalent expertise. They arise from having to balance egalitarian ideals with those of individual self-determination. These issues will now be considered in more detail.

—8—

Philosophical considerations

INTRODUCTION

Issues which have arisen in the previous chapters are about general assumptions, ideas and values. These are by nature philosophical and deserve some consideration in this book. In many respects, special needs education highlights and exemplifies many of the dilemmas which arise generally within education. This could lead to general discussions about current concerns in the philosophy of education. However, this is neither my intention nor within my competence. In this chapter, I intend to discuss several specific areas arising from discussions in previous chapters which call for some clarification: (a) the nature of special educational needs, (b) the theoretical and causal significance of attributing 'learning difficulties' and (c) the place of equality in this field.

THE CONCEPT OF SPECIAL EDUCATIONAL NEEDS

Separating needs from provision

In Chapter 1 we saw how the concept of special educational needs came to be introduced: to replace that of handicap as a conceptual integration which covers children in special and ordinary schools, to provide more positive terminology and to highlight the variable and interactive nature of learning difficulties. Though the implications of using the notion of special educational needs have been subject to particular kinds of sociological critique (Tomlinson, 1985), there has been little conceptual analysis of the notion itself. That there has been some need for this is apparent in the 1981 Act evaluation study (Goacher et al., 1988), in which it was found that the notion did present difficulties in practical use. This is reflected, in particular, in how special educational needs are formulated in statements, and in how needs can be identified separately from provision. As Powell and Booker (1987) observe, there are problems in trying to express needs independently of the provision required to meet them. The 1981 Act Schedules, Regulations and Circular 1/83 did not resolve or clarify the matter. The argument of Powell and Booker is that the concept of need should embrace both the state of the child and the provision required. This position is consistent with a conceptual analysis of need in terms of:

- a norm or standard;
- the fact that the standard is not being achieved;
- the fact that what is said to be needed really is the relevant condition of achieving the standard (Dearden, 1972).

According to Dearden's analysis, identifying a need implies that some condition is necessary for achieving a standard. In other words, what is needed is provision to meet that need. If this is a correct analysis of the need concept, then advice about special educational needs will necessarily involve advice about provision required. This makes it difficult to understand why professionals are supposed to distinguish between the child's special needs and the provision required.

Optimal versus available provision

The attempted separation of needs from provision can be seen as a way of distinguishing between what a child would ideally require given his or her characteristics and circumstances and what provision is actually available. The separation is a means of trying to fit provision to the child rather than the child to the available provision. Yet the concept of needs seems to confuse the matter by referring to provision and not to the child's characteristics and circumstances. In fact, this is what was intended in introducing the concept of need, in order to refocus attention on what can be done for the child, what can be provided. However, in doing this, attention is drawn away from the prior issue of the child's current functioning and circumstances, possibly as these might involve certain kinds of deficit. The Dearden analysis of need implies that there would be three key elements to identifying needs:

- a description of the child's strengths, weaknesses and circumstances of learning;
- goals which are relevant for the child in view of this description;
- optimal means for achieving these goals.

Circular 1/83 (para. 4) came close to making these distinctions, but the suggested format for the statement nevertheless still confounds them. It is inaccurate to refer to the description of child functioning and circumstances as his or her needs as this comprises only the initial condition for identifying needs.

The goals which are relevant for the child are derived from the general aims and goals for all children and are adapted to the individual characteristics of the child. As noted in previous chapters, learning outcomes depend on the interaction of teaching and learning resources. In assessing a child's strengths and weaknesses it is the child's learning resources and constraints which are identified, as far as that can be validly done. The optimal means for achieving the individually relevant goals will take account of what teaching and other resources are available. It is the goals and the means aspects of the needs identification which are usually referred to as provision. This is where there is a connection between needs and provision. The advice to professionals to separate needs from provision should therefore be reformulated as advice to distinguish between the optimal provision needed by the child on the one hand, and the provision that is currently available on the other.

Evaluative and descriptive aspects of the special educational needs concept

If the concept of educational needs is so complex, what advantage is there in using such a concept? Dearden (1972) argues that 'need' is a deceptively attractive concept because it serves two critical functions. Firstly, because of the connection between needs and desires, it can promise to solve the motivational problems in education. If education is considered in terms of needs, then it may appear that learners would desire to learn. However, this is illusory as needing something does not entail that a person desires it. Secondly, the concept of need appears 'to offer an escape from arguments about values by means of a straightforward appeal to the facts empirically determined by the expert' (p. 60). Dearden's point is that need concepts offer no such escape. Attributing an educational need to a child implies that some educational goals or standards are judged valuable. Needs cannot simply be described as being true or false. They indicate what is valuable; not what is, but rather what ought to be.

However, needs statements are not simply evaluative, they also involve a descriptive component. It is a descriptive or empirical question whether the norm or standard has been attained and whether the condition said to be needed will in fact attain the standard. Dearden's point is that empirically based knowledge from psychology and sociology is relevant to these descriptive aspects of need but not to the normative or evaluative aspect. This has an important bearing on the relationship between professionals and clients. Teachers and psychologists, for example, through their professional knowledge have some justification in pronouncing on whether a norm has been attained and on the effectiveness of conditions to attain norms. This is what constitutes their professional expertise. They go beyond their authority when they presume to settle questions of norms without the participation of the client. It is in this sense that defining special educational needs requires the collaboration of clients, as professionals are not contracted to be arbitrators of educational values. This is not to say that professionals do not or should not make value judgements, but that there are other legitimate value positions.

It is also relevant to this discussion to consider the concept of 'equivalent expertise' mentioned in Chapter 7 in relation to the parent–professional partnership. This notion attempts to legitimise partnership in terms of knowledge. Yet the attempt fails to recognise that partnership is not just a question of sharing technical expertise. If it were, then parental claims to expertise would be limited to concrete knowledge and information rather than to generally applicable principles and knowledge claimed by professionals. Partnership is, instead, relevant to parent–professional relationships in terms of settling educational value judgements. It is also evident that, to the extent that there are differences in these evaluative aspects of identifying special educational needs, partnership is problematic. The significance of this analysis of educational need is to make the value or interest issues explicit. This addresses those sociological analyses of special needs education which question whose needs and interests are involved in this field (Barton and Tomlinson, 1984). From the above analysis it is clear that special educational needs as a concept are related to issues of value and interests. There is therefore no question of opposing an interest versus a needs view of the field. The two are interconnected. Fundamental questions about what educational values and interests are worthwhile, and about the relationship between individual and social values, are at the heart of the special needs concept. This analysis leads back inevitably to basic questions about the nature of education.

'Special' in the concept of special educational needs

A certain amount of disquiet about the use of the term 'special' has been noted. This is expressed in claims that all children are special, and that therefore all children have special educational needs. This reference to 'special' as a common characteristic of all children is an attempt to emphasise the individuality of all children, that from one viewpoint no two children are alike. It is aimed primarily at redressing the discrimination and devaluation of those with exceptional characteristics. This has been recently expressed in the recommendation that we refer to individual rather than special needs:

> all of us in the education service should seek to eradicate the use of all forms of labels, including the now fashionable 'special needs', recognising that they are essentially discriminatory. Instead, we should find ways of acknowledging the individuality of each pupil, that all children experience learning difficulties and that all can experience success.
>
> (Ainscow and Tweddle, 1988, p. 69)

I have already discussed some of the issues connected with this kind of position. In a later section of this chapter, the question of individuality in describing and explaining learning difficulties will be considered. For the present discussion, I want to propose a different conception of 'special' which is not necessarily devaluing. Special can also refer to something out of the ordinary, different or exceptional in the frequency sense of having a low incidence. This is what is implied in much of the Warnock Report's use of the term, and it is explicit in the 1981 Education Act formulations of special as what is 'different from' or 'additional to' the ordinary.

The notion of special as exceptional is not without its difficulties or risks, but it captures what is usually meant by the term. Labels like 'special' are not in themselves discriminatory; it is how they are used and for which purposes that can connect them with discrimination and devaluation. Phrases like 'special children' can lead to typing children in a way that can ignore what they have in common with 'ordinary' children and how they are different from each other — their individuality. This possibility does not undermine the advantage of the term. Special, in the exceptional sense, refers to additional educational requirements which some children share with other children. As such it represents a kind of educational requirement which some children have in common. Special does not refer to how one child is different from all other children; nor is it inconsistent for two children who are different in many respects to have the same special educational needs. Special educational needs are not therefore the same as individual needs. A child's individual educational needs go beyond her or his special educational needs in identifying those educational needs which are unique to that child. The position that all children's educational needs are unique, a position of radical individuality, will be discussed in the next section.

The full significance of interpreting special as exceptional becomes clearer if children with special educational needs were taken to include children with very high general and specific learning abilities. That special educational needs have come to be associated with educational needs deriving from interactions involving disability and personal difficulties is not conceptually necessary. That special educational need has also been defined in the 1981 Education Act to exclude children who have additional educational requirements on account of English being a second language also reinforces the identification of special needs with disability. What underlies the discrimination and devaluation associated with special educational needs relates to attitudes towards disability and difficulties, not just to the term itself.

'Educational' in the concept of special educational needs

The final point in this section concerns the significance of the term 'educational' in the concept of special educational needs. As I have mentioned in previous chapters, recent developments in the field represent the growth of an educational perspective towards disability and difficulty. The force of the term 'educational' captures this link to general educational and curricular perspectives. However, this can be an obstacle to the wider integration of perspectives on children's needs, which go beyond the educational to include health and welfare needs. The risk is that the term 'educational' in the concept of special educational needs inhibits the links which have to be made between education, health and welfare positions.

The special educational needs framework introduced by the Warnock Report complicated matters by introducing another conceptual framework which has to be translatable into health and social welfare frameworks. My argument in Chapter 5 was that it is unclear to what extent a common curriculum framework can and should include deficit-focused goals and programmes. Similarly, there is uncertainty about the overlap of educational and welfare goals. That there might be is crucial to the linking of health, personal welfare and educational frameworks and to the problems of managing inter-professional relationships between social workers, therapists, doctors and teachers. Taking the relationships between health and educational frameworks, for example, from one viewpoint it does not matter whether rehabilitative or corrective goals are called educational or health goals. What does matter, however, is that the overlap between education, health and welfare services is recognised and that the balance between developmental, adaptive and corrective goals is managed both conceptually and professionally. This is a formidable professional issue which I discussed in Chapter 7.

THE INDIVIDUALITY OF LEARNING DIFFICULTIES

The fall of the general and the rise of the individual case

The Warnock Report, in recommending the abolition of handicap categories, was advocating an orientation which focuses on the individual child's learning difficulties. This was motivated by concerns that handicap categories did not deal with differences between individuals coming within any category and that a general category did not provide clear-cut indications of how to teach an individual. This focus on individuality also enabled children with exceptional learning characteristics to be seen as individuals in the way that all children are individuals. This challenges the stereotyping of children with special educational needs. In previous chapters, I have questioned whether an interactive model of special educational needs can abandon general categories of within-child and environmental causal factors. My intention in this section is to consider some of the conceptual and epistemological grounds for challenging a non-categorising approach to learning difficulties.

The identification of within-child causal factors fell increasingly into disrepute as the validity of prediction came under more scrutiny. The assessment measures which had been used to identify general factors were applied in circumstances and to groups for which they were not designed or initially validated. Even in cases where predictive validities were relatively high for future learning outcomes, these predictions were for groups and did not necessarily enable accurate prediction for some individuals. This called into question the value of identifying general within-child factors (Lindsay and Wedell, 1982), particularly if there seemed to be little prospect of correcting the identified deficits.

In interpreting this situation, higher-level theoretical assumptions and orientations come into operation. One orientation is to abandon the search for general within-child factors which affect future learning. Predictive failure is turned into a virtue by arguing that in any case the point of prediction is to enhance learning and that this can be done by focusing on particular individuals and specific learning outcomes. This orientation was discussed in Chapter 6 as the objectives orientation, as one which focuses on what is alterable within specific situations for individual learners. The other orientation is not to abandon the search for general factors, but to widen and intensify the search. This would involve including environmental and developmental factors which interact with child factors, and using factors which are not too distant from the outcomes to be predicted (Keogh and Becker, 1974).

Nomothetic and idiographic orientations

These two orientations represent two distinct and rival methodological approaches to research in education and in the human sciences more generally. The orientation which continues the search for general factors is often referred to as nomothetic. The nomothetic approach aims to establish general concepts and principles which apply across a range of individuals and situations. Such concepts and principles are derived empirically from groups of individual cases and are then applied to other cases. It is this application of the general case which enables some prediction and possibly some degree of intervention and control. The nomothetic approach is the traditional scientific approach.

The orientation which abandons the search for general factors in favour of understanding and explaining individual cases in specific situations is often called idiographic. Idiographic approaches are concerned with the individuality of learning difficulties as no two individual cases are seen as alike and therefore nothing general can be said about individuals. Allport (1960) explained the idiographic position as a quest for 'laws that tell us how uniqueness occurs'.

What underlies the differences between nomothetic and idiographic approaches is the fundamental question of the degree of similarity and and difference which is perceived between different individuals. As it has been said, 'Every man is in certain respects, a) like all other men; b) like some other men; c) like no other men' (Kluckhohn et al., 1959). The idiographic orientation focuses on how people are like nobody else. This emphasis is associated with the conditions of professional practice which require work with individuals. Practitioners need to explain individual cases, and it is this which prompts the search for such explanations.

The idiographic orientation takes several distinct forms in education-related research. One form, represented by Skinnerian psychology, is explicitly anti-theoretical but pro-experimental analysis. It is anti-theoretical in implying that there is no explanatory place for general concepts which are inferred from direct evidence. The experimental analysis is in relation to specific behaviours in specific situations. This form of idiographic research has been strongly represented in behavioural approaches in the special needs field, referred to in Chapter 6. The other form is associated with the illuminative–ethnographic research tradition discussed in Chapter 4. With this form of idiography, case studies are used to illustrate particular points. Concepts in this tradition are developed via concrete experience, which requires that they be communicated through case studies. These concepts are sensitising in the sense of giving a general direction in approaching empirical instances. They lack clear-cut specifications of attributes which enable a definite identification of an instance of a class. Their use is to enable others to generalise from the case to their own experience — to illuminate their experience (Elliott, 1978). Though the illuminative and radical behavioural forms of idiography take differing positions about scientific analysis, they share a common focus on the individual case. It is also notable that they represent the two currently influential approaches to research in the special needs field. As I have indicated before, this can be attributed to the practicality ethos in special needs education.

Nomothetic and idiographic orientations as complementary

Over the years, some researchers have dismissed the radical versions of idiographic and nomothetic approaches (Lewin, 1936; Gage, 1985; Frank, 1986). They argue that the natural sciences are not exclusively nomothetic, if by that it is meant that individual cases are not relevant to the formulation and alteration of general concepts and principles. Idiographic description and knowledge can negate general principles and it plays as significant a role in the natural as in the social sciences. In both there is an interplay between the general and the individual case. Individual cases can be illuminated and explained by using the general case, so long as there is sufficient knowledge of the particular situation to which it is applied. The general case abstracted from concrete situations can also be tested and altered in the light of idiographic knowledge. The very search for principles which explain individuality involves the search for general knowledge about how individual uniqueness arises.

If, as Frank argues, idiographic knowledge of individuals and nomothetic generalisations are essential to systematic explanation, then what can account for the methodological controversy? One reason for the controversy is that, in psychology, nomothetic knowledge has traditionally derived from highly controlled, laboratory-based research, while idiographic knowledge derives from practitioner and applied work. Those primarily concerned with general principles have been less interested in applying them. The controversy may therefore be partly about who does research and where it is done. The move to more naturalistic research approaches has involved a switch to the detailed rich descriptions of individual cases. However, it would be mistaken to believe that such idiographic knowledge can be readily applied to different cases without identifying some general concepts, trends and relationships.

The flight from nomothetic research orientations can also be attributed to a lack of confidence in establishing general principles and concepts, which finds expression in criticisms of positivism in the social sciences. McIntyre (1981) has distinguished between the search for generalisations in the social sciences and the traditional account given of these general principles. His argument is that social scientists have aspired to generalisations which parallel those in the physical sciences, namely those which:

• do not tolerate counter-examples;
• have strict restrictions on applicability;
• enable systematic application to hypothetical instances.

These positivist aspirations have not been met, he contends, but that should not undermine the value or possibility of social science generalisations. Failure in prediction for the social sciences need not lead to disgrace.

McIntyre's point is that predictive failure has created a professional problem for social scientists in their advisory capacities, i.e. as applied social scientists, because claims to expertise were thought to require framing in strong positivist terms. His view is that research can search for generalisations to enlighten practice but that there needs to be recognition of the limits of prediction in human affairs. There are various sources of systematic unpredictability in human affairs, such as pure contingency. This degree of unpredictablity does not imply, however, that phenomena cannot be explained after the actions or events; nor is it incompatible with a principle of determinism.

Implications for explaining learning difficulties

The implication of these considerations for explaining learning difficulties is to endorse the joint use of nomothetic and idiographic orientations. Individual case analyses are as important as large-scale studies of multiple interactive factors that determine learning outcomes. The search for general predictive factors is compatible with some degree of predictive failure, but the search for factors needs to go beyond the identification of deficits to include environmental and other within-child assets and deficits.

The compensatory interaction model of learning difficulties (Wedell, 1980) has been proposed in the context of accounting for predictive difficulties. However, such compensatory processes for child deficits do entail general processes which can be investigated nomothetically. To do so, certain additional assumptions need to be made explicit. One assumption is that the outcomes of interactions between resources and deficits within children and between children and their environments depend on the degree or level of causal factors. For example, the more severe a deficit, the less likely it is that a strong resource will affect the outcome. Environmental and child resources would also be expected to have most impact on outcomes with less severe child deficits. This analysis leads to an acknowledgement of some limits to compensatory potential in an interactionist model.

The level of generality to be used in describing deficits and resources will depend on the descriptive level at which learning outcomes are identified. If learning outcomes are described at general levels which involve the aggregation of various component outcomes, an analysis of causal factors into deficits and resources will similarly need to be described at such general aggregated levels. However, if there are wide disparities between the components making up general outcome and entry factors, then the level of descriptions for these factors may need to be altered to a more specific level. The point is that there is no inherent reason for using any particular level of description. The levels will depend on the nature of the phenomena being represented and the scope of explanation or prediction being sought.

Reference to within-child and environmental factors in terms of resources and deficits may be seen as treating them in an all or none way. This may seem inconsistent with their representation as a matter of degree and as forming dimensions or continua which do not lend themselves to simple divisions between deficits and resources. Setting cut-offs along a dimension is not a simple matter, though this does not make it an arbitrary matter. The end positions of a continuum are distinct and lend themselves to categoric styles of differentiation. Differentiation becomes more difficult towards the middle of the dimension. The fact that some degree of uncertainty exists in this range needs to be acknowledged explicitly, particularly in practical settings. However, when cut-off points are used in this range then they should at least be selected on the basis of predicting the outcomes under consideration. As I argued in Chapter 2, setting cut-off points along a dimension is arbitrary only if an absolute cut-off is sought. Such certainty is not available in systematic research.

To conclude this section, it is worth restating that the purpose of identifying general categories of environmental and child factors is to enable the broad anticipation of future educational outcomes. This aim provides a continuing challenge in the form of identifying accurate and useful factors which operate over different time scales and situations. To abandon this nomothetic search is to give up the opportunity to consider systematically the degree and extent to which causal factors can be altered. When a deficit is identified as relatively stable, unalterable, consistent across situations and severe, this can have shocking and painful emotional consequences. However, it need not mean that educational progress is

impossible. Knowledge of a deficit can be used tentatively to identify the broad possibilities and limits for progress, which enables
the choice of positive and feasible learning objectives and teaching
procedures. My contention is that the retreat from nomothetic
approaches is associated ironically with a positive egalitarian social
commitment which aims to promote educational progress for all.
Some of the value issues associated with this form of egalitarianism
will be discussed in the next section.

EQUALITY AND SPECIAL EDUCATIONAL NEEDS

Equality as a self-evident educational value

The value attached to equality in special needs education has been
highlighted in various parts of this book. In this section, I plan to
discuss some of the difficulties both conceptual and evaluative
associated with the principle of equality in this field. The case for
equality in education has usually been taken as axiomatic and self-
evident (Entwistle, 1978). Although there have been conservative
commentators who have been anti-egalitarian, the educational
debate has been strongly influenced by egalitarians. Equality and
equality of opportunity are often invoked as basic principles to
justify the principles of comprehensive schooling and special
needs integration. When invoked they have the function of drawing a justification to an end. It is in this sense that equality has
an axiomatic function. If questioned, equality and equality of
opportunity are presented as fair or just. I will discuss some of
these issues as they relate to special needs education.

Equal opportunity not sufficient for special educational needs

In the recent thrust towards equal opportunities policies in several
LEAs, the assumption has been that equal opportunities are about
disadvantages associated with class, sex and race. The Fish Report,
Educational Opportunities for All? (1985), distinguished between
'providing equal opportunities' and 'ensuring equal access to
them'. The point is that children with disabilities and significant
difficulties need sustained help to make use of opportunities which
may be provided for all. It is interesting that in linking special
needs issues to those of equality of opportunity, the Fish Report
finds it necessary to distinguish bween access and opportunity.
In other contexts, these two terms are not distinguished but are
taken as interchangeable (Reid and Hodson, 1987). The Fish argument can be interpreted as meaning that there are certain children
whose learning characteristics inhibit them in using ordinarily

provided opportunities. This is significant because it recognises that learning outcomes do not depend only on providing educational opportunities; the personal resources to use these opportunities are also important. The Fish position is that positive action is needed to help some make use of ordinarily available opportunities.

However, the Fish position on equal access is complicated by differences which exist between different kinds of special educational need. This complication arises out of the different kinds of obstacle to educational progress, which bear directly on questions of equality. Children with motor or sensory disabilities who have the intellectual resources to benefit from ordinary educational opportunities can be denied these opportunities on account of what can be seen as irrelevant characteristics. By comparison, children with intellectual disabilities do not have the intellectual resources to benefit from ordinary educational opportunities as they are normally defined. The kinds of adaptation required in these two broad cases are different in a significant way. Adaptation in the first case is of access to valued learning outcomes, whereas adaptation in the case of intellectual disabilities is of the valued outcomes themselves. In Warnock terms, these are modifications of educational level. That there will be different positions taken in these two areas of special needs can be related to differences found in positions towards equality of opportunity and equality of outcome. These considerations raise a set of related questions about equality in general; the relation between equality of opportunity, equality of outcome and the principle of positive discrimination or action; and the basis for equality as a social and education principle.

Equality of opportunity and of outcome

As many social and political commentators have explained, the principle of equality presents notorious difficulties and is subject to easy criticism and parody. This is particularly relevant to special needs education if the basis for the new developments in the field depends on egalitarian principles. There can be serious doubts about whether literal, exact and universal equality of outcome is admirable or desirable, even if it were possible. By contrast, equality of opportunity has attained a degree of support across the political spectrum. However, as a consensus concept, equality of opportunity functions to conceal underlying differences in value orientation. In education, its appeal has been in the evident unfairness and wastefulness of lost opportunity for those children with ability to benefit from high levels of achievement. It is closely connected with the idea of social mobility and as such also has appeal to the politically conservative who favour social efficiency. From a radical left-wing position, equality of opportunity takes the social system as it is, reinforces competition and can be seen as promoting inequality of outcome. Equality of opportunity in this view provides equal chances to become unequal. It is related to the principle of meritocracy in which decision making, with its associated privilege and socio-economic power, is in the hands of those with ability, knowledge and energy. Although the merito-cratic principle has been criticised for providing a social safety-valve and for ultimately making inequality seem justified (Bour-dieu and Passeron, 1977), it is not generally endorsed by all con-servatives, some of whom suspect that it even threatens traditional social structures.

It is therefore strange that, despite the radical left-wing criticisms of meritocracy and equality of opportunity, the concept has been so prominent in recent progressive educational debates and move-ments. Perhaps equality of opportunity was a more politically appealing notion in the 1980s in the context of radical government policies which promoted the values of liberty and choice. It is also less problematic than the concept of equality of outcome or results. In educational terms, equality of outcome implies that in some way people should become equal as a result of their schooling. What is involved in practice here is quite unclear: whether it involves everyone achieving the same educational level, and whether it requires a process of low minimum outcomes for all — what some call disparagingly a levelling-down process. It is rel-evant to this discussion that equality of outcome is usually about outcomes which are outside educational experience as such. It is about the impact of educational outcome on occupational and social status. As such, equality of educational outcome is about the wider issues of social equality, in which some of the demands placed on the educational system may be more appropriately placed on other social sub-systems, such as health and housing.

This raises the question of the limits of equality, both of oppor-tunity and of outcome. Though equality of educational outcome will be promoted by greater equality of opportunity, this depends on the initial availability of educational opportunities. Where there is already universal schooling, more school opportunities may have less effect on producing more equal educational outcomes. This is where background factors associated with social and family experiences have a critical contribution to inequalities both of opportunity and of outcome. To the extent, therefore, that these factors are not directly under the influence of schooling, the prom-ise of equal opportunity and equal outcome in education is likely to be unfulfilled.

Nurture and nature

As Entwistle (1978) notes, the notion of equality of opportunity is itself somewhat misleading as it is often concerned with opportunity rather than with equal chances or outcomes. However, as I argued with respect to the distinction in the Fish Report between equal opportunity and equal access, some learners need to be helped to use the provided opportunities. This implies that there are learner characteristics, whether of attitude or ability, which are relevant to using opportunities. The idea that learner resources or capacities can affect the use of educational opportunities is a highly charged one for the very reason that it bears directly on questions of equality.

When differences or inequalities in learner resources are identified there are differing approaches to their origins. Egalitarian positions tend to adopt nurturist or environmentalist causal analyses, with the implication that inequalities in learner resources and outcomes are socially determined and are therefore open to social intervention and removal. Right-wing positions tend to adopt a nativist causal analysis, with the implication that inequalities in learner resources are natural, biologically determined and not alterable. Even with the current emphasis on the interaction of nature and nurture, the balance of these broad classes of causal factors in determining individual differences is still associated with ideological positions. What is at issue in this debate is the extent to which environmental opportunities can account for differences not only of educational outcomes but also of educationally relevant learner characteristics.

The search for environmental explanations of differences in learner resources and outcomes derives partly from the false assumption that environmental factors are more open to change than genetic inherited factors. In fact, the growth of genetic explanations and techniques opens the prospect of altering inherited factors. In some cases it might prove easier to implement interventions aimed at genetic than at environmental causal factors. Environmental interventions often require changes in other people's behaviour, something which can be difficult to effect. Of course, the prospect of genetic engineering raises disturbing fears about manipulation and abuse, but the point is that all interventions to alter causal factors which influence human characteristics can infringe human rights, whether such interventions are biological, psychological or social.

Environmental explanations are also significant in that they imply that the origins of differences in valued characteristics are not inherent, built-in or natural. Environmental explanations can be thought to protect us from a belief in a natural human moral hierarchy, where some people are naturally better than others. Yet this commitment to secure fair treatment and respect for all is not necessarily supported by searching for environmental accounts. That valued characteristics may have some significant inherited origins does not imply that those with more of these characteristics are morally better people. Those with more abilities, for example, may have more to contribute and may under certain conditions receive more rewards, but this does not mean that they deserve these rewards, in a moral sense. Their personal resources are not deserved in the sense of their being responsible for them. For similar reasons, those with disabilities do not deserve their personal characteristics. The ethical position is that characteristics for which one is not responsible are not subject to moral evaluation. However, the corollary is that there are certain human differences which cannot be attributed or reduced only to environmental factors. To recognise and accept this presents a considerable challenge to some widespread beliefs.

Other egalitarian moves

The egalitarian emphasis on equalising opportunities and outcomes also finds expression in two moves. One is to consider equality of outcome in relation to groups rather than individuals; the other is to reinterpret valued educational outcomes in a way that might make them open to more children. The move to focus on equality of outcome for groups, as between boys and girls, blacks and whites, middle and working class, is difficult to justify even if it has political appeal. To accept equal group outcomes implies that vast inequalities between individuals within social groups are acceptable. This has the effect of treating individuals only in terms of their group membership, which goes against the principle that irrelevant matters such as social class, gender and ethnic origin should not have a bearing on educational access or opportunity. The focus on group outcomes can also be consistent with a meritocratic assumption that individual differences within groups are attributable to innate differences. This implies that equal opportunities are concerned with improving the outcomes for those children with ability to achieve higher educational levels. This implication begs the question discussed above of the origin of individual differences.

The second egalitarian move is to broaden and redefine what counts as valued educational outcomes. The best-known recent version of this (Hargreaves, 1982) involves a critique of the traditional emphasis on written propositional knowledge. Hargreaves recommends a broader focus on applied and practical knowledge and skills, personal and social skills and affective outcomes, such as commitment to learning. What underlies the critique of traditional scholastic knowledge is a genuine concern to adapt educational aims and outcomes to changing social and human needs. However, there is also an element of making achievement possible for a wider range of children. This is a valid move to the extent that such achievements are genuinely valued by those involved, such as parents, teachers, learners and employers. But whether the relevant learner resources for these alternative outcomes are distributed any differently from those for written knowledge is an open question. Those identified as having high levels of the relevant resources or abilities may be different children from those identified as having high scholastic abilities, but this does not remove the prospect of an unequal distribution of these alternative resources, whatever their origins.

This discussion illustrates the intractability of the equality question which stems from uncertainties about the causal analyses of learner resources, the relative contribution of opportunities and learner resources to educational outcomes, and definitions of what count as desirable outcomes. These issues have been debated for many centuries and promise to continue to be a source of major social debate with a considerable impact on the nature of education, including special needs education.

Equality and the evaluation of human characteristics

In some recent conceptions of integration for children with special educational needs, the emphasis has been on eradicating discrimination against children with disabilities and promoting equal participation in ordinary schools (Booth, 1988). It is interesting that this advocacy assumes that 'discrimination against handicapped people is a consequence of values which reward and applaud people for their talents and physique' (Booth, 1983, p. 21). This is a different interpretation of discrimination from that implicit in the advocacy of equality of opportunity. In the latter case, discrimination is a consequence of preventing children from receiving the best schooling on account of irrelevant gender, social or economic factors. Here, however, discrimination hinges on differentiation which is not educationally significant. Booth's position is more radical in questioning the values which determine what is counted as educationally significant. Discrimination in this interpretation involves the principle of equality of value: 'in schools which operate according to such a principle, attempts are made to reduce devaluation of pupils according to their sex, background, colour, economic or class position, ability, disability or attainment' (p. 116).

This position is at the core of the ideological debates about equality. It expresses a commitment, that equality is basically an ethical rather than a factual issue. It expresses the commitment to the moral equality or fellowship of all. Yet it is strange that such a commitment is seen to imply that evaluating human performances, actions or characteristics is in itself dehumanising and demeaning. Such an interpretation denies fundamental human distinctions between what is valuable and what is not. This can hardly be the intention behind a moral principle of human equality. If such a principle means anything, it assumes that equality is an equality of positive evaluation, of finding what is good, not of denying the possibility of evaluation in case there may be some negative evaluation. For this reason a radical interpretation of the principle of equality of value can dehumanise in the sense of denying human tendencies to value certain states or characteristics.

Equality and human dignity

What underlies the radical interpretation is a profound anxiety about devaluing and humiliating human beings, an anxiety which is apparent in much egalitarian discourse. What is not appreciated in this approach to devaluation is that there are crucial distinctions between evaluating what people do and say, their specific characteristics, and evaluating them as persons overall. The ethical challenge of equality is to distinguish between aspects of personality and personality or personhood overall. A child with a severe disability, for instance, also has other characteristics. Identifying a characteristic as a disability has evaluative implications because it assumes that there is a lack of disposition to a valued outcome. Yet this does not justify evaluative implications for the person overall. Having an intellectual retardation is not grounds for moral evaluation of the person involved.

When evaluation is linked and attributed to formal administrative selection and placement processes, there is a risk of confusing different levels of evaluation. Evaluation can take place personally within a specific interpersonal context and it can occur as administrative action directed at groups of people. Though the formal social and the informal personal levels of evaluation are related, there is no simple correspondence between them. There is scant evidence, for example, that children educated in special schools have general negative evaluations of themselves as people (Burns, 1982). Secondly, the concept of devaluation is emotive in that it evokes a sense that low evaluation or negative evaluation is inherently bad. It equates devaluation with extreme forms of rejection and contempt, which are not necessarily implied in negative or low evaluation. On the contrary, it is negative evaluation which makes it possible to analyse problems and situations in order to improve matters.

Nothing in what has been discussed denies that there are many extreme and unacceptable examples of devaluation. My point is that the existence of contempt for humanity does not necessitate the abandonment of all evaluations. The fact that people make evaluations should not be the issue. The issues should rather concern what is valued, how values are used and how values are related to each other. Equality means that we all have the same basic right to fair treatment *whatever* our abilities or disabilities. As Midgley argues, 'the inequalities in our capacities really do become sinister if we make a foolish assumption which apparently is often made — namely, that testing people's capacities is somehow a suitable way of assessing their essential worth' (1981, p. 35).

Removing unjustifiable inequalities

The force and appeal of equality derives from conditions of inequality which limit people's lives and their fulfilment. These inequalities are unacceptable because they strike many of us as grossly unfair or unjust. However, there is a difference between eradicating unjustifiable inequalities and promoting 'complete equality'. Following the arguments of Rawls (1971), justice does not imply equality; the question is rather the extent to which inequality is unjust. This approach requires the justification of inequalities. According to Rawls, inequalities can be justified only if they are shown to have advantages for the less advantaged. This means that there is no unfairness in greater benefits for a few provided that the situation of those less fortunate is improved. Rawls's scheme is based on the notion of what people deserve. Inequalities of natural endowment are not deserved and are seen therefore to call for redress: the compensation for initial inequalities. However, it is clear that there are no definitive criteria for what are unjustifiable inequalities, or for how much redress and who should receive redress for initial inequalities. Although this implies that there will be different opinions on the matter, the important point is to consider inequalities from the perspective of public or collective benefit.

Without this kind of rationale, there can be no basis for justifying positive action on behalf of children with special educational needs. Yet it is also clear that the problems involved in deciding who has special needs derive from uncertainties about who deserves compensatory or additional special educational resources. These problems are inherent in formulating principles in terms of groups but having to apply such principles to individual cases. There seems, therefore, to be no escape from the uncertainties of deciding on both the size of the group to receive additional provision and whether individuals are to be considered as part of the group. This point takes the discussion back to the argument in the earlier chapters about the problems of identifying special educational needs. It appears that these problems are not merely scientific empirical matters but ones concerned with evaluative principles.

In concluding this section, it follows from the above discussion that simple justifications of the normalisation or integration of children with special educational needs in terms of equality of respect are problematic. Having respect for someone implies amongst other things crediting the person with some autonomy to decide about and to exercise some control over his/her life. Autonomy may be best enhanced by a life which permits choice in a controlled environment, where serious failure is avoided. This could lead to policies where some degree of separate provision is advisable. What matters here is who decides about the best ways of enhancing autonomy. Where a decision is made for someone with a disability without consultation there are serious risks that this very decision is itself a denial of respect. The point is that equality of respect implies some crediting of personal choice or self-determination which may result in decisions to opt for some degree of separate provision. A radical egalitarian position which denies values such as those of self-determination can be self-defeating and dangerous.

Conclusion: the 1988 Education Reform Act and the future

INTRODUCTION

Although there was little reference to special educational needs in the original Education Reform Bill, one of the notable aspects of its passage through Parliament was the concern expressed for children with special needs in both Houses and from all parties (Rowan, 1988). Despite this, there has been much anxiety in special needs circles about the possible negative effects of the Education Reform Act on the developing system of special provision and the developments associated with the 1981 Education Act. It is too early, however, to know with any confidence about its specific effects. By the time of writing this book, the subject working parties on mathematics, science and English had reported, some circulars and orders had been issued, the National Curriculum Council (NCC) and School Examinations and Assessment Council (SEAC) were in operation and the development of standard assessment tasks for 7-year-olds was well under way. This is an early stage in the implementation of a radical and complex piece of legislation. Nevertheless, the general principles and requirements of the different elements which will have a bearing on special needs education are known. This makes it possible to consider, albeit tentatively, the likely impact of the Act in general terms.

I do not intend to outline the key elements of the 1988 Act or to comment in any depth on its relationship to the 1981 Act and current ideas and practices in the special needs field. Wedell (1988a, 1988b) has done this recently and it will be done by others. It would also not be in keeping with the orientation of this book to consider general underlying issues and dilemmas in the field. My intention is rather to consider how some of the points which have been raised in the previous chapters bear on some of the principles and provisions of the 1988 Act. As this book is concerned with reappraising special needs education, it is relevant to consider how such a reappraisal informs an initial evaluation of the 1988 Act. I will summarise the key themes and issues raised in each chapter and then discuss how they relate to aspects of the Education Reform Act provisions.

THE CONCEPTUAL ORIGINS OF SPECIAL EDUCATIONAL NEEDS

I argued in Chapter 1 that the introduction of the concept of special educational needs by the Warnock Report represented a positive move in the education of children with difficulties. By focusing on what was to be provided to meet needs, the emphasis was away from child deficiencies. By drawing attention to the child's assets and to the influence of the environment, a more sophisticated model of causation was endorsed. However, a basic confusion in the Warnock attitude to categorisation in this field was also identified. In recommending that handicap categories be abandoned, the Warnock Report confounded administrative categories of special educational provision with categories of child disorder and difficulty. This abolition represented a repugnance towards pejorative terms like 'subnormality'. These terms were replaced by softer terms with less stigmatising and distancing connotations, but the new terms, 'special educational needs' and 'learning difficulties', with their qualifiers, 'specific', 'moderate' and 'severe', were nevertheless still categories.

The 'abandonment of categories' was identified with philosophical assumptions which gave precedence to knowing about individuals rather than knowing through the use of general concepts. As I argued in a later chapter, there is no necessity to choose between idiographic, individually based assumptions and nomothetic assumptions based on general concepts and principles. This implies that a concern for the individual with special needs is compatible with the use of general categories. This was put more positively in the argument that an interactive model depended on the use of appropriate categories. Another aspect of abandoning categories was identified as a rejection of medically based terms. This was apparent in the coining of the more educationally relevant term, 'learning difficulties'. What underlies the Warnock position, it was argued, was really the promotion of the integrated conceptual framework which brought together the different terms by which children with difficulties in ordinary and special schools are referred to. An integrated conceptual framework was seen as a significant way to promote integration, which I have identified as the main positive feature of the 1981 Act and the Warnock Report.

As regards the 1988 Act, it is interesting to note that the Bill made some reference to 'categories' of children with special educational needs. In response to criticism this was later amended to refer to 'cases or circumstances'. Although this amendment illustrates that it is important to maintain the use of the Warnock and 1981 Act terminology and not to slip back to 1944 Act language, this sensitivity about the use of the term 'category' does indicate that the confusions discussed in Chapter 1 are still current in the field. In this respect it is clear that the phrase 'children with special educational needs' has a critical function in the implementation of 1988 Act in identifying where special considerations and exceptions are needed. The term 'special educational needs' has important administrative functions, suggesting that the claim that the 1981 Act 'abandoned categories' needs to be interpreted in a more sophisticated way.

CLASSIFICATION OF CHILDHOOD DIFFICULTIES

In Chapter 2 there was an examination of broad issues connected with identifying special educational needs. It was argued that the criticism of the special needs concept as conflating normative with non-normative conditions was not well founded. Where there is agreement about the presence of a condition this is not always associated wth organic causation. Disagreements about the presence of conditions are found mostly in cases where difficulties are intermediate along a continuum of severity. This means that there is no clear relationship between the organic–functional distinction and whether conditions are normative or not. All difficulties or disorders are normative in the sense of being identified in relation to social norms about personal functioning. Disagreements arise in relation to what is valued in terms of personal functioning, how the difficulties are conceptualised and explained, and which occupational groups are to be responsible for working with the different areas of difficulties. According to this analysis, the problem of setting thresholds for special educational needs is inherent at intermediate points along a continuum of difference. However, thresholds are not arbitrary in the sense that they could be set anywhere. Where there is uncertainty in setting thresholds, this requires openness in the negotiation between the parties involved in attributing special needs. Where disagreements do arise this is often associated with the financial, resource and responsibility implications of identification.

The advantages of a general systems framework were outlined in Chapter 2 in relation to conceptualising human disorder and difficulty at more than one level of analysis. This involves seeing units at each level of analysis both as parts of higher-level units and as wholes in their own right within a theoretical hierarchy.

This kind of framework makes it possible to avoid the parallel errors of reducing all disorder and difficulty to a biological level of explanation and enlarging disorders to a sociological level of explanation. Causal factors can, in principle, be found at several levels of analysis and the exaggerated conflict of biological versus psychological versus sociological can be avoided.

The usual definition of an 'interactionist' framework by contrast to a 'within-child' framework requires further elaboration from a general systems perspective. Within-child factors can refer to physiological or psychological processes, and they are not inherent in the individual in the sense of being unalterable. From a general systems perspective the characterisation of models as 'interactionist' versus 'within child' can be seen to reflect an interest in redressing the balance away from biomedical assumptions of disorder and towards psycho-social assumptions. The main point of the discussion in Chapter 2 was to suggest that redressing the balance can go too far in denying the presence of biological factors.

Although much of the discussion in Chapter 2 does not relate directly to specific aspects of the new changes to the educational system, the position on thresholds for identification of special educational needs is relevant to the establishment of the national assessment procedures. With the introduction of attainment targets in the different National Curriculum subjects and the assessment of children on a unitary system of ten levels of attainment, there are questions about how this might affect the identification of children with special needs. There has been little recent research about the procedures and criteria used in the 1980s for identifying those with moderate learning difficulties. However, there is anecdotal evidence to indicate that, with the increasing use of criterion-referenced assessments and the reduced popularity of IQ tests in some LEAs, there has been more diversity of criteria for the identification of children with moderate learning difficulties. This diversity may also be attributed to differences in LEA policy on what additional resources are made available in ordinary schools. The identification process depends as much on the LEA's response to learning difficulties as on the learning characteristics of a child. Nevertheless, it is likely that with nationally set attainment targets and levels there will be less variation between schools and LEAs in the criteria used to identify children with learning difficulties. This does not imply that the new assessment procedures, which will establish a series of graded attainment levels, will remove all uncertainties about thresholds. What constitutes a significantly below average attainment level will still involve decisions about threshold setting.

Where the ten-level system will probably affect identification is at the floor of the attainment levels. The Black Committee (Task

Group on Assessment and Testing; TGAT, 1988) recommended that the average 7-year-old attainment level be used to define level 2 on the ten-level scale. This means that the below average attainment for 7-year-olds will have to be defined as level 1. It is not known exactly how many 7-year-olds will score at level 1 on the different attainment targets but it is likely that a sizeable proportion will not even score at level 1. It is also too early to know what effect this low floor will have on the identification of learning difficulties, but it does appear even at this stage to have been a mistake not to define more levels for below average attainment for 7-year-olds. If this required a system with more than ten levels then this could have been recognised in the interests of all children.

THE 1981 EDUCATION ACT

In Chapter 3 I discussed the difficulties with the implementation of the 1981 Education Act. Some of these were attributed to the ethos which is sensitive about general categories. The main significance of the Act was seen in the provisions for integration rather than in the 'abolition of categories'. The 'abolition' was interpreted as the separation of the delivery of special services from the usual location of delivery in special schools and units. Linked to this interpretation was a rejection of the false dichotomy between interactive and within-child models of special educational needs. An interactive approach, it was suggested, depended on the use of general categories of child and environmental factors for decisions about future educational provision. That there are areas of uncertainty about the use of general concepts and cut-offs in the identification of special needs was not seen to undermine the basic principle. Such uncertainties ought to be recognised and openly communicated to all parties involved and the consequences handled as positively as possible.

A confusion about the meaning of the term 'special educational provision' was also discussed. Its definition in the 1981 Act in terms of provision which is additional to or different from what is 'generally made' was interpreted as referring to what was provided to the 'normal majority', and not to the place of availability. This led to the proposal that special educational provision be considered in terms of three dimensions: the kind of different/ additional provision, the location of the provision (where it is available) and the authorisation for the provision (who determines the provision). The administrative difficulties involved in the statutory assessment and decision-making procedures for statements of special educational needs were also discussed in terms of proposals for reducing dependence on statutory procedures. This could take the form of improving administrative and professional effectiveness and efficiency, initiating short cuts to resource allocations or establishing allocations to schools rather than through individuals. Whatever the form, there is a need to reconcile several principles: protecting additional resources, ensuring maximum non-segregation and meeting individual needs. It was suggested that, in the context of the 1988 Act provisions for the local management of schools, more specific statutory duties with clearer conditions and criteria should be placed on schools to protect the interests of children with special educational needs. More specific national guidelines about LEA and school procedures for special needs decision making were also recommended.

The statutory assessment procedures of the 1981 Act have to accommodate the changes associated with the introduction of the National Curriculum. In particular, this involves the need to adapt the current advice about children's educational needs to take account of the provisions for exempting children from aspects of the attainment targets, programmes of study and assessment arrangements (section 18 of the Education Reform Act). How these modifications and disapplications will be determined and how they will be incorporated in statements has not yet been clarified, despite the new Circular 22/89, which revises Circular 1/83 on the workings of the 1981 Act. As with Circular 1/83, LEAs and schools need greater clarification and guidance on procedures and criteria. Amongst the uncertainty there may be one positive spin-off from the changing climate in the education system. There may be a recognition of the need for more specificity in the procedures and criteria for decision making in this field.

INTEGRATION

In Chapter 4 I discussed some integration issues with a particular focus on the social aspects of the organisation of special education services. The issues which underlie different starting points and assumptions were mentioned, whether integration was about desegregation or non-segregation, and integration as a means or process and not as an end in itself. This led to a discussion of the reconciling and the social–political approaches to integration and of the tensions which can arise in attempting to offer individual choice and administer a complex system of services. That so much of current thinking about integration and special needs education generally is in terms of individual functioning was used as an entry into a brief discussion of some sociological perspectives.

The contribution of a sociological perspective on special needs education and integration/segregation was endorsed. It was argued, however, that much of the current sociology of special education is associated with particular social values which emphasise the damaging effects of social differentiation. Sociological analysis, it was argued, does not necessarily imply that the interests of those with impairments and difficulties are incompatible with other social interests. Much of the sociology of this field is also practised from socially critical positions which ignore the contributions of other levels of analysis. The biological and psychological are often conflated in the process of attributing to these disciplines the function of legitimising an unjust social system. The concept of differentiation was then discussed in connection with social value questions. Educational differentiation was interpreted as damaging when differences in opportunities and social rewards are seen as unjust. Some differentiation in provision, it was noted, does not imply overall differences in personal and social value.

Much of the current research in integration in the United Kingdom was interpreted as promoting integration, with little attempt to test out the limits to educating children with special needs in ordinary schools as they operate in practice. The predominant use of qualitative and single case methodologies in the United Kingdom was linked to philosophical positions about the nature and function of social research. A case was made for a more flexible and combined use of idiographic and nomothetic approaches, and for the value of comparative studies to inform, not determine, decisions about teaching methods and placement.

The main conclusion of the chapter was that the principles of integration are not incompatible with some degree of separate teaching, whether in special units, classes or schools. This position related to the argument in Chapter 5 for a feasible and flexible common curriculum framework which enables some specialisation of goals and teaching procedures. It was concluded that, where separate provision is necessary, integration requires the linking of the different sectors, the interaction of staff and of learners, and the sharing of materials and facilities.

The future of integration has looked uncertain over the last few years, partly as the commitment at a national level has been mixed. The legislative duties to integrate have been too general to promote a consistent and systematic move towards reviewing and developing provision at LEA level. The lack of additional central resources, in the form of educational support grants, for example, has been symbolic of the weak government commitment. Funded schemes to stimulate developments in which schools commit themselves with the support of parents and teachers to extending their teaching resources for children with special needs have been sadly missing. It is in this context that the provisions of the 1988 Act could set back the tentative moves towards educating children with special needs in ordinary schools. This depends to some extent, however, on how the 1988 Act provisions are implemented, particularly in the context of the local management of schools.

The provisions for local management involve delegating budgets to all secondary schools and primary schools with 200 or more pupils. Special schools will not be included unless authorities want them to be so. LEAs must delegate salary, material and equipment costs, but they cannot delegate certain central services and administrative costs, such as education support grants, and inspector/ adviser and LEA training grants. LEAs may delegate funds for services such as child guidance, educational welfare, statements and units for children with special needs, and peripatetic and advisory teachers. There will be strong pressures on LEAs to delegate funds for the special needs support services, as LEAs will be required to retain only 10 per cent, reducing to 7 per cent, of the general schools budget. The formula for delegating to schools will also include additional funds for children with special needs.

Local management of schools requires governors and head-teachers to make financial decisions at a school level with the aim of enabling schools to be more responsive to educational needs. There have been many specific criticisms of the general scheme: for example, about the capability of schools to manage funds and the weighting given in formulas for allocation to smaller schools and to schools with experienced teachers. Although these issues have a bearing on special needs matters, the ones relevant to this discussion concern the use of the scheme to enable the education of children with special needs in ordinary schools. One of the main dangers of local management is that provision for the wider special needs group will be undermined once schools are paying for support and advisory services. These fears relate to the work of LEA-based support and psychological services. Schools may plan to use their delegated funds for children with special needs, but in the context of an overall scarcity of funding, there will be difficult decisions about how to spend school funds. In this situation, provision for special needs could come under pressure and be cut back. By locating financial decision making at school level, the relative merits of alternative forms of expenditure will be more apparent and this could lead to re-evaluation of special needs spending. The result could be a situation in which special educational provision becomes marginalised unless schemes for using these delegated funds are developed.

One way of ensuring the continuity and development of special needs services would be for ordinary schools to collaborate in clusters to share some of their special needs funds. Some of the delegated funds could be used for individual school provision with the rest being pooled by a group of schools to develop resources for special needs which could not be met by one school alone. The LEAs could play a significant role in the establishment of shared teaching resources by delegating the discretionary funds on the condition that schools enter such arrangements. In fact, the principle of the local management of schools is central to the development of more locally based and integrated special services. Schools could not take more responsibility for special educational needs without some mechanisms for devolving financial responsibility to them. The local management principle is also relevant to the development of services in ordinary schools for the smaller group of children otherwise educated in special schools. Special funds could be ear-marked to extend provision for children with statements, in addition to special needs funds which are part of the general allocation.

It can be concluded that the local management of schools could in principle be used positively to extend the capability of schools to provide for special educational needs, even if in practice this form of it turns out to undermine provision. The major determining factors here are the overall level of finance, the specific weighting given for special needs in the delegation formula and the quality of commitment and management at both school and LEA levels. It is likely that there will be initial difficulties in the transition into local management, but it is important that there should be plans for developing the financial and management systems which will enable as many children with special needs as possible to be educated in ordinary schools.

COMMON CURRICULUM FOR SPECIAL EDUCATIONAL NEEDS

In Chapter 5 I discussed some of the dilemmas and difficulties connected with a common curriculum for all children. It was argued that the formulation of educational aims should be in general terms to have general applicability, but not be so general that it provides no guidance about what is worth developing. The challenge of reconciling the attainment of educational aims with having common aims also depends on not pitching the demands of educatedness too high and on distinguishing between different levels of describing educational intentions. Following this line of argument, it was concluded that educational aims could be the same for virtually all children, and that this was compatible with a degree of differentiation of more specific intentions (goals and objectives) and methods at school or class level. Differentiation was seen as necessary if a common curriculum framework was to be relevant to the diversity of individual children. This requires a flexible set of common curriculum areas which do not take up all the available school time and therefore allow some specialisation.

It was also suggested that some current conceptions of curriculum modification for special educational needs did not address the difficulties of reconciling common curricula with individual differences. The trend towards playing down the differences in content and method for some children with special needs was observed to fit oversimplified notions of a common curriculum for all. A model was presented which incorporated both common and specialist curricular areas. Modification or adaptation could focus on either the environment or the child, or both. Adaptations to the environment to provide alternative forms of access to the common curricular areas, for example, involve equipping the child with access skills which are additional or special to the child. This means not only that changes are made to adapt the environment to the child, but that the child has also to adapt to external demands. Another aspect of adapting the child to external demands was identified in those programmes which have rehabilitative or restorative goals. Such programmes are specialist and do not form part of ordinary school programmes. Although these programmes can raise false hopes, if they are effective they should have a place in special needs education and ought to be accommodated within a flexible curriculum framework. The proposed model of curriculum modification implies some difficult decisions about resource availability under conditions of scarcity. There is, for example, a limit to the time available for schooling. More time spent on common goals means less for specialist ones.

It is a mark of the marginal importance attached to recent developments in areas such as multicultural and special educational needs that the legislation for a National Curriculum has paid relatively little attention to these aspects of education. In the special needs case, the 1988 Act has established a general provision for modifying or disapplying the curriculum and assessment but the details involved are still being worked out. Most of the considerations have been about attainment targets, programmes of study and assessment arrangements, starting from the perspective of the average child. This has its positive side if children with special needs can be included in the general scheme. In this sense, the National Curriculum can be seen as representing a formal entitlement for children with special needs to participate in areas of learning which are common to other children. However, entitlements can be double edged, particularly if the entitlement is to something which is not relevant to the needs of particular children. In such cases entitlements can turn into rigid impositions.

Much of the initial and continuing criticism of the National Curriculum is connected with these rigidity and irrelevancy issues. This has been apparent in the concern that most of the school curriculum in practice would consist of the nationally defined curriculum and that there would therefore be little time for other curricular areas and for cross-curricular work, let alone curricular developments. From the perspective of children with special educational needs, particularly those with the comparatively more severe difficulties (the 2 per cent), these rigidities arise from not taking sufficient account of the diversity of individual learner resources and attainments in the initial considerations for designing a National Curriculum. This is shown in the legislative provision for modifying and disapplying, where no clear initial public indication is given of when and how these exemptions will be applied (Norwich, 1989).

A related concern about the National Curriculum provisions is that establishing the possibility of disapplying the curriculum for a minority of children with special needs — those with severe learning difficulties, for example — signifies that some children will be excluded from a National Curriculum which is supposed to be for all. Some critics have likened this to the pre–1970 system in which children with severe learning difficulties were not the responsibility of the education service, a system which implied that they were not 'educable'. Although this response probably exaggerates the likely effects of the disapplication powers, there ought to be government guidelines on the matter. For example, what parts of the National Curriculum can be disapplied and how will alternatives be formulated? A legislative Act, such as the Education Reform Act, lays out broad provisions which have to be worked out in more detail in orders, regulations and circulars. The lack of specific central guidelines on these matters just as the National Curriculum is first introduced into schools only reinforces suspicions that special needs issues continue to be a low government priority.

These points need to be seen in the context of the basic orientation to curriculum embodied in the Education Reform Act. As other commentators have noted (Lawton and Chitty, 1988), the National Curriculum is an assessment-based curriculum. By this is meant that curricular targets are defined with a primary focus on how attainment can be assessed. There is less emphasis on the complex process of curriculum development and design, with the careful linking and translating of broad, general into increasingly specific and more concrete intentions at different levels in the education system. By leaving out this critical process, important aspects of the curriculum are ignored: for example, cross-curricular themes and topics, curricular ownership and development, and social–emotional aspects of learning. In this respect the National Curriculum expresses a strong centralist and directive approach. The focus on attainment targets and assessment derives mainly from the government's wish to raise national educational attainment levels. It is based on the belief that the wider use of assessment information by those with a stake in schools will increase accountability and raise standards. It is a policy which plays down the contribution of teaching resources, in the form of facilities and personnel, to raising standards. For this reason it lacks credibility.

DESIGNING TEACHING AND ASSESSMENT

In Chapter 6 I attempted to show how different and sometimes opposite perspectives on curriculum design and assessment are interrelated. I argued that design questions involve the processes both of specifying learner outcomes and of identifying principles of procedure — even though the relative emphases on these two basic aspects could vary. This involved abandoning a unitary approach to learning, such as radical behaviourism, and adopting a broader concept of learning objectives and outcomes. It also recognised that teaching methods or procedures can lead to multiple learning outcomes and that the co-ordination of teaching processes with learning outcomes is central to the design issue.

A similar attempt was made to interrelate task analytic with learner analytic approaches to assessment. This was based on questioning the assumptions that learner characteristics are general, fixed and assessable by traditional norm-referenced tests. The alleged opposition between criterion- and norm-referenced assessment orientations was similarly criticised. In pointing out several misconceptions about these orientations, it was suggested that all assessment involves both a comparative and a domain specification element. When the emphasis is more on formulating the domain or criterion in specific terms, assessment can be referenced against attaining or not attaining the specific objective. When the domain is formulated in general terms, assessment cannot be referenced against a specific objective, but is referenced against a well-defined typical performance.

The distinction between formative and summative assessment was queried for not dealing explicitly with the anticipatory or predictive use of assessment. It was argued that it was more useful to see assessment in terms of monitoring and summarising progress at different levels of specificity within courses and at the end of courses. This assessment can be used to alter teaching approaches or to move on to another, perhaps the next, stage of learning at these different levels. Whatever the case, assessment would have no use unless it implied some prediction about learning. On the basis of this reasoning, an interactionist approach which focuses on learner, task and learning environment was suggested. This includes explicit analysis of learner characteristics in specific teaching contexts in a way that goes beyond assessing specific learner performances to inferring more general characteristics. Although this approach is not well developed, the assumptions were elaborated in a schematic model. This model takes account of the functions of assessment in (a) adapting objectives and teaching procedures within a common curriculum framework and (b) deciding on exceptional adaptations in response to teaching and learning difficulties.

The Task Group on Assessment and Testing (TGAT) distinguished between formative, diagnostic, summative and evaluative purposes of assessment in their initial report (TGAT, 1988). Consistent with much current professional opinion, priority was given to the formative purposes. Assessment procedures designed specifically for summative purposes were seen to be relevant only at age 16, otherwise summative purposes could be met by aggregating assessments used for formative purposes. In view of the discussion in Chapter 6, there are difficulties with this position. It overlooks the practical difficulties of summarising specific classroom-based assessments for important summative functions during the process of schooling, such as decisions about subject options and special educational provision. In this respect the TGAT position which underpins the National Curriculum oversimplifies the functions of assessment.

The TGAT proposals have little to say about the formative use of assessment information at different stages of learning, or for whom the information is useful. The emphasis on formative assessment can be seen to derive from the importance attached to assessment in classroom teaching for teachers and learners. However, assessment also has a use for those involved in longer-term and broader educational decisions. This includes parents and those who manage and advise schools. The significance of the public reporting of attainment levels as part of the National Curriculum would be hard to appreciate without taking account of the broader use of assessment information during the period of schooling.

Although the TGAT report was welcomed with some relief by certain educationalists, it seems that the proposals are couched in terms which do not register fully the difficulties of setting up a unitary system to serve diverse purposes. This system of assessing attainment seems to imply continuous assessment as part of class teaching, which can then be aggregated with information from standard assessment tasks into profile components and made available at the reporting ages. Questions of how teacher assessments will be related to assessment on standard tasks and of whether genuine ongoing teacher assessments will be used for aggregating at the reporting times have yet to be addressed. It is likely, for practical reasons, that teacher assessments which are to be used for reporting purposes will be done in addition to the usual ongoing informal assessments. If so, this will increase the time used for assessment activities and generally reduce time for learning activities. There may also be difficulties in spreading out National Curriculum teacher assessments over a period of time and not having them just before reporting times.

One of the usual criticisms of externally based assessment procedures, that they are unrelated to the curriculum and tend to distort it, applies less to this scheme, as the assessment is supposed to monitor progress through the levels of nationally set attainment targets. However, the effect is to shift some of the difficulties to basic curriculum questions about what attainments are worth pursuing and how they are formulated. The position taken by the DES and National Curriculum Council is to give greater weight to knowledge, understanding and skill attainments than to application, communication and personal quality ones. Although there are difficulties in assessing these latter areas of attainment, it is better to include them as attainment targets as a way of protecting a broader concept of educational attainment. But it would require some way of describing levels of progression other than the unitary ten-level scheme.

By the criteria of a behavioural objective the attainment levels defined in the National Curriculum are general descriptions of varied kinds of outcome. These will require further translation into specific concrete terms to be useful for devising assessment items. This point is connected to the step size between the different levels of progression within an attainment target. As mentioned before, from the perspective of progress for children with learning difficulties these may be broad step sizes. Particularly at the lower levels of attainment there could have been more levels to enable some 7-year-old children with learning difficulties to be placed on the scale. Although the broad framework can accommodate a range of special educational needs, it is unlikely to be able to include all children with such needs.

There have been no indications at the time of writing about how the assessment procedures will be adapted for children with special needs. With the development of the national assessment procedures it is possible, however, that the general direction of statutory assessment for identifying children with special needs could change. This possibility for change arises as the new assessment procedures should provide a range of broadly defined curriculum-based indications of attainment. This will make it possible for the additional assessment performed by psychologists to focus more on learner and teaching factors which underlie these attainments. The suggestions in Chapter 6 for teaching-based assessments of learner processes and characteristics are more likely to be developed in the context of education in the 1990s.

A final point on the theme of assessment concerns the principle of reporting the results of the national assessments. As mentioned before, the very purpose of having an elaborate assessment system is to make the assessment information available to parents and others interested in the educational system. It has been widely predicted that this will have the effect of increasing pressures on schools to take the individual results of low attainers out of the overall school results. This could lead to more children being considered for temporary exemptions (section 19) and statements which would exempt them from parts of the National Curriculum and assessment procedures. However, to anticipate this tendency does not entail any specific conception of how the use of the modification and disapplication provisions will influence the reporting of schools results. At present it is still unclear how the attainment results of children with statements will be reported at school level, whether as part of a separate section on children with special needs, as part of the overall age-based reporting, or not at all.

The proposals for reporting assessment results represent a crude method of providing consumer information. The attainment levels of children do not indicate adequately the effectiveness of a school, as many critics of the 1988 Act have argued. Not only do starting levels have to be taken into account, but there are other broader performance indicators of which informed parents would need to be aware. These points were discussed by the TGAT committee, which decided to recommend that reporting be of unadjusted raw attainment levels in the context of an account of background information about the school.

Many of the fears about the negative effects of the assessment procedures have to be seen in the context of the level of financing in local authority schools. Whether competitiveness between schools will be promoted by these changes will depend partly on these resourcing factors. Whether schools will be less willing to exercise fully their responsibilities for all children and to include more children previously placed in special schools will depend on the future relationships between schools. In the context of major changes in local government finance and the squeeze on public service finance over the last decade, it is likely that the national assessment information will be neither of a high quality nor on balance used in more positive ways.

PROFESSIONAL ISSUES

In Chapter 7 I discussed some of the conflicts and dilemmas of professionalism in the special needs field. The difficulties which arise from differences between professional groups, such as training, conceptual and language frameworks, were mentioned, as were differences within the broader group of teachers. The relationships between specific professional groups and parents were seen to be influenced by relationships between different professional groups themselves. Inter-professional difficulties were discussed in terms of achieving mutual understanding and the appreciation of the contributions of other groups. This depends itself on some clarity about the professional role and the scope and effectiveness of particular services.

Several examples of inter-professional relationships were discussed to illustrate these points. The relationship between therapeutic professionals and teachers was seen to depend amongst other factors on the co-ordination of therapeutic goals and procedures with educational ones. The relationship between educational psychologists and advisory/support teachers illustrated how changing roles in one group need to be co-ordinated with roles in other groups. The relationship between special needs teachers and teachers in ordinary schools raised some questions about the advantages and disadvantages of occupational specialisation. A significant role was identified for central and local government in promoting the co-ordination of different professional services. A balance needs to be achieved between respecting some degree of professional autonomy and the representation of the wider public interest — in this case, client interest.

The 1988 Act can be interpreted as a significant attempt to redress the balance of influence between educationalists and the clients of the educational service, the parents, in order to improve the quality of schooling. Parents will receive information about their children's attainment levels in different areas of the curriculum. Parents will be able to vote for schools to opt out of LEA administration and financing, and there will be more scope for parents to send their children to schools of their choice. When these provisions are considered in the context of greater parental representation on school governing bodies, which will have increased powers with the local management of schools, there can be little doubt about the intention to involve parents in the process of schooling. Whether these major changes will enhance the quality of education in schools is a very complex question which depends partly on factors outside the scope of the 1988 Act. The fears of many critics are based on the belief that schools will go into more competition with each other and that some less popular schools will decline in the process. The role of LEAs in the overall planning of local services will be reduced and the disparity of services will widen.

Many of these fears are particularly relevant to provision for children with special educational needs. With the increased influence of parents overall there is a serious risk that parents of children with special needs, as a minority, will find that they have less influence in practice on the kind and quality of services for their children. The opportunity for all parents to exercise more choice as individuals may not result in better quality provision for children with special needs. One of the functions of an LEA has traditionally been to mediate the conflicting interests of different groups and to protect standards for all. With less local authority influence to counter and regulate the influence of different parents and schools, these minority interests could be overlooked. This position does not deny a constructive role for some competition between schools. What is at issue is whether individual interests are played out on the basis of meaningful information about schooling and educational attainments. What is needed is a system in which individual interests can accommodate collective interests which take account of the education needs of all children.

CONCLUDING COMMENTS

In Chapter 8 three broad areas of general relevance were discussed: the concept of special educational needs, the individuality of learning difficulties, and equality as a social and educational value. In some respects the analyses of these topics represent the key argument of this book. Overall the position taken has been one which calls for a more critical and balanced perspective in the field, one which avoids exaggerated polarities between different conceptions and values.

I have argued that the concept of special educational needs does depend on concepts such as disability and impairment. Paralleling this is the position that an interactionist view cannot be fully realised without a commitment to some general categories of child and environmental assets and deficits. This is also connected to epistemological questions about the role of general concepts and principles in coming to know about individuals — the relationship between idiographic and nomothetic orientations in the social sciences. The allied question of how to select research methodologies in this field also arises in this context. Another main strand of the argument has been the indispensability of different disciplines and levels of analysis and explanation. This was presented in terms of the conceptual and explanatory value of social, psychological and biological explanations, with the implication that these relatively separate perspectives need to accommodate their frameworks to each other. The simple polarisation of medical and educational models was also criticised for confounding models defined in terms of professional practice and interests with those defined in terms of levels of analysis.

As regards the question of a common curriculum for all or virtually all children, I questioned the belief that it can be realised only in common schools and classrooms. The implementation of a common curriculum has to take account of the diversity of learner characteristics and the flexibility needed to translate general value orientations into specific practices. Some degree of curricular specialisation is compatible with a flexible common curriculum orientation for all. This position is particularly relevant to some children with special educational needs who may need additional or different programmes, some of which might be focused on adapting the child to the environment. Questions of the design of teaching were similarly not portrayed in terms of simple polarities between process or product approaches. This kind of analysis was also applied to questions of assessment, where the relationship between norm- and criterion-referenced assessment approaches was identified.

One way of summarising the main theme of this book is in terms of a commonly found style of dichotomous thinking in this field. I have tried to argue that thinking in terms of global oppositions and polarities between certain positions oversimplifies matters. This is not to imply that there are no answers to questions or working resolutions to basic dilemmas. It is rather to suggest that understanding derives from seeing connections and complementarity between positions, although there may be continuing tensions between them. This is most relevant to some of the social value positions taken in this and the wider educational field. This understanding can lead to an appreciation that dignity in learning for all does not depend only on equality, but can also arise from being treated as having autonomy and through some sense of belonging to a valued learning community.

References

Ainscow, M. and Tweddle, D. (1979) *Preventing Classroom Failure*. Chichester: John Wiley & Sons.

Ainscow, M. and Tweddle, D. (1988) *Encouraging Classroom Success*. London: D. Fulton.

Allport, G. W. (1960) *Personality and Social Encounter*. Boston, Massachusetts: Beacon Press.

Arter, J. A. and Jenkins, J. R. (1979) Differential diagnosis — perspective teaching: a critical appraisal. *Review of Educational Research* **49** (4), 517–55.

Bantock, G. H. (1973) *Culture, Industrialisation and Education*. London: Routledge & Kegan Paul.

Barton, L. and Tomlinson, S. (1984) *Special Education and Social Interests*. London: Croom Helm.

Bloom, B. (1976) *Human Characteristics and School Learning*. New York: McGraw-Hill.

Board of Education (1929) *Report of the Mental Deficiency Committee* (Wood Report). London: HMSO.

Board of Education (1934) *Report of Committee of Inquiry into Problems Relating to Partially Sighted Children*. London: HMSO.

Booth, T. (1988) 'Challenging conceptions of integration'. In Barton, L. (ed.), *The Politics of Special Educational Needs*. London: Falmer Press.

Booth, T. and Potts, P. (1983) *Integrating Special Education*. Oxford: Basil Blackwell.

Bourdieu, P. and Passeron, J. C. (1977) *Reproduction in Education, Society and Culture*. London: Sage.

Bradley, L. and Bryant, P. (1985) *Children's Reading Problems*. Oxford: Basil Blackwell.

Brennan, W. K. (1987) *Changing Special Educational Needs*. Milton Keynes: Open University Press.

Bunn, T. (1987) Sociological perspectives on special education, part 1. *Educational Psychology in Practice* **2** (4), 5–10.

Burns, R. D. (1982) *Self Concept Development and Education*. London: Holt, Rinehart & Winston.

Burt, C. (1921) *Mental and Scholastic Tests*. London: B. King & Son.

Carlberg, C. and Kavale, K. (1980) The efficacy of special versus regular class placement for exceptional children: a meta-analysis. *Journal of Special Education* **14** (3), 295–309.

Carrier, J. G. (1984) 'Comparative special education: ideology, differentiation and allocation in England and the US'. In Barton and Tomlinson (1984).

Case, R. and Bereiter, C. (1984) From behaviourism to cognitive behaviourism to cognitive development: steps in the evolution of instructional design. *Instructional Science* **13**, 141–58.

Chapman, E. K. and Stone, J. M. (1988) *The Visually Handicapped Child in Your Classroom*. London: Cassell.

Coard, B. (1971) *How the West Indian Child is Made Educationally Subnormal in the British School System: The Scandal of the Black Child in Schools in Britain*. London: Beacon Press.

College of Speech Therapists (1988) Discussion paper. London: College of Speech Therapists.

Cottam, P. (1985) 'The practice outside Hungary'. In Cottam and Sutton (1985).

Cottam, P. and Sutton, A. (1985) *Conductive Education: A System for Overcoming Motor Disorders*. London: Croom Helm.

Crick, B. (1984) *Socialist Values and Time*. Fabian Tract 495. London. Fabian Society.

Croll, P. and Moses, D. (1985) *One in Five: The Assessment and Incidence of Special Educational Needs*. London: Routledge & Kegan Paul.

Cunningham, C. C. (1983) 'Early support and intervention: HARC Infant Project'. In Mittler, P. and McConachie, H. (eds) *Parents, Professionals and Mentally Handicapped People: Approaches to Partnership*. London: Croom Helm.

Davie, R., Butler, N. and Goldstein, H. (1972) *From Birth to Seven: The Second Report of the National Child Development Study*. London: Longman.

Dearden, R. F. (1972) 'Needs in education'. In Dearden, R. F., Hirst, P. H. and Peters, R. S. (eds) *A Critique of Current Educational Aims*. London: Routledge & Kegan Paul.

DES (Department of Education and Science) (1978) *Special Educational Needs* (Warnock Report). Cmnd 7212. London: HMSO.

DES (1984) *Organisation and Content of the 5–16 Curriculum*. London: HMSO.

DES (1988a) *The National Curriculum: Mathematics for Ages 5–16*. London: HMSO.

DES (1988b) *The National Curriculum: Science for Ages 5–16*. London: HMSO.

DES (1988c) *The National Curriculum: English for Ages 5–11*. London: HMSO.

Dessent, T. (1987) *Making the Ordinary School Special*. London: Falmer Press.

DHSS (Department of Health and Social Security) (1976) *Fit for the Future* (Court Report). Cmnd 6684. London: HMSO.

Eisner, E. (1969) 'Instructional and expressive educational objectives: their formulation and use in the curriculum'. In Popham, W. J. (ed.) *Instructional Objectives*, AERA Monograph 3. Chicago, Ill.: Rand McNally.

Elliott, J. (1978) 'Classroom research: science or commonsense?' In McAleese, R. and Hamlyn, D. (eds) *Understanding Classroom Life*. Slough: NFER.

Engel, G. L. (1977) The need for a new medical model: a challenge for biomedicine. *Science* **196** (4286), 129–36.

Engelman, S. and Carnine, D. (1982) *Theory of Instruction*. New York: Irvington Publications.

Entwistle, H. (1978) *Class, Culture and Education*. London: Methuen.

Etzioni, A. (1969) *The Semi-Professions and Their Organisations*. New York: Free Press.

Evans, J., Everard, K. B. E., Friend, J., Glaser, A. Norwich, B. and Welton, K. (1989) *Decision Making for Special Needs: A Resource Pack*. London: London University Institute of Education.

Faupel, A. (1986) Curriculum management: teaching curriculum objectives. *Educational Psychology in Practice* **2** (2), 4–15.

Feuerstein, R., Rand, Y. and Hoffman, M. B. (1979) *The Dynamic Assessment of Retarded Performers: The Learning Potential Assessment Device*. Baltimore: University Park Press.

Fish Report (1985) *Educational Opportunities for All?* London: ILEA.

Ford, J., Mongon, D. and Whelan, M. (1982) *Special Education and Social Control*. London: Routledge & Kegan Paul.

Frank, I. (1986) 'Psychology as a science: resolving the idiographic–nomothetic controversy'. In Valsiner, J. (ed.) *The Individual Subject and Scientific Psychology*. New York: Plenum Press.

Frith, U. (1985) The usefulness of the concept of unexpected reading failure: comments on reading retardation revisited. *British Journal of Developmental Psychology* **3**, 15–17.

Gage, N. L. (1985) *Hard Gains in the Soft Sciences: The Case of Pedagogy*. CEDR Monograph. Bloomington, Indiana: Phi Beta Kappa.

Gagné, R. M. (1985) *The Conditions of Learning*, 4th edn. New York: Holt Rinehart & Winston.

Galloway, D. M. (1985) *Schools, Pupils and Social Educational Needs*. London: Croom Helm.

Galloway, D. M. and Goodwin, C. (1979) *Educating Slow Learning and Maladjusted Children: Integration or Segregation?* Harlow: Longman.

George, V. and Wilding, P. (1984) *Ideology and Social Welfare*. London: Routledge & Kegan Paul.

Gipps, C., Goldstein, H. and Gross, H. (1985) Twenty per cent with special needs: another legacy from Cyril Burt? *Remedial Education* **20** (2), 73–5.

Goacher, B., Evans, J. Welton., J. and Wedell, K. (1988) *Policy and Provision for Special Educational Needs: Implementing the 1981 Education Act*. London: Cassell.

Golby, M. and Gulliver, J. (1979) Whose remedies, whose ills? A critical review of remedial education. *Journal of Curriculum Studies* **11** (2), 137–47.

Goode, W. J. (1969) 'The theoretical limitations of professionalisation'. In Etzioni (1969).

Goodison, L. (1987) Integration: whose ideal? *New Society* (10 July).

Graham, P. (1980) 'Epidemiological studies'. In Quay, H. C. and Werry, J. S. (eds) *Psychopathological Disorders of Childhood*. Chichester: John Wiley & Sons.

Guildford, J. P. (1967) *The Nature of Human Intelligence*. New York: McGraw-Hill.

Hargreaves, D. H. (1982) *The Challenge of the Comprehensive School*. London: Routledge & Kegan Paul.

Haynes, J. (1971) *Educational Assessment of Immigrant Pupils*. Slough: NFER.

Hegarty, S. (1987) *Meeting Special Needs in Ordinary Schools: An Overview*. London: Cassell.

Hegarty, S. and Evans, P. (1985) *Research and Evaluation in Special Education*. Windsor: NFER-Nelson.

Hegarty, S., Pocklington, K., and Lucas, D. (1981) *Educating Children with Special Educational Needs in the Ordinary School*. Slough: NFER.

Hegarty, S., Pocklington, K. and Lucas, D. (1982) *Integration in Action: Case Studies in the Integration of Pupils with Special Educational Needs*. Slough: NFER.

Helier, C. (1988) Integration: a need for positive experience. *Educational Psychology in Practice* **4** (2), 75–9.

Hindley, C. B. and Owen, C. F. (1978) The extent of individual changes in IQ for ages between 6 months and 17 years in a British longitudinal sample. *Journal of Child Psychology and Psychiatry* **19** (4), 387–95.

Hodgson, A., Clunies-Ross, L. and Hegarty, S. (1984) *Learning Together: Teaching Children with SEN in the Ordinary School*. Windsor: NFER-Nelson.

Honzik, M. P., MacFarlane, J. W. and Allen, L. (1948) The stability of mental test performance between 2 and 18 years. *Journal of Experimental Education* **17**, 309–24.

Howell, K. W., Kaplan, J. S. and O'Connell, C. Y. (1979) *Evaluating Exceptional Children: A Task Analysis Approach*. Columbus, Ohio: Merrill.

Hutt, M. L. and Gibby, R. G. (1976) *The Mentally Retarded Child: Development, Education and Treatment*, 3rd edn. Englewood Cliffs, NJ: Prentice-Hall.

Illich, I. (1977) *Disabling Professions*. London: Marion Boyers.

Jones, N. (1983) 'The management of integration: the Oxfordshire experience'. In Booth and Potts (1983).

Jowett, S., Hegarty, S. and Moses, D. (1988) *Joining Forces: A Study of Links Between Special and Ordinary Schools*. Windsor: NFER-Nelson.

Kaufman, A. S. (1980) *Intelligent Testing with the WISC-R*. New York: Wiley Interscience.

Kelly, A. V. (1982) *The Curriculum: Theory and Practice*. London: Harper.

Kelly, G. (1955) *The Psychology of Personal Constructs*. New York: Norton.

Kennedy, I. (1980) Unmasking medicine. *Listener* (6 November).

Keogh, B. and Becker, LD. (1974) Early detection of learning problems: questions, cautions and guidelines. *Exceptional Children* (5–11 September).

Kluckhohn, C. Murray, H. A. and Schneider, D. J. (1959) *Personality in Nature, Society and Culture*. New York: Knopf.

Lawton, D. (1988) 'Ideologies of education'. In Lawton and Chitty (1988).

Lawton, D. and Chitty, C. (1988) *The National Curriculum*. Bedford Way Paper No. 33. London: University of London Institute of Education.

Lewin, K. (1936) *Principles of Topological Psychology*. New York: McGraw-Hill.

Lightfoot, W. (1948) *The Partially Sighted School: An Exposition and Study of the Methods Used in England for Educationally Defective Children*. London: Chatto & Windus.

Lindsay, G. and Wedell, K. (1982) The early identification of educationally 'at risk' children revisited. *Journal of Learning Disabilities* **15** (4), 212–17.

Lubovsky, V. I. (1981) Basic principles of special education in the USSR. *Unesco Prospects*, 444–7.

Lunt, I. and Sheppard, J. (1986) Participating parents: promise and practice. *Educational and Child Psychology,* **3** (3).

McConkey, R. (1985) *Working with Parents: A Practical Guide for Teachers and Therapists.* London: Croom Helm.

MacDonald Ross, M. (1975) 'Behavioural objectives: a critical review'. In Golby, M., Greenwald, J. and West, R. (eds) *Curriculum Design.* London: Croom Helm.

McIntyre, A. (1981) *After Virtue: A Study in Moral Theory.* London: Duckworth.

Madden, N. A. and Slaven, R. E. (1983) Mainstreaming students with mild handicaps: academic and social outcomes. *Review of Educational Research* **53** (4), 519–69.

Madden, P. (1987) Social workers: Parents' future friends? *Special Children* **8,** 14–15.

Mager, R. F. (1962) *Preparing Instructional Objectives.* Palo Alto, California: Fearon.

Marchesi, A. (1986) Project for integration of pupils with special needs in Spain. *European Journal of Special Needs Education* **1** (2), 125–33.

Mawer, P. and colleagues (1983) *Data-Pac: An Interim Report.* Birmingham: University of Birmingham Department of Educational Psychology.

Midgley, M. (1981) 'Freedom and heredity'. In *Heart and Mind.* London: Methuen.

Mittler, P. (1979) *People Not Parents.* London: Methuen.

Morgan, M., Calman, M. and Manning, N. (1985) *Social Approaches to Health and Medicine.* London: Croom Helm.

Mortimore, P. (1988) *School Matters: The Junior Years.* Wells: Open Books.

Norwich, B. (1988) 'Educational psychology services in LEAs: what future?' In Jones, N. and Sayer, J. (eds) *Management and the Psychology of Schooling.* London: Falmer Press.

Norwich, B. (1989) Adapting the National Curriculum: exploring the complexities. *British Journal of Special Education* (September).

Nuttall, D., (1989) 'National assessment: will reality match aspirations?' Unpublished paper from conference, 'Testing Times' (8 March).

Oliver, M. (1985) The integration–segregation debate: some sociological considerations. *British Journal of Sociology of Education* **6** (11) 75–91.

Overton, W. F. (1984) 'World views and their influence on psychological theory and research'. In *Advances in Child Development and Behaviour,* vol. 18. London: Academic Press.

Posner, C. J. and Strike, K. A. (1976) A categorisation scheme for principles of sequencing content. *Review of Educational Research* **46** (4), 665–90.

Potts, P. (1983) 'What difference would integration make to the professional?' In Booth and Potts (1983).

Powell, J. and Booker, R. (1987) Needs, provision and the wider context in the 1981 Education Act: a challenge to current practice. *Educational Psychology in Practice* **33,** 34–9.

Quay, H. C. (1980) 'Classification'. In Quay, H. C. and Werry, J. S. (eds) *Psychopathological Disorders of Childhood.* Chichester: John Wiley & Sons.

Rawls, J. (1971) *A Theory of Justice.* Cambridge, Massachusetts: Harvard University Press.

Raybould, E. C. (1984) 'Precision teaching and pupils with learning difficulties: perspectives, principles, practices'. In Fontana, D. (ed.) *Behaviourism and Learning Theory in Education*, British Journal of Educational Psychology Monograph No. 1, 43–7.

Rectory Paddock School (1981) *In Search of a Curriculum: Notes on the Education of Mentally Handicapped Children*. Sidcup: Robin Wren Publications.

Redmond, P., Evans, P., Ireson, J. and Wedell, K. (1988) Comparing the curriculum process in special (MLD) schools: a systematic qualitative approach. *European Journal of Special Needs Education* **3** (3), 147–60.

Reid, D. J. and Hodson, D. (1987) *Science for All: Teaching Science in the Secondary School*. London: Cassell.

Rowan, P. (1988) Cause for concern. *Times Educational Supplement* (29 July).

Russell, P. (1986) 'The Education Act 1981'. In Cohen, A. and Cohen, L. (eds) *Special Educational Needs in the Ordinary School*. London: Harper.

Rutter, M. (1977) 'Classification'. In Rutter, M. and Hersov, L. (eds) *Child Psychiatry: Modern Approaches*. Oxford: Blackwell Scientific.

Rutter, M., Cox, A., Tupling, C., Berger, M. and Yule, W. (1975) Attainment and adjustment in two geographical areas: 1. prevalence of psychiatric disorder. *British Journal of Psychiatry* **126**, 493–509.

Rutter, M., Maughan, B., Mortimore, P. and Ouston, J. (1975) *15,000 Hours*. Wells: Open Books.

Rutter, M. Tizard, J. and Whitmore, K. (1970) *Education, Health and Behaviour*. Harlow: Longman.

Rutter, M. and Yule, W. (1975) The concept of specific reading retardation. *Journal of Child Psychology and Psychiatry* **16**, 181–97.

Sandow, S. and Stafford, P. (1987) *An Agreed Understanding: Parent–Professional Communication and the 1981 Education Act*. Windsor: NFER-Nelson.

Sattler, J. M. (1982) *The Assessment of Children's Intelligence and Special Abilities*, 2nd edn. Boston, Massachusetts: Allyn & Bacon.

Sayer, J. (1985) *What Future for Secondary Schools?* London: Falmer Press.

Select Committee Report (1987) *Special Educational Needs: Implementation of the Education Act 1981* (Education, Science and Arts Committee). London: HMSO.

Shapiro, H. S. (1980) Society, ideology and the reform of special education: a study of the limits of educational change. *Education Theory* **30** (3), 211–23.

Share, D. and Silva, P. A. (1986) The stability and classification of specific reading retardation: a longitudinal study from age 7 to 11. *British Journal of Educational Psychology* **56** (1), 32–40.

Shayer, M. and Beasley, F. (1987) Does instrumental enrichment work? *British Journal of Educational Research* **13** (2), 101–21.

Skilbeck, M. (1984) *School Based Curriculum Development*. London: Harper Education.

Solity, J. and Bull, S. (1987) *Bridging the Curriculum Gap*. Milton Keynes: Open University Press.

Stenhouse, L. (1975) *An Introduction to Curriculum Research and Development*. London: Heinemann.

Sutherland, G. (1984) *Ability, Merit and Measurement: Mental Testing and English Education 1880–1946*. Oxford: Clarendon Press.

Sutton, A. (1986) Conductive education: a challenge to integration. *Educational and Child Psychology* **3** (2), 5–12.

Swann, W. (1983) 'Curriculum principles for integration'. In Booth and Potts (1983).

Szasz, T. (1961) *The Myth of Mental Illness*. New York: Harper & Row.

Tansley, A. E. and Gulliford, R. (1960) *The Education of Slow Learning Children*. London: Routledge & Kegan Paul.

TGAT (Task Group on Assessment and Testing) (1988) *Report* (Black Report). London: DES.

Thomas, D. (1985) The determinants of teachers' attitudes to integrating the intellectually handicapped. *British Journal of Educational Psychology* **55**, 251–63.

Thomas, G. (1986) Integrating personnel in order to integrate children. *Support for Learning* **1** (1), 19–27.

Tomlinson, S. (1982) *A Sociology of Special Education*. London: Routledge & Kegan Paul.

Tomlinson, S. (1985) The expansion of special education. *Oxford Review of Education* **11** (2), 157–65.

Tomlinson, S. and Barton, L. (1984) 'The politics of integration'. In Barton and Tomlinson (1984).

Topliss, E. (1979) *Provision for the Disabled*. Oxford: Basil Blackwell/Martin Robertson.

van der Wissel, A. and Zegers, F. E. (1985) Reading retardation revisited. *British Journal of Developmental Psychology* **3**, 3–9.

Vislie, L. (1982) *Integration of Handicapped Children in Compulsory Education in Norway*. Paris: OECD/CERI.

von Bertalanffy, L. (1968) *General System Theory*. New York: George Braziller.

Vygotsky, L. S. (1978) *Mind in Society*. Cambridge, Massachusetts: Harvard University Press.

Wedell, K. (1980) 'Early identification and compensatory interaction'. In Knights, R. M. and Bakker, D. J. *Treatment of Hyperactive and Learning Disordered Children: Current Research*. Baltimore University Park Press.

Wedell, K. (1983) Assessing special educational needs. *Secondary Education Journal* **13**, 14–16.

Wedell, K. (1986) Cluster. *Times Educational Supplement* (19 September), 47–8.

Wedell, K. (1987) Personal communication with author.

Wedell, K. (1988a) 'The national curriculum and special educational needs'. In Lawton and Chitty (1988).

Wedell, K. (1988b) The new Act: a special need for vigilance. *British Journal of Special Education* **15** (3), 98–101.

Weiss, P. (1969) 'The living organism: determinism stratified'. In Koestler, A. and Smythies, J. R. (eds) *Beyond Reductionism*. London: Macmillan.

Welton, J. (1983) Implementing the 1981 Education Act. *Higher Education* **12**, 597–607.

Welton, J., Wedell, K. and Vorhaus, G. (1983) *Meeting Special Educational Needs: 1981 Act and Its Implications*. Bedford Way Paper no. 12. London: University of London Institute of Education.

Westmacott, E. and Cameron, R. J. (1981) *Behaviour Can Change*. Basingstoke: Macmillan Education.

Wheldall, K. and Merrett, F. (1984) *Positive Teaching: The Behavioural Approach*. London: Unwin.

Whitaker, P. S. (1988) How much education — what sort of psychology? *Educational Psychology in Practice* **3**, 11–16.

White, J. (1982) *The Aims of Education Restated*. London: Routledge & Kegan Paul.

Wilson, J. and Cowell, B. (1984) How should we define handicap? *Special Education: Forward Trends* **11** (2), 33–5.

Wolfendale, S. (1983) *Parental Participation in Children's Development and Education*. London: Gordon & Breach Science Publications.

Wolfendale, S. (1986) Routes to partnership with parents: rhetoric or reality? *Educational and Child Psychology* **3** (3), 19–28.

Wolfensberger, W. (1972) *The Principle of Normalisation in Human Services*. Toronto: National Institute of Mental Retardation.

Woods, R. (1987) *Development and Assessment in Education and Psychology: Collected Papers 1967–78*. London: Falmer Press.

Yola, C. and Ward, J. (1987) Teachers' attitudes towards the integration of disabled children in regular schools. *The Exceptional Child* **34** (1), 41–55.

Ysseldyke, E. and Salvia, J. (1978) *Assessment in Special and Remedial Education*. Boston, Mass.: Houghton Mifflin.

Yule, W. (1981) 'The epidemiology of psychopathology'. In Lahey, B. B. and Kazdin, A. E. (eds) *Advances in Clinical Psychopathology*, 4. New York: Plenum Books.

Yule, W. (1985) Comments on van der Wissel and Zegers. *British Journal of Developmental Psychology* **3** (1), 11–15.

Name Index

Ainscow, M. 8, 88, 89, 93, 94, 100, 105, 134
Allport, G. W. 137
Arter, J. A. 84

Bantock, G. H. 76
Barton, L. 8, 19, 34, 56, 59, 133
Beasley, F. 83
Becker, L. D. 136
Bereiter, C. 105
Booker, R. 130–1
Booth, T. 53, 56, 146
Bourdieu, P. 60, 143
Bradley, L. 84
Brennan, W. K. 81
Bryant, P. 84
Bull, S. 89, 93, 100, 105
Bunn, T. 59
Burns, R. D. 147
Burt, C. 26

Cameron, R. J. 88
Carlberg, C. 66
Carnine, D. 91
Carrier, J. G. 60
Case, R. 105
Chapman, E. K. 83
Chitty, C. 160
Coard, B. 23
Cottam, P. 84, 119
Cowell, B. 15
Croll, P. 10
Cunningham, C. C. 128

Dearden, R. F. 131, 132
DES (Department of Education and Science) 6, 7, 9, 15, 53, 73, 80
Dessent, T. 48, 49, 54, 123

Eisner, E. 93
Elliott, J. 138
Engel, G. L. 29

Engelman, S. 91
Entwistle, H. 141, 144
Etzioni, A. 112
Evans, J. 35, 125

Faupel, A. 99
Feuerstein, R. 83, 107
Ford, J. 60
Frank, I. 138
Frith, U. 23

Gage, N. L. 138
Gagné, R. M. 98
Galloway, D. M. 17, 27, 65
George, V. 75
Gibby, R. G. 73, 74
Gipps, C. 26
Goacher, B. 33, 34, 35, 48, 115, 127, 130
Golby, M. 86
Goode, W. J. 113
Goodison, L. 57, 58
Goodwin, C. 65
Graham, P. 28
Guildford, J. P. 22
Gulliford, R. 76
Gulliver, J. 86

Hargreaves, D. H. 58, 65, 74, 75, 145
Haynes, J. 107
Hegarty, S. 53–4, 55, 57, 65, 66, 69, 82
Helier, C. 57
Hindley, C. B. 21
Hodgson, A. 66
Hodson, D. 74, 141
Honzik, M. P. 21
Howell, K. W. 100
Hutt, M. L. 73, 74

Illich, I. 128

Jenkins, J. R. 84

Jones, N. 68
Jowett, S. 67

Kaufman, A. S. 21
Kavale, K. 66
Kelly, A. V. 88, 92, 94, 97
Kelly, G. 95
Kennedy, I. 28
Keogh, B. 136
Kluckhohn, C. 137

Lawton, D. 75, 160
Lewin, K. 138
Lightfoot, W. 12
Lindsay, G. 136
Lubovsky, V. I. 64
Lunt, I. 126

McConkey, R. 126
MacDonald Ross, M. 91
McIntyre, A. 139
Madden, N. A. 66
Madden, P. 111
Mager, R. F. 90
Marchesi, A. 68
Mawer, P. 91
Merrett, F. 89, 93
Midgley, M. 63, 148
Mittler, P. 56
Morgan, M. 28
Mortimore, P. 67
Moses, D. 10

Norwich, B. 121, 160

Oliver, M. 58, 59, 60–1
Overton, W. F. 95
Owen, C. F. 21

Passeron, J. C. 60, 143
Posner, C. J. 96
Potts, P. 53, 116, 127
Powell, B. 130–1

Quay, H. C. 28

Rawls, J. 148
Raybould, E. C. 92
Redmond, P. 99
Reid, D. J. 74, 141
Rowan, P. 150
Russell, P. 33
Rutter, M. 7, 9–10, 13, 19, 20, 22, 26, 67

Salvia, J. 100

Sandow, S. 57, 126, 127
Sattler, J. M. 21
Sayer, J. 123
Shapiro, H. S. 61
Share, D. 23
Shayer, M. 83
Sheppard, J. 126
Silva, P. A. 23
Skilbeck, M. 96
Slaven, R. E. 66
Solity, J. 89, 93, 100, 105
Stafford, P. 57, 126, 127
Stenhouse, L. 93
Stone, J. M. 83
Strike, K. A. 96
Sutherland, G. 25
Sutton, A. 64, 84, 119
Swann, W. 35, 82, 90, 99
Szasz, T. 29

Tansley, A. E. 76
Thomas, D. 66
Thomas, G. 67
Tizard, J. 7, 10
Tomlinson, S. 8, 18, 19, 23, 34, 56, 58, 59, 60, 61, 62, 111, 114, 115, 130, 133
Tweddle, D. 8, 88, 89, 93, 94, 100, 105, 134

van der Wissel, A. 23
Vislie, L. 49
von Bertalanffy, L. 3, 30
Vygotsky, L. S. 64, 107

Ward, J. 66
Wedell, K. 15, 16, 33, 38, 70, 94, 136, 139, 150
Weiss, P. 30
Welton, J. 33, 124
Westmacott, E. 88
Wheldall, K. 89
Whitaker, P. S. 91
White, J. 73, 76
Whitmore, K. 7, 10
Wilding, P. 75
Wilson, J. 15
Wolfendale, S. 126, 128
Wolfensberger, W. 54
Woods, R. 24

Yola, C. 66
Ysseldyke, E. 100
Yule, W. 20, 22, 28

Zegers, F. E. 23

Subject Index

Adaptive behaviour
  assessing 21
Aims, educational
  and the common curriculum 73–5,
    158–9
Alternative access programmes 85
Assessment 100–10, 153–4, 161–5
  criterion-referenced 100, 101–3,
    153, 161
  curriculum-based 88, 100–1
  dependability of 19–26
  and educational
    psychologists 121–2
  formative 100, 101, 104–5, 161, 162
  of intellectual difficulties 21–2
  norm-referenced 88, 101–4, 161
  psychiatric 20–1
  of reading difficulties 22–3
  social and ethnic bias in 23–6
  summative 104, 161, 162
Australia
  studies of integration 66
Autonomy, personal 149, 167

Behavioural approach see Objectives
  approach
Behavioural difficulties, children with
  categorisation of 10, 62
  control systems 60
  and integration 67, 69
  provision for 47–8
Bias in assessment 23–6
Biomedical model 29
Bio-psycho-social model 30
Black Committee 153–4

Categories and categorisation 151–2
  and 1981 Education Act 37–9, 51
  abolition of 6–17, 154
  alternatives to 8–9
  and individual needs 12
  and interactive approach 39–41

and multiple disabilities 10–12
  negative use of 42
  problems with 6–7
  and resource allocation 13–14
  and Warnock Report 6–14, 15, 16,
    33
Central government initiative 68–9
Cerebral palsy, children with 84
Child causal factors (within-child
  factors)
  and interactive approach 41–3, 136,
    153, 154
  and learner analysis 100
  and learning difficulties 140
City Technology Colleges 76
Common curriculum see Curriculum
Compensatory interactive model
  of learning difficulties 139–40
Comprehensive schooling
  and educational aims 78
  and hidden curriculum 77
  and inequality 141
  and integration 54, 65
  and special needs education 34, 60,
    69
Conductive education 84, 86, 119
Conflict theories 59
Court Report (child health services)
  on disability and handicap 27–8
Criterion-referenced assessment 100,
  101–3, 153, 161
Cross-service interaction
  and 1981 Education Act 36
Curriculum
  common 69, 72–87, 158–61, 167
  and integration 63
  and specialised goals 84–7
  designing and
    implementing 88–110
  differentiation 79–81, 159
  hidden 77
  modification 79–81, 82–3, 159

national   52, 76, 153, 155, 159–61,
   162, 163, 164
social aspects of   77–8
Curriculum-based assessment   88,
   100–1

DATA PAC   91
Deficit-focused programmes   83–4,
   135
Developmental curriculum   80, 81
Differentiation   60, 61, 62–3, 156
   curricula   79–81, 159
   negative and positive aspects   63–4
Disability
   Court Report definition of   28
   identification of special needs
      with   135
Disruptive behaviour, children with
   provision for   47–8
DISTAR   91
Dyslexia   22

Education Act (1944)   9, 37, 38, 51, 152
Education Act (1976)   34
Education Act (1981)   3, 7, 33–52, 68,
   150, 151, 154–5
   background and principles   33–5
   concept of 'special'   134, 135
   concept of special education
      needs   37–9
   evaluation of   35–7
   and integration   67, 151
   legal categories of special education
      need   43–4
   and parents   128–9
   and professionals   115, 116
   significance of   50–1
   and special education needs   130
   support services   121
Education Reform Act (1988)   1, 3, 48,
   70, 150–1, 155, 159, 160, 164
   and integration   67
   and parent/professional
      relationships   165–6
   and speech therapists   117
Educational psychologists
   and advisory teachers   120–2, 165
   assessments by   20
   and behavioural objectives   89
   as professionals   114, 115, 116
   training and qualifications   120
Egalitarianism *see* Equality
Emotional difficulties, children with
   categorisation of   10, 61–2
   and integration   67, 69

Environmental factors   3
   and categories of handicap   15–16
   and equality   144–5
   interaction with child causal
      factors   41–2, 136
   in learning difficulties   140
   possibility of altering   40–1
Epidemiological approach   19–20
Epilepsy, children with   10
Equality   141–9
   and differentiation   62–3, 63–4
   and educational aims   74, 75
   and evaluation of human
      characteristics   146–7
   and human dignity   147–8
   of opportunity   56, 71, 74, 141–3,
      144
   of outcome   142–3
   removing unjustifiable
      inequalities   148–9
   of value   56, 146–7
ESN (M) category
   social construction of   59–60
Ethnic bias
   in IQ tests   22, 23–5
Exclusionist view of psychiatry   28
Expressive objectives   93

Family therapy   125–6
Fish Report   35, 37, 55, 115, 141–2, 144
Formative assessment   100, 101,
   104–5, 161, 162
Functional integration   54, 55
Functional theories   59
Funding
   and assessment   164–5
   Education Support Grants   68, 156
   of special needs education   157–8

General systems approach   3, 30–1,
   32, 62, 87, 152–3
Goals, curricular
   common and specialised   84–7
Grants *see* Funding

Handicap
   Court Report definition of   28
   see also Categories and categorisation
Health professionals   111, 116, 117,
   118
   and cross-service interaction   36
   intervention by   86
   and psychiatric assessments   20–1

Idiographic orientations   137–9, 156,
   166

Illness, attitudes to 30
Individualism 58–9
  and categories of handicap 12
  and common curriculum 78
  and educational aims 75
  and equality 145, 148–9
  and integration 62, 151
  and learning difficulties 136–41
  and special education needs 134
Instructional objectives 93
Instrumental Enrichment (IE) 83–4,
    86, 123
Integration 53–71, 155–8
  and 1981 Education Act 51, 151
  conceptions and
      misconceptions 53–4
  critique of theories 61–3
  evaluating 65–7
  forms of 54–5
  legislative provision for 67–70
  and social values 78
  sociological perspectives 58–61
  and special education teachers 123
Intellectual difficulties, children with
  assessing 21–2
  and equal opportunities 142
Interactive approach
  to special education 16, 39–43, 136,
      153, 154, 162, 166
  to special education needs 16,
      39–43
IQ (Intelligence Quotient)
  as assessment method 21–2, 23–5,
      103, 153
  cut-off points 21, 26

Kelly's Personal Construct Theory 95

Labelling
  and categories of handicap 8, 14
Learner analysis approach 100,
    105–6, 161
Learner characteristics
  teaching assessment of 106–8
Learner outcome objectives 93
Learning difficulties, children with
  concept of, in Warnock Report 8–9
  and curriculum 79
  definition of, in 1981 Education
      Act 38–9
LEAs (Local Education Authorities)
  and 1981 Education Act 34, 36, 43,
      44, 46, 47, 51, 52
  and 1988 Education Reform Act 166
  and education officers 115

  and funding of special
      education 157, 158
  and health professionals 116
  and parents 127
  and speech therapists 117–18
Locational integration 54–5, 61

Maladjustment
  definition of 10
Medical models 60, 167
  for identifying disabilities 27–8, 32
  learner analysis as 100
Meritocracy 143, 145
Moderate learning difficulties, children
    with 61
  and integration 66, 69
  problems of identifying 26, 153
  structured objectives approach
      for 99
  support teaching of 124
Modified curriculum 80–1
Motor difficulties, children with 69
Multiple disabilities
  categorisation of children
      with 10–12

National Curriculum 52, 76, 153, 155,
    159–61, 162, 163, 164
National Curriculum Council (NCC),
    150, 163
Needs, special education
  concept of 130–5, 151–2
New Zealand 23
Nomothetic orientations 137–9, 156,
    166–7
Norm-referenced assessment 88,
    101–4, 161
Normative/non-normative conditions,
    18–19, 27, 28, 62, 152

Objectives approach 136
  and curriculum implementation 88,
      89–99
  and educational psychology 121
Organismic psychological theory 95,
    96

Parents
  and 1981 Education Act 33, 34, 35,
      36, 37, 43, 48
  and 1988 Education Reform Act 165,
      166
  and integration 57, 58
  and professionals 111, 115, 126–9,
      132–3, 165–6
  and psychiatric assessments 20

Partially sighted children 12
Peto Institute, Hungary 119
Physical disabilities 7, 15
Physiotherapists 116
    and teachers 119
Portage pre-school programme 68,
    125–6
Positivist theories 59
Process approaches
    and curriculum implementation 88,
        92, 93–7
    and educational psychology 121
Professional associations 112, 113,
    125
Professionals 111–29, 165–6
    and 1981 Education Act 37
    autonomy of 112–13
    cross-service interaction by 36
    inter-professional
        relationships 114–26, 135, 165
    and parents 111, 115, 126–9, 132–3,
        165–6
    psychiatric assessments by 20–1
Provision of special education
    decision-making in 45–8
    defining 44–5, 154–5
    and needs 130–2
Psychiatric assessment 20–1
Psychiatry
    identifying disorders through 28–9
Psychological approaches 62
Psychologists *see* Educational
    psychologists

Reading backward (RB) 22, 23
Reading difficulties
    assessing 22–3
'Reconciling' approach to
    integration 56
Rectory Paddock School 83
Reductionist view of psychiatry 29
Rehabilitative programmes 86, 87,
    159
Relative approach
    to special education needs 16,
        39–41
Resource allocation
    and 1981 Education Act 37, 49–50
    and categories of handicap 13–14
Restorative programmes 86, 159

School organisation
    clusters of schools 70
    local management of schools 70,
        157–8

SEAC (School Examinations and
    Assessment Council) 150
Sensory impairments, children
    with 69
    alternative access programmes 85
Severe learning difficulties, children
    with 4, 160
    relative nature of 40
    structured objectives approach
        for 99
Sex ratio differences
    in assessment of reading
        difficulties 23
Social bias
    in assessment 23–6
Social–emotional goals
    and the identification of learning
        difficulties 15
Social integration 54, 55
Sociological perspectives
    critique of 61–2
    on integration 58–61, 155–6
Soviet Union 64–5
Spain 68
Special, use of term 133–5
Special schools 24
    and 1981 Education Act 38
    and categories of handicap 17
    and common curriculum 76, 77
    defence of 57–8
    dissatisfaction with 65
    generic 69
    and local management of
        schools 157
    modifications to curricula 82–3
    and multiple disabilities 11–12
    and negative evaluation 147
    in the Soviet Union 64–5
    and special educational
        provision 47
    teachers 116
Specific learning difficulties 4
    and integration 67
Specific reading retardation
    (SRR) 22–3
Speech therapists 116
    and teachers 117–19
Spina bifida, children with 84
Statementing 43, 44, 48–9, 117
    and exemption from National
        Curriculum 164
Stigma
    and categorisation 14
Summative assessments 104, 161, 162

Task analysis 90, 105–6, 161

Teachers
  attitudes to integration 66
  and curriculum implementation 96
  and educational
      psychologists 120–2, 165
  as professionals 113
  and psychiatric assessments 20
  special needs 114, 118
    and ordinary teachers 122–4, 165
  and therapists 117–20, 165
Teaching methods
  in objectives approach 91–2
TGAT (Task Group on Assessment and
    Testing) 162, 164
Therapeutic professions
  intervention by 86

United States 21, 65, 66–7

Visually impaired children
  modifications to curricula 83

Warnock Report 53, 151
  and categorisation 6–14, 15, 16, 33,
    151
  concept of 'children with learning
    difficulties' 8–9, 151
  concept of 'special' 134
  on curricular modifications 84, 87
  on educational aims 73, 75
  and individuality 136
  and integration 37, 151
  'named person' proposal 115
WISC-R test 21
Within-child factors *see* Child causal
    factors
Wood Committee (1929) 9
World Health Organisation
  International Classification of
    Diseases (ICD9) 28

Zone of next development 107